Ultimate Python Polars for Data Analytics

Transform Your Large-Scale Data into High-Performance Analytics with Python Polars

Sunny Khilare

www.orangeava.com

First Published: March 2026

Published By: Orange Education Pvt Ltd, AVA®

Address: 9, Daryaganj, Delhi, 110002, India

275 New North Road Islington Suite 1314 London,
N1 7AA, United Kingdom

ISBN (PBK): 978-93-49887-35-0
ISBN (E-BOOK): 978-93-49887-33-6

Scan the QR code to explore our entire catalogue

www.orangeava.com

Get a Free eBook

We hope you're enjoying your recent book purchase! Your feedback is incredibly valuable to us and helps other readers discover books that truly make a difference.

If you found this book useful or enjoyable, we'd greatly appreciate it if you could leave a short review with a 5-star rating on Amazon. Your review supports our work and allows us to reach more learners worldwide.

As a thank-you, we're happy to offer you a **free digital copy of this book** plus a **30% discount code** for your next purchase on our official websites:

www.orangeava.com

www.orangeava.in (For the Indian Subcontinent).

☑ **How it works:**

Leave your review on Amazon, take a screenshot of the confirmation or use the following link to submit the claim and email it to **info@orangeava.com.** Once received the required detail, we will send your rewards within 24 hours, **along with one month free subcription to the book on AVA SkillShelf!**

Claim Form
https://rebrand.ly/4d2477

Thank you for your support—it truly means a lot to us.

Colored images

Please follow the links or scan the QR codes to download the ***Code Bundles and Images*** of the book:

https://github.com/orgs/ava-orange-education/repositories

The code bundles and images of the book are also hosted on ***https://rebrand.ly/p6qrn9m***

In case there's an update to the code, it will be updated on the existing GitHub repository.

Errata

We take immense pride in our work at **Orange Education Pvt Ltd,** and follow the best practices to ensure the accuracy of our content to provide an indulging reading experience to our subscribers. Our readers are our mirrors, and we use their inputs to reflect and improve upon human errors, if any, that may have occurred during the publishing processes involved. To let us maintain the quality and help us reach out to any readers who might be having difficulties due to any unforeseen errors, please write to us at:

errata@orangeava.com

Your support, suggestions, and feedback are highly appreciated.

Dedicated to

My Parents, for Shaping
My Values, and to My Wife, for Her
Unwavering Support During the Creation of This Book.

About the Author

Sunny Khilare is an experienced data professional with a strong background in data analysis, data engineering, and high-performance data processing using Python. He holds an engineering degree, and has built a career focused on designing scalable, efficient, and production-grade data solutions across complex data environments.

With nearly a decade of experience in analytics and data systems, Sunny has worked on a wide range of problems including data quality frameworks, analytics platforms, performance optimization, and large-scale data processing. His work has involved designing solutions for data validation, anomaly detection, latency analysis, and processing large volumes of structured and semi-structured data.

Sunny's technical expertise spans Python, Polars, Pandas, DuckDB, PyArrow, SQL, and cloud-based data pipelines. He has developed frameworks capable of processing tens of gigabytes of data efficiently, with a strong emphasis on performance tuning, lazy execution, and clean data architecture.

Passionate about modern data tools and knowledge sharing, Sunny actively explores advanced topics such as query optimization, streaming execution, and extending Python data frameworks using Rust. Through this book, Sunny Khilare aims to help data professionals build faster, scalable, and maintainable data pipelines using Polars.

About the Technical Reviewer

Pritish Swain has more than 15 years of experience across B2C and B2B domains, specializing in Data Science and Analytics as well as large-scale digital transformation initiatives. He has designed and delivered data-driven solutions across diverse industries, including online travel platforms, manufacturing, energy sector, and airports.

Leveraging advanced analytics and AI/ML, Pritish has led high-impact analytics programs that drive operational efficiency and strategic decision-making. He brings extensive experience working with senior leadership and C-suite stakeholders, contributing to enterprise-wide strategy discussions and long-term capability-building initiatives.

Currently, Pritish leads Data Analytics at Pratt & Whitney, where he is responsible for building a Global Capability Center (GCC). His focus includes developing high-performing teams, embedding analytics into core business processes, and driving sustainable business value through data-driven and digital transformations.

Acknowledgments

Writing this book has been a long and rewarding journey, and it would not have been possible without the support, guidance, and encouragement of many individuals and organizations.

I would like to begin by expressing my sincere gratitude to everyone who supported me throughout my educational journey. The teachers, mentors, and well-wishers who nurtured my curiosity, and encouraged my analytical thinking that played a vital role in shaping my foundation.

I am equally thankful to the many people who guided me throughout my corporate journey. I have been fortunate to work with leaders, mentors, and peers who challenged my thinking, shared their knowledge generously, and helped me grow both technically and professionally. Their insights into real-world data problems, system design, and performance engineering deeply influenced the practical perspective presented in this book.

I would also like to acknowledge my previous organizations and colleagues for providing environments that encouraged learning, experimentation, and innovation. The problems I encountered, the systems I worked on, and the collaborations I was part of directly inspired many of the examples and approaches discussed in this book. I am grateful to the colleagues who shared ideas, reviewed approaches, and supported me during demanding projects.

My sincere thanks goes to the technical reviewers and editors who helped refine this manuscript. Their detailed feedback, critical observations, and commitment to clarity significantly improved the quality, accuracy, and readability of the content.

Finally, I am deeply grateful to everyone who encouraged me throughout this journey, directly or indirectly. This book is a reflection not only of my work but also of the collective support and wisdom I received along the way.

Preface

Modern data systems demand speed, scalability, and efficiency. As datasets grow larger and workflows become more complex, traditional data-processing tools often struggle to keep up with performance and memory constraints. This gap has led to the emergence of new-generation data frameworks designed to handle large-scale data workloads more effectively. Polars is one such framework—built in Rust, designed for performance, and optimized for modern hardware.

This book was written to provide a comprehensive, practical, and production-oriented guide to using Polars for data analysis and data engineering workflows. It is intended for readers who want to move beyond basic DataFrame operations and learn how to design high-performance, scalable, and maintainable data pipelines using Polars.

The journey begins with a clear introduction to Polars, its core philosophy, and the features that distinguish it from traditional libraries such as Pandas. Early chapters focus on building a strong foundation—understanding Polars' data structures, configuration options, and input/output capabilities—ensuring readers gain confidence in working with the framework from the ground up.

As the book progresses, readers are guided through increasingly advanced data transformation techniques, including grouping, joining, reshaping, window functions, and working with nested data. Dedicated chapters explore data visualization, SQL integration, and extending Polars through user-defined functions and high-performance Rust plugins using PyO3. These topics bridge the gap between exploratory analysis and real-world, production-grade data processing.

Special emphasis is placed on performance and scalability. Polars' lazy execution model, query optimization engine, streaming mode, and GPU support are explained in detail, helping readers understand not just how to write code, but why certain approaches perform better. Profiling, optimization, and testing techniques are covered to ensure readers can confidently deploy Polars-based solutions in demanding environments.

The later chapters focus on applied use cases, including market data analysis, machine learning workflows, and big data processing using cloud platforms such as Google Cloud. These chapters demonstrate how Polars integrates seamlessly with modern data ecosystems, enabling efficient ETL pipelines, analytics, and model development.

This book is written for data analysts, data engineers, quantitative analysts, and Python developers who want to leverage Polars for high-performance data processing. While prior experience with Python and DataFrames is helpful, the book is structured to gradually build expertise—from fundamentals to advanced topics—making it accessible to both intermediate users and experienced professionals.

By the end of this book, readers will have a deep understanding of Polars' capabilities, best practices for performance optimization, and the confidence to apply Polars effectively in real-world data-intensive applications. My hope is that this book serves not only as a learning resource, but also as a long-term reference for building fast, scalable, and efficient data workflows with Polars.

DID YOU KNOW

Did you know that Orange Education Pvt Ltd offers eBook versions of every book published, with PDF and ePub files available? You can upgrade to the eBook version at **www.orangeava.com** and as a print book customer, you are entitled to a discount on the eBook copy. Get in touch with us at: **info@orangeava.com** for more details.

At **www.orangeava.com**, you can also read a collection of free technical articles, sign up for a range of free newsletters, and receive exclusive discounts and offers on Print Books and eBooks.

PIRACY

If you come across any illegal copies of our works in any form on the internet, we would be grateful if you would provide us with the location address or website name. Please contact us at **info@orangeava.com** with a link to the material.

ARE YOU INTERESTED IN AUTHORING WITH US?

If there is a topic that you have expertise in, and you are interested in either writing or contributing to a book, please write to us at **business@orangeava.com**. We are on a journey to help developers and tech professionals to gain insights on the present technological advancements and innovations happening across the globe and build a community that believes Knowledge is best acquired by sharing and learning with others. Please reach out to us to learn what our audience demands and how you can be part of this educational reform. We also welcome ideas from tech experts and help them build learning and development content for their domains.

REVIEWS

Please leave a review. Once you have read and used this book, why not leave a review on the site that you purchased it from? Potential readers can then see and use your unbiased opinion to make purchase decisions. We at Orange Education would love to know what you think about our products, and our authors can learn from your feedback. Thank you!

For more information about Orange Education, please visit **www.orangeava.com**.

Table of Contents

CHAPTER 1
Introduction to Polars

"Every company has big data in its future and every company will eventually be in the data business."

Thomas H. Davenport

Introduction

Data is a byproduct of human actions, interactions and reactions. The way we experience the world can be expressed through the data we generate. With the advent of the internet, there has been a tremendous increase in data volumes over the years. Data professionals use this data to make data-driven decisions and enhance their products, strategy, and operations.

De facto industry-leading libraries such as Pandas have helped professionals analyze the data. With an increase in the data volume, the limitations of such libraries are becoming apparent. This is where Polars comes in. It is a lightning-fast dataframe library which can handle larger datasets and demanding workflows. Polars is written in Rust and optimized for parallelism. It can handle large amounts of data compared to other traditional dataframe libraries. It can be used to create flexible, scalable and elegant data solutions. Polars is slowly becoming a top choice for professionals who want to take their workflows to the next level.

This book will help you master Polars with ease. Hence, whether you are a data analyst, data scientist, or data engineer, you will learn how to use Polars for data wrangling with large datasets and build scalable workflows.

Structure

In this chapter, we will discuss the following topics:

- Introduction to Polars
- Key Features of Polars
    - Apache Arrow Backend
    - Apache Arrow Data Types
    - Parallelization
    - Query Optimization
- Comparison with Other Dataframe Libraries
- Installation of Polars in Python Environment
    - Our First Dataframe with Polars

Introduction to Polars

Polars started as an open-source project in 2020. The vision for it was to make it an easy-to-use dataframe library which does not compromise performance. Developed using Rust, Polars currently supports four languages, which are Python, Rust, R and Node.js. Polars provides seamless integration with Python, which allows users to work with data from various sources such as CSV, Parquet, and JSON. Whether you are performing simple analysis or building intricate data pipelines using the cloud, Polars is designed to handle large-scale data processing with speed, flexibility, and ease. Polars shines in single-node operations, while existing libraries such as Pandas are single-threaded and utilize only RAM and do not incorporate any DBMS concepts in their operation. Polars overcomes these inefficiencies with parallelism, cache optimization, and query engine.

Key Features of Polars

Now, we will cover the important features of Polars that set it apart from other dataframe libraries.

Apache Arrow Backend

Apache Arrow is an open-source, cross-language development platform designed to accelerate data processing and analytics. It provides a standardized, columnar memory format that optimizes the way data is stored and accessed in memory. This columnar structure is ideal for analytical workloads, as it allows for efficient vectorized execution and better cache locality. This makes data processing faster and more efficient. Arrow is engineered to handle large-scale data with high performance, which is crucial for modern big data applications.

One of Arrow's key features is its ability to facilitate fast, zero-copy data interchange between different programming languages and systems (Refer to *Figure 1.1*). By providing a common memory layout, Arrow allows data to be shared between frameworks, such as Python, R, Java, and C++, without the need for serialization or deserialization. This eliminates the overhead associated with traditional data transfer methods and results in substantial performance improvements when you are moving data across different systems or languages.

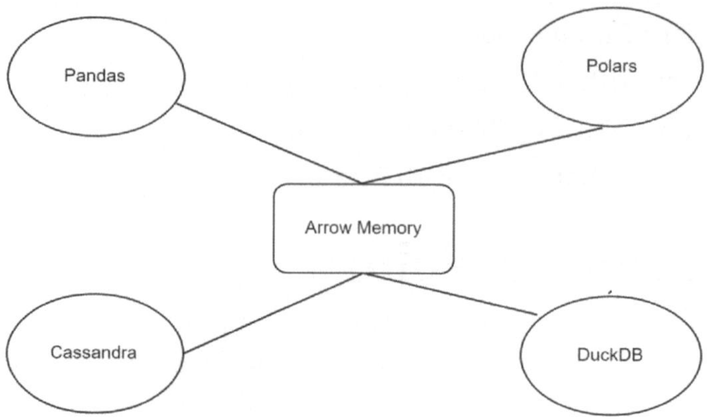

Figure 1.1: *Apache Arrow Zero Copy*

Instead of creating a copy of data and then converting it for a target representation system utilizing Apache Arrow backend can freely transfer data between them.

Arrow's columnar memory format serves as the foundation for several data processing libraries and tools, including Apache Parquet and Polars (Refer *Figure 1.2*). It plays a crucial role in enabling interoperability between various data tools and frameworks, which makes it an essential part of the modern data ecosystem. By providing a unified, efficient memory representation, Apache Arrow not only speeds up data processing but also simplifies data handling, which empowers data engineers and analysts to work more effectively across multiple platforms.

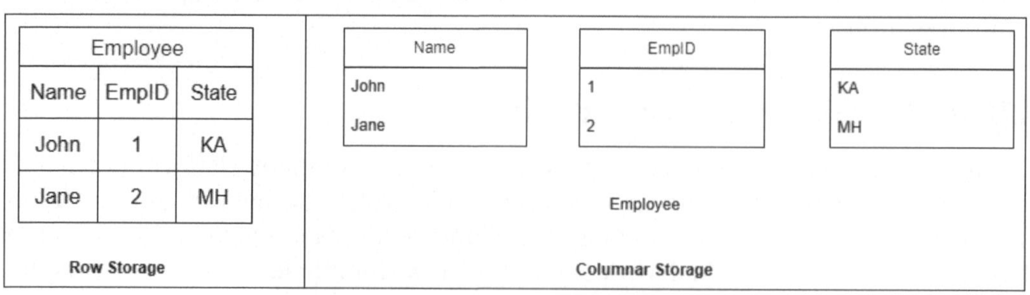

Figure 1.2: *Apache Arrow Columnar Storage*

Columnar storage is better than raw storage for analytical queries because it allows for faster access to specific columns and reduces the need to read unnecessary data. It offers higher compression rates due to the similarity of data within columns, which saves storage space. It excels in read-heavy workloads, especially when only a few columns are queried. Columnar databases enable faster aggregations and calculations by optimizing the data retrieval process. This makes columnar storage ideal for OLAP systems and big data analytics.

Apache Arrow leverages Single Instruction, Multiple Data (SIMD) to optimize data processing, particularly for vectorized operations on large datasets. Its columnar storage format is well-suited for SIMD, as it allows entire columns to be processed simultaneously, rather than individual elements (Refer *Figure* 1.3). This increases performance by enabling faster operations such as filtering and aggregation. Additionally, the columnar layout improves cache utilization and instruction parallelism, which makes Arrow highly efficient for analytical workloads. By taking advantage of SIMD, Arrow accelerates data manipulation, particularly on modern CPUs that are designed to handle vectorized operations.

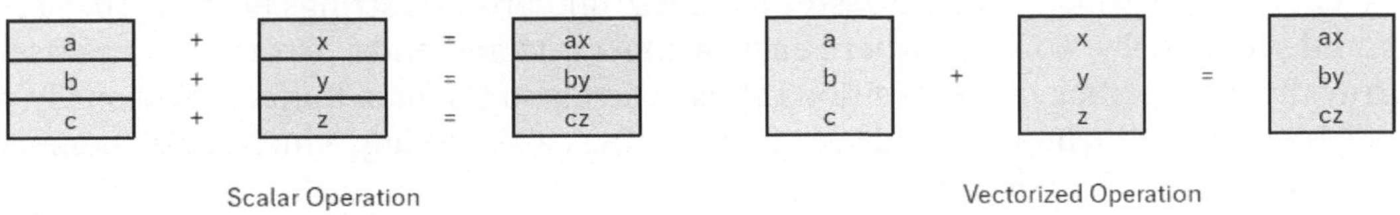

***Figure* 1.3**: *Apache Arrow Vectorized Operations*

Instead of adding elements one by one to each other in a scalar fashion, we add two columns using a single instruction. This results in a vectorized operation.

Apache Arrow Data Types

Apache Arrow provides a rich set of data types tailored for high-performance, in-memory columnar data processing. Its primitive types include integers, floating-point numbers, and booleans, which align closely with traditional data structures while offering precise control over bit widths (for example, int32, float64). Arrow further supports advanced scalar types such as decimal for fixed-point precision, which is often required in financial applications. Its string and binary types enable user to handle text and raw data efficiently and support both variable-length and large-scale storage for datasets with significant size variations. These data types are optimized for analytical tasks and leverage a columnar layout for improved CPU and memory performance.

Numeric Array

In Apache Arrow, numeric arrays are designed with a focus on both performance and clarity, while representing data. Each numeric array contains the actual data values (such as numbers stored as f32 for 32-bit floating-point or u64 for 64-bit unsigned integers) in a data buffer. Alongside this, Arrow always includes a validity buffer, which is a small array of bits. Each bit in the validity buffer indicates whether a corresponding value in the data buffer is valid or missing. This design keeps the memory overhead minimal because only a single bit is used for each value to track its validity.

This approach offers a clear advantage over libraries such as Pandas. In Pandas, missing data is often represented by special values such as NaN for floats, which can be confusing because NaN could mean either "missing data" or "not a number." Arrow, by contrast, makes a clear distinction between valid but undefined values (such as NaN) and genuinely missing data, which ensures more accurate data handling and less ambiguity.

Arrow String Array

The memory layout of an Arrow LargeString array is optimized for performance and efficiency. All the string data is stored in a single continuous block of memory (called the data buffer), which makes it faster to access and process strings because they are stored sequentially. To know where each string starts and ends, Arrow uses an offset array that keeps track of the positions of each string in the data buffer. Additionally, a null-bit buffer is included to indicate if any strings are missing, which saves memory by using only one bit per value.

In contrast, Pandas handles strings as Python objects, which means that each string will be stored separately in memory. This contributes to more memory overhead because each object includes additional metadata about its type. While accessing strings in Pandas, the program jumps around in memory to fetch each string, which can slow things down because it leads to cache misses (when data is not readily available in fast memory).

While Arrow is faster for reading strings due to its sequential layout, it has a drawback. If you filter or select values from an Arrow string array, the entire string data might need to be copied. This is slower and uses more memory. In Pandas, only pointers (references to the string data) are copied, which make such operations faster and less memory-intensive. However, the trade-off is that Pandas' scattered memory layout is less efficient for tasks such as sequential reading.

Parallelization

With CPUs no longer getting significantly faster due to physical limits (end of Moore's Law), modern computers now rely on multiple cores to handle tasks in parallel. Polars is designed to make the best use of this parallelism, as it splits tasks across multiple cores to speed up data processing. Some tasks are naturally easy to run in parallel because they do not need communication or sharing of data between threads. Polars takes advantage of these tasks, such as aggregating columns in a DataFrame or applying functions in group-by operations. Each thread can process its part independently, which makes these operations highly efficient.

Many data operations such as grouping or joining rely on creating hash tables. But splitting these tasks across threads is tricky, if each thread builds its own hash table, the results will need extra work to combine, which can cause delays (synchronization phase).

Sharing one hash table with all threads causes a bottleneck because threads wait for access (locking), which makes parallelism ineffective.

Polars avoid these problems with a lock-free hashing algorithm. Instead of threads waiting on each other:

- Each thread calculates hashes for its data and decides which thread should handle each key. This is based on a simple rule: hash value % thread count.
- This guarantees each thread has unique keys in its hash table.
- Once all threads finish, the results are combined quickly, which makes hashing both parallel and efficient.

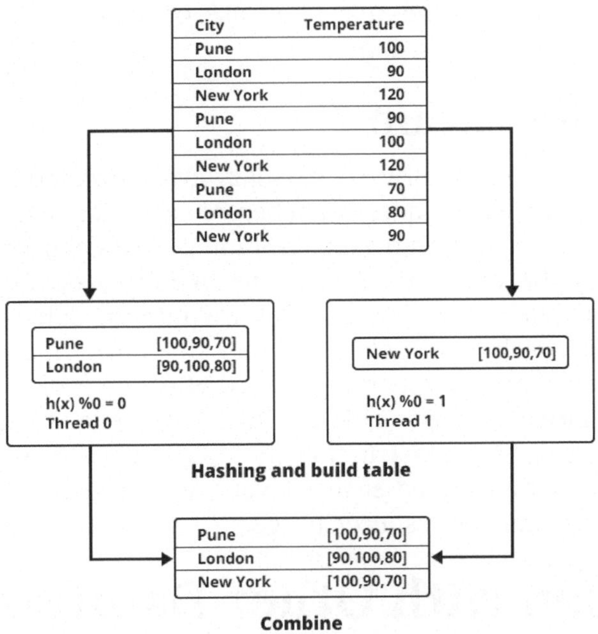

***Figure 1.4**: Lock Free Hashing*

The expression hash_value % thread_number is commonly used in hash-based partitioning to distribute data or tasks across multiple threads in a balanced manner. Here is a detailed explanation:

- **Hash Value:** A hash function takes an input (such as a data element or key) and produces a numeric value (the "hash value") that uniquely represents the input.

The hash value is deterministic as the same input yields the same hash, but it appears as random for varied inputs.

- **Modulo Operation (%):** The modulo operation computes the remainder when the hash value is divided by the total number of threads (thread_number). This ensures that the result is always in the range [0, thread_number - 1].
- **Thread Assignment:** The result of hash_value % thread_number determines the thread responsible for processing that particular data element. Each result corresponds to a thread ID (for example, 0, 1, 2, ..., thread_number - 1).

Key Benefits:

- **Even Distribution:** After assuming that the hash function distributes values uniformly, the modulo operation ensures that data or tasks are evenly spread across all threads.
- **Deterministic Mapping**: The same input will always map to the same thread, which will bring about consistency in task allocation.

This innovative approach ensures maximum use of parallelism, while avoiding the delays of synchronization and locking.

Query Optimization

Query optimization in Polars is driven by its lazy evaluation model, which allows the framework to analyze the entire query plan before execution and apply optimizations for efficiency. When using lazy frames (LazyFrame), Polars constructs a logical query plan that describes the data transformations. Before executing the plan, Polars applies optimizations such as predicate pushdown (filtering data early in the pipeline), projection pushdown (selecting only necessary columns), and join simplifications (optimizing the way datasets are merged). Additionally, Polars benefits from its columnar memory model and uses efficient Rust-based execution to process data in parallel, while leveraging Single Instruction, Multiple Data (SIMD) operations for faster computation. These optimizations enable Polars to handle large datasets with high performance while minimizing resource usage.

Comparison with Other Dataframe Libraries

Polars is a high-performance DataFrame library designed to handle large datasets efficiently, while leveraging modern hardware features such as multi-threading and Single Instruction Multiple Data (SIMD). While Pandas, Dask, and PySpark are widely used, Polars stands out with its focus on performance, simplicity, and a unique query engine inspired by SQL. The following is a comparison of Polars with these libraries (Refer *Table 1.1*):

Polars versus Pandas

Performance

Polars is significantly faster than Pandas for large datasets because of their columnar memory layout, lazy evaluation, and multi-threaded execution. Pandas processes data row by row, which is less efficient for analytical workloads.

Scalability

Pandas struggles with datasets larger than memory. Polars, on the other hand, uses memory-efficient techniques and can handle out-of-core computations with tools such as Arrow or by chunking data.

API and Features

Both libraries have intuitive APIs, but Polars introduces additional features such as lazy frames for query optimization and parallel execution.

Polars versus Dask

Parallelism

Dask provides parallelism by splitting data into smaller Pandas-like DataFrames, while Polars natively supports multi-threading and SIMD for faster computation. Polars' built-in parallelism is easier to use compared to Dask's chunk-based setup.

Ease of Use

Polars is simpler to work with as it does not require manual tuning of partitions or task graphs such as Dask.

Scalability

Dask is designed for distributed computing and scales well across clusters. Polars is more suited for single-machine environments but is optimized to handle large datasets efficiently within that constraint.

Polars versus PySpark

Performance

For single-machine workloads, Polars outperforms PySpark due to its optimized execution model and lack of overhead from distributed systems. However, PySpark excels in distributed environments and scales effortlessly across multiple nodes.

Ease of Use

PySpark has a steeper learning curve, requiring knowledge of Spark internals. Polars, with its Pythonic API, is more beginner-friendly and integrates seamlessly into Python workflows.

Deployment

PySpark is ideal for big data and distributed systems. Polars shines in scenarios where performance on a single machine is critical without the complexity of a distributed setup.

Metric	Polars	Pandas	Dask	PySpark
Execution Model	Multi-threaded, SIMD	Single-threaded	Parallel (Chunked Pandas)	Distributed
Performance	Fastest for single machine	Slower for large data	Good for medium workloads	Best for distributed systems
Scalability	Single machine, large data	Limited by memory	Scales across a cluster	Designed for distributed
Optimizations	Lazy evaluation, Arrow-based	None	Task graph optimizations	Optimized for distributed ops
Best Use Case	Single-machine, large data	Small to medium data	Medium to large-distributed	Large-scale distributed

Table 1.1: *Polars versus Incumbent Dataframe Libraries*

Polars versus Pandas

To compare the execution times of Polars and Pandas. We will be creating a dataframe with 10 million rows using Pandas and Polars, with two columns: id (containing random integers between 1 and 100) and 9 value columns (containing random float values).

- Perform a groupby operation on the id column and calculate the following aggregations for each of the 9 value columns:
  - Sum
  - Mean
  - Max
  - Min
- Measuring the execution time of these operations using timeit to compare the performance between Pandas and Polars.

Pandas: A straightforward, single-threaded approach for performing the groupby aggregation, which is suitable for small-to-medium datasets, but is potentially slower with larger datasets like 10 million rows.

Polars: It uses LazyFrames for deferred execution, which optimizes the computation by deferring the operation and optimizing the execution plan. This makes Polars much faster than Pandas for large datasets, as it can leverage multi-threading and efficiently manage memory.

Now let us perform a simple comparison of Pandas and Polars. We will generate 10 million rows of data, with random integers between 1 and 100 for the ids column and random float values for 9 values columns using numpy. A seed is set for reproducibility of the random values, as shown here:

```
import numpy as np
# Set random seed for reproducibility
np.random.seed(42)
# Generate 10 million rows
ids = np.random.randint(1, 101, size=10_000_000)  # Random integers
between 1 and 100
values = np.random.rand(10_000_000, 9)  # Random float values, 9 value
columns
```

Now, we will create a Pandas DataFrame with 9 value columns and an id column, and then perform a groupby operation on the id column. We will also calculate the sum, mean, max, and min for each value column.

```
import pandas as pd
import timeit
# Create the Pandas DataFrame
df_pandas = pd.DataFrame(values, columns=[f'value_{i}' for i in range(1,
10)])
df_pandas['id'] = ids
# Measure the execution time for groupby operation
pandas_time = timeit.timeit(lambda: df_pandas.groupby('id')[['value_1',
'value_2', 'value_3', 'value_4', 'value_5',
                                                                 'value_6',
'value_7', 'value_8', 'value_9']].agg(['sum', 'mean', 'max', 'min']),
number=5)

print(f"Pandas execution time: {pandas_time} seconds")
```

Now, we will perform the same operation using Polars Lazyframe, as shown here:

```
import polars as pl
import timeit
# Create the Polars LazyFrame
df_polars_lazy = pl.LazyFrame({f'value_{i}': values[:, i-1] for i in
range(1, 10)}).with_columns(pl.lit(ids).alias('id'))
# Measure the execution time for groupby operation
polars_lazy_time = timeit.timeit(lambda: df_polars_lazy.group_by('id')
.agg([pl.col(f'value_{i}').sum().alias(f'sum_value_{i}') for i in
range(1, 10)] +
                                      [pl.col(f'value_{i}').mean().
alias(f'mean_value_{i}') for i in range(1, 10)] +
```

```
                                              [pl.col(f'value_{i}').max().
alias(f'max_value_{i}') for i in range(1, 10)] +
                                              [pl.col(f'value_{i}').min().
alias(f'min_value_{i}') for i in range(1, 10)])
                                        .collect(), number=5)

print(f"Polars LazyFrame execution time: {polars_lazy_time} seconds")
```

The execution times for the groupby operation with aggregation on a dataset of 10 million rows show a clear performance advantage which Polars has over Pandas. Pandas took 7.76 seconds, while Polars, using a LazyFrame, completed the same task in 4.06 seconds. This significant difference in execution time demonstrates the efficiency of Polars, especially with large datasets. Polars' ability to optimize computations using lazy execution and leverage multi-threading allows it to outperform Pandas, which is single-threaded and may struggle with large data sizes. The results underline the benefits of using Polars for data processing tasks that involve larger volumes of data.

The preceding example presents a simple case of benchmarking for groupby operations between Pandas and Polars. However, in real-world scenarios, benchmarking data processing frameworks involves considering various factors to get accurate, reliable, and meaningful results. Some of the key considerations include:

- **Data Size:** Benchmarking should be done with different dataset sizes (small, medium, large) to understand how frameworks scale.
- **Memory Usage:** Monitor memory consumption alongside execution time, as some libraries may perform faster, but use more memory.
- **Data Complexity:** Complex data types (for example, nested structures, string manipulations) can impact performance differently across libraries.
- **Concurrency/Parallelism:** For multi-threaded or distributed frameworks, measure performance with varying numbers of threads or worker nodes.
- **Hardware/Environment**: Benchmark results can vary based on the machine's CPU, memory, and storage configuration, as well as the software environment.
- **Data Preprocessing**: Preprocessing steps (such as cleaning, transformation, or feature engineering) should be considered, as they can affect the overall performance.
- **I/O Operations:** Consider disk read/write operations, if working with large datasets stored on disk (rather than in memory).
- **Latencies:** Measure latency for individual operations to identify bottlenecks that can affect the overall performance.
- **Algorithmic Optimizations**: Some frameworks may have built-in optimizations, while others may require manual fine-tuning (for example, indexing, caching).

- **Real-World Workflows**: Benchmark real-world tasks (for example, joins and complex aggregations) rather than isolated operations to capture performance under practical workloads.

Considering all these factors ensures that the benchmark results accurately reflect the performance of data processing frameworks in a production environment. We will cover these in depth in the upcoming chapters.

Installation of Polars in Python Environment

Now, we will cover how to install Python and Polars on your machine. If you would like to follow along with the book then you can install all the packages from the requirements file provided in the repository.

1. **Install Python**

   Step 1: Download and install Python from the official Python website.

   Visit https://www.python.org/downloads/.

   Choose the appropriate installer based on your operating system (Windows, macOS, Linux).

   Windows: Make sure to check the box "Add Python to PATH" during installation for easier access via the command line.

   macOS/Linux: Python should already be installed on your system by default, but if not, you can install it using Homebrew (for macOS) or the package manager (for Linux, sudo apt; install python3 for Ubuntu).

   Step 2: Verify the Python installation as follows:

   ```
   python --version
   Or for Python 3:
   ```

   ```
   python3 -version
   ```

2. **Install Polars**

   Once Python is installed, follow these steps to install Polars:

   Step 1: Open your terminal/command prompt.

   Step 2: Install Polars using pip (Python's package installer):

   ```
   pip install polars
   ```

   Or for Python 3 specifically, use:

   ```
   pip3 install polars
   ```

Step 3: Verify that Polars is installed correctly by running the following:

```
import polars as pl
print(pl.__version__)
```

This will print the version of Polars, while confirming the installation.

Note: *You can also install Polars with all optional dependencies via the following command:*

```
pip install 'polars[all]'
```

If you are expecting to encounter a row count > 4.2 billion, then you can consider using the following command for installation:

```
pip install polars-u64-idx
```

Our First Dataframe with Polars

The code reads a CSV file directly into a DataFrame using the pl.read_csv() function. This loads the data immediately and allows you to work with it without the need for lazy evaluation. The first 5 rows of the DataFrame are printed using df.head(), which provides a quick preview of the data. This approach is simple and efficient for cases where you want to perform immediate operations on the dataset.

```
import polars as pl

# Step 1: Define the path to the CSV file
csv_file_path = r"C:\Polars-book\Chapter1\\"+'large_dataframe.csv'  #
Replace with your actual file path

# Step 2: Read the CSV file using Polars
# Polars reads the CSV file and loads it into a DataFrame by default
df = pl.read_csv(csv_file_path)

# Step 3: Print the first 5 rows (head) of the DataFrame
print(df.head())
```

Output:

shape: (5, 10)

col_1 --- f64	col_2 --- f64	col_3 --- f64	col_4 --- f64	…	col_7 --- f64	col_8 --- f64	col_9 --- f64	col_10 --- f64
-1.182901	-2.467077	0.869938	0.022906	…	0.304478	0.012752	0.804861	1.718607
-0.170019	0.365224	-0.086186	0.81293	…	-1.029503	0.54984	0.62414	1.206564
-0.142156	0.006468	-0.70849	-0.458606	…	2.396807	1.330939	-1.342845	0.874591
0.11241	-0.058192	0.675886	0.739299	…	-0.852386	-0.242498	0.634894	0.693562
-0.274246	-0.679662	0.596456	0.46892	…	-1.822351	0.969387	-0.800207	-0.787063

Figure 1.5: *Preview of Dataframe Using df.head()*

Conclusion

Polars is a high-performance dataframe library designed for modern data processing needs. It outperforms traditional libraries such as Pandas for large-scale data operations due to its parallel execution, efficient memory usage, and innovative features such as lazy evaluation. With its simple API, high-performance backend, and ability to handle large datasets efficiently, Polars is well-positioned for data-intensive tasks in both academic and industry settings. In the next chapter, we will explore the foundational data types in Polars, including Series and DataFrames for efficient data handling. We will cover optimized numeric and temporal types for high-performance calculations and precise date/time management. Additionally, we will discuss nested and string data types for handling complex and textual data efficiently.

Key Takeaways

- **Polars**: It is an open-source dataframe library designed for high performance, especially with large datasets. It started in 2020 and was developed using Rust, with Python being one of its primary interfaces. Polars focuses on fast, parallelized execution with memory-efficient data processing, which makes it well-suited for both single-node and large-scale data tasks.
- **Performance and Scalability**: Pandas is a widely used dataframe library but is single-threaded and less optimized for large datasets. Polars improves upon this by utilizing parallelism, SIMD (Single Instruction Multiple Data), and Apache Arrow backend for better memory utilization and faster execution.

  While Pandas struggle with memory-intensive operations, Polars efficiently handles large datasets, often outperforming Pandas in operations such as groupby, aggregation, and complex transformations.
- **Apache Arrow Integration**: Polars leverage the Apache Arrow columnar memory format, thereby optimizing both storage and computation. Arrow's memory layout is designed for high-performance analytical queries, with zero-copy data exchange and efficient storage. This enables faster access to specific columns and supports vectorized execution for more efficient data manipulation, especially in large-scale datasets.
- **Lazy Evaluation:** Polars introduces LazyFrames, allowing deferred execution. This enables query optimization, parallel execution, and efficient computation, which helps in minimizing unnecessary operations.
- **Parallelization**: Polars fully exploit multi-core CPUs, distributing tasks across threads to process data in parallel. It avoids common issues such as synchronization and locking, which results in maximum performance.

- **Comparison with Other Libraries**:
  - **Pandas**: Best for small to medium datasets, but slower and memory-intensive for larger datasets. It does not utilize parallelism or advanced optimizations.
  - **Dask:** Focuses on parallelism and scalability but requires manual tuning of partitions and task graphs. It is ideal for larger distributed workloads, but can be more complex than Polars.
  - **PySpark**: Suited for distributed computing and large-scale operations across clusters. However, it has more overhead for single-node tasks compared to Polars, which excels in local data processing with minimal overhead.

Polars can be installed easily with pip, which makes it accessible for Python users. You can install the library with pip install Polars, and verify the installation by importing the library and checking the version. Additionally, you can install Polars with all the optional dependencies for enhanced functionality and better handling of large row counts.

Exercises

1. Benchmarking Polars versus Dask: In this chapter, we have performed a simple benchmarking comparison between Polars and Pandas. Now, perform a similar comparison between Polars and Dask. Measure the execution time for similar operations (for example, creating a DataFrame, groupby aggregation, and so on.), and note down your observations on:
   - Execution Time
   - Memory Usage (If Possible)
   - Ease of Use
2. Working with JSON Data:
   - Create a DataFrame from the JSON file provided in this chapter's repository.
   - After loading the data into a Polars DataFrame, try to export it to CSV format and confirm the process by checking the file.
   - Make sure to check for any challenges or nuances you encounter, while converting from JSON to CSV.

CHAPTER 2
Core Concepts of Data Frames and Data Structures

"Data that is organized is knowledge; knowledge that is applied is wisdom."

Unknown

Introduction

In data analysis, the choice of data structures can significantly impact the efficiency and flexibility of your workflows. Polars, a high-performance DataFrame library, offers a robust set of foundational data types designed to handle diverse and complex data seamlessly. This chapter will act as a comprehensive guide to these data types and will help you unlock the full potential of Polars in your analytical projects.

By mastering these data types, you will be able to master the tools to manipulate and analyze data efficiently and pave the way for advanced applications and deeper insights. Thus, whether you are working with numbers, timestamps, hierarchical data, or text, this chapter will provide the foundational knowledge required to use Polars effectively.

Structure

In this chapter, we will discuss the following topics:

- The Rise of DataFrames
- Series and DataFrame Representation
  - Polar Data Types
  - Numeric Data Types
  - Temporal Data Types

- Nested Data Types
- String Data Types
- Other Data Types

The Rise of DataFrames

In the realm of data analysis and manipulation, DataFrames have emerged as a critical structure due to their versatility and efficiency. They provide a tabular, column-oriented format, which makes them intuitive to use and well-suited for representing structured data.

Let us have a look at the advantages and disadvantages of DataFrames over other data representations:

Human-Readable Representation:

- DataFrames organize3 data into rows and columns, akin to spreadsheets or database tables. This makes them easy to read and understand for users.
- It simplifies exploration and analysis by offering a clear and intuitive format for both analysts and developers.

Efficient Handling of Heterogeneous Data:

- Unlike traditional arrays or matrices, DataFrames allow columns to store data of different types (for example, integers, st.rings, dates).
- This flexibility is essential for real-world datasets, which often include mixed data types.

Columnar Operations for Speed and Simplicity:

- DataFrames enable vectorized operations, which allows users to perform calculations on entire columns without writing explicit loops.

Seamless Integration with Data Pipelines:

- DataFrames integrate easily with various data sources (for example, databases, CSV files, APIs) and can become the foundation for more complex transformations.
- Their compatibility with modern data ecosystems makes them indispensable for ETL (Extract, Transform, Load) processes.

Advanced-Data Manipulation and Analysis:

- DataFrames support a wide range of operations such as grouping, aggregating, filtering, and joining datasets.
- This makes them far more powerful than basic data structures such as dictionaries, arrays, or lists.

Rich Ecosystem of Tools and Libraries:

- Libraries like Polars, Pandas, and Apache Arrow build on the DataFrame concept and offer tools for visualization, machine learning, and statistical analysis.
- This ecosystem results in seamless workflows, from preprocessing to final insights.

Here is a comparison table of different data representation methodologies:

Feature	DataFrames	Arrays	Dictionaries	SQL Tables
Human Readability	High (tabular format)	Low	Medium	High (relational)
Heterogeneous Data	Yes (column-specific)	No	Yes	Yes
Performance	Optimized for operations	High for numerical	Medium	High but static
Ease of Use	Intuitive and flexible	Requires indexing	Requires keys	Requires SQL queries
Ecosystem	Extensive (tools/libraries)	Basic (math ops)	Limited	Static for analytics

Table 2.1: *Dataframes Vs Other Data Representations*

DataFrames are more than just a convenient way to store data; they are a gateway to efficient, scalable, and versatile data analysis. Their ability to handle heterogeneous data, perform high-speed operations, and integrate with modern ecosystems makes them a cornerstone of data science and engineering workflows. Thus, by leveraging DataFrames, analysts can focus on deriving insights rather than managing data complexities.

Series and DataFrame Representation

A Series is the building block of a DataFrame and represents a one-dimensional array of data with a labeled index. Think of a Series as a single column in a DataFrame. It can hold data of a single type (for example, integers, floats, strings, or objects). Moreover, its labeled index makes it more versatile and powerful than a simple array.

For example, in Polars, a Series is essentially a sequence of values with an associated index. It is demonstrated here:

Index	Value
0	20
1	30
2	40
4	10

Table 2.2: *A Series*

The ability to focus on individual Series within a DataFrame allows for granular control over data and facilitates more precise transformations and calculations. This modular nature of Series makes them invaluable for breaking down complex datasets into manageable components.

One of the defining features of a Series is its labeled index, which provides a unique and intuitive way to access specific data points. Unlike arrays that rely on raw numerical indices, a Series leverages meaningful labels, which makes accessing data easier and more readable. This labeled indexing system also supports various data types such as numerical values, strings, and timestamps. This attribute makes Series highly adaptable to diverse analytical needs. Beyond being a simple column, a Series is versatile enough to stand alone for smaller datasets or intermediate calculations. Therefore, it often serves as a temporary structure during transformations or filtering tasks.

The importance of a Series extends to its role in visualization and other downstream applications. In many data visualization workflows, a Series can directly feed into tools for plotting, which simplfies the process of creating charts or graphs for one-dimensional data. This avoids the need for converting single columns into full DataFrames, which saves both time and computational resources. Furthermore, the ability to store and process data efficiently ensures that a Series is not just a passive container, but an active participant in data manipulation, as it provides the foundation for more complex operations and insights.

While a Series is a component of a DataFrame, their relationship is symbiotic. A DataFrame can be seen as a "container" that organizes multiple Series, while each Series acts as an independent yet interconnected entity. This modularity allows DataFrames to benefit from the simplicity of Series while extending their capabilities to multi-dimensional data analysis. Understanding how to transition between these two structures (by extracting Series from a DataFrame or combining multiple Series into a DataFrame) is a crucial skill in advanced data manipulation.

By leveraging the unique strengths of both Series and DataFrames, analysts and engineers can efficiently manage, analyze, and visualize structured data. This can also help them create insights that drive informed decision-making. You can consider the following example:

```
import polars as pl

# Create three Series
series1 = pl.Series("ages", [25, 30, 35, 40])          # Integer
series
series2 = pl.Series("heights", [5.8, 6.0, 5.5, 5.9])    # Float series
series3 = pl.Series("names", ["Alice", "Bob", "Charlie", "David"])  #
String series

# Create a DataFrame using the Series
df = pl.DataFrame([series1, series2, series3])
```

```
# Print the resulting DataFrame
print(df)
shape: (4, 3)
┌──────┬─────────┬─────────┐
│ ages ┆ heights ┆ names   │
│ ---  ┆ ---     ┆ ---     │
│ i64  ┆ f64     ┆ str     │
╞══════╪═════════╪═════════╡
│ 25   ┆ 5.8     ┆ Alice   │
│ 30   ┆ 6.0     ┆ Bob     │
│ 35   ┆ 5.5     ┆ Charlie │
│ 40   ┆ 5.9     ┆ David   │
└──────┴─────────┴─────────┘
```

Explanation

- **Series Creation**
  - series1 is an Integer series representing ages.
  - series2 is a Float series representing heights.
  - series3 is a String series representing names.
- **DataFrame Creation**
  - These three Series are passed into the pl.DataFrame() function, which combines them into a single DataFrame.
- **Result**: The final DataFrame has three columns: ages (integer), heights (float), and names (string), where each corresponds to one of the Series that were created earlier.

This approach demonstrates how to create individual Series and then combine them into a DataFrame in Polars, thus enabling flexible data structure creation.

Polars Data Types

Polars provides a robust framework for data manipulation and analysis by offering a comprehensive range of data types. These data types are designed to handle diverse real-world datasets efficiently while ensuring compatibility with modern analytical needs. Unlike traditional data structures, Polars leverage strong typing to optimize memory usage and computation speed, which makes it ideal for handling large-scale datasets. Its data types include numerical types for handling integers and floating-point values, temporal types for managing dates and times with precision, and string types for efficient text processing. By explicitly defining these types, Polars ensure faster operations, better error handling, and more predictable behavior in data workflows.

What sets Polars apart from others is its support for advanced and specialized data types such as nested types. This allows for hierarchical or complex data structures, and categorical types, which are then optimized for repeated textual data in large datasets. These types enable users to store and process data with varying levels of granularity while maintaining scalability and performance. Moreover, the type-awareness of Polars ensures compatibility with its high-performance query engine. This ability allows users to perform transformations, aggregations, and filtering operations seamlessly.

Let us now explore various Polars data types.

Numeric Data Types

Polars offers a comprehensive set of numeric data types designed to handle numerical values with high performance and precision. These data types are fundamental for mathematical computations, statistical analysis, and machine learning (ML) workflows. Polars supports both integer and floating-point types and also caters to different levels of precision and memory efficiency. Integer types range from 8-bit to 64-bit, which bring about flexibility in handling small integers efficiently or representing large numbers without overflow. Floating-point types (32-bit and 64-bit) ensure the accuracy required for scientific computations and financial modeling, where precision is a critical attribute.

One of the key advantages of Polars' numeric data types is their seamless integration with its query engine, which enables efficient vectorized operations. This design allows for optimized performance during complex operations like aggregations, transformations, and mathematical calculations. Polars also support null values in numeric columns and facilitates robust handling of missing or incomplete data.

Polars provide a variety of numeric data types, where each is tailored for specific use cases based on range, precision, and memory requirements. These types are essential for handling numerical data efficiently in large-scale data analysis. Here is a list of Polars' numeric data types with examples:

- **Integer Types**
    - **Int8**: A signed 8-bit integer, ranging from -128 to 127

      Example: [-128, -45, 0, 45, 127]
    - **Int16**: A signed 16-bit integer, ranging from -32,768 to 32,767

      Example : [-32768, -100, 0, 100, 32767]
    - **Int32**: A signed 32-bit integer, ranging from -2,147,483,648 to 2,147,483,647

      Example : [-2147483648, 0, 100000, 2147483647]

- **Int64:** A signed 64-bit integer, which is capable of representing very large numbers

  Example: [-9223372036854775808, 0, 1000000000000,9223372036854775807]

- **UInt8:** An unsigned 8-bit integer, ranging from 0 to 255

  Example: [0, 45, 100, 200, 255]

- **UInt16**: An unsigned 16-bit integer, ranging from 0 to 65,535

  Example:[0, 500, 10000, 65535]

- **UInt32**: An unsigned 32-bit integer, ranging from 0 to 4,294,967,295

  Example: [0, 100000, 2000000000, 4294967295]

- **UInt64**: An unsigned 64-bit integer used for very large positive numbers

  Example: [0, 1000000000000, 18446744073709551615]

- **Floating-Point Types**
  - **Float32**: A 32-bit floating-point number, which supports decimal values with limited precision

    Example: [0.0, 3.14, -1.23, 100000.5]

  - **Float64:** A 64-bit floating-point number, which offers higher precision for scientific or financial computations

    Example: [0.00001, -12345.6789, 3.1415926535, 1e10]

When selecting the right numeric data type, it is essential to consider the nature of the data and the specific requirements of the analysis. Integer types should be used when dealing with whole numbers, as they are efficient in terms of memory usage and computational speed. For datasets that require precision with decimal values, floating-point types are the better choice, as they allow for more accurate calculations with fractional numbers. Smaller bit-width types, such as Int8 or UInt8, are ideal when you are working with data that fits within narrower ranges. This is because they optimize performance and reduce memory consumption. On the other hand, for datasets that require high precision or need to handle very large values, larger types like Int64 or Float64 should be used, as they can represent a wider range of numbers and offer greater accuracy. However, this gain is observed at the cost of increased memory usage. Understanding these trade-offs is crucial for optimizing both performance and resource utilization in data processing.

We can summarize numeric data types of Polars as follows:

Sr No	Data Type	Signed/ Unsigned	Bit Width	Range	Use Case	Memory Utilized (per value)
1	**Int8**	Signed	8	-128 to 127	Small integers with minimal memory usage	1 byte
2	**Int16**	Signed	16	-32,768 to 32,767	Medium-range integers	2 bytes
3	**Int32**	Signed	32	-2,147,483,648 to 2,147,483,647	General-purpose integers for large datasets	4 bytes
4	**Int64**	Signed	64	-9,223,372,036,854, 775,808 to 9,223, 372,036,854,775,807	Very large integers	8 bytes
5	**UInt8**	Unsigned	8	0 to 255	Positive small integers, memory efficiency	1 byte
6	**UInt16**	Unsigned	16	0 to 65,535	Medium-range positive integers	2 bytes
7	**UInt32**	Unsigned	32	0 to 4,294,967,295	Large positive integers, e.g., ID columns	4 bytes
8	**UInt64**	Unsigned	64	0 to 18,446,744, 073,709,551,615	Very large positive integers	8 bytes
9	**Float32**	Signed	32	~ ±3.4e38	Decimal values with limited precision	4 bytes
10	**Float64**	Signed	64	~ ±1.8e308	High-precision decimal values, scientific data	8 bytes

Table 2.3: *Numeric Data Types*

Here is an example of a Polars DataFrame with numerical data types:

```
import polars as pl

# Creating a DataFrame with Integer and Float columns
df = pl.DataFrame({
    "ages": [25, 30, 35, 40],          # Integer column
    "heights": [5.8, 6.0, 5.5, 5.9]   # Float column
})

# Printing the DataFrame
print(df)
```

Output:

```
shape: (4, 2)
┌──────┬─────────┐
│ ages ┆ heights │
│ ---  ┆ ---     │
│ i64  ┆ f64     │
╞══════╪═════════╡
│ 25   ┆ 5.8     │
│ 30   ┆ 6.0     │
│ 35   ┆ 5.5     │
│ 40   ┆ 5.9     │
└──────┴─────────┘
```

Temporal Data Types

Polars provides robust temporal data types to handle date and time values efficiently, while enabling precise operations and analysis in time-sensitive data applications. Temporal data types are crucial for a wide range of tasks such as time series analysis, financial modeling, event tracking, and data logging. Polars offers specialized types for representing dates, times, and timestamps, where each is optimized for high performance and ensures accuracy in handling temporal data.

The primary temporal data types in Polars are Date, Time, Duration, and Datetime. The Date type represents calendar dates without any associated time, which makes it ideal for scenarios like tracking dates of events or transactions. The Time type, on the other hand, captures specific times of the day without reference to a particular date, and is useful for situations such as recording event durations or schedules. The Datetime type combines both date and time information, which allows for precise representation of points in time that is essential for time series data or for tracking events that occur at specific times. The Duration data type in Polars is used to represent time intervals or differences between two timestamps.

Here are the Polars code examples for each of the primary temporal data types that demonstrate how to work with these types in Polars

The Date type is used to store calendar dates. You can create a Date column in a Polars DataFrame by using `pl.date()`, as shown here:

```
import polars as pl

# Create a DataFrame with date strings (must be in YYYY-MM-DD format)
df_date_strings = pl.DataFrame({
    "event_date_str": ["2024-06-01", "2024-02-15", "2024-12-25"]
})

# Use .with_columns and .cast(pl.Date) to convert the string column to a
Date column
```

```
df_date_casted = df_date_strings.with_columns(
    pl.col("event_date_str").cast(pl.Date).alias("event_date")
).select("event_date") # Keep only the new Date column

print("\n--- Using String Dates with .cast(pl.Date) ---")
print(df_date_casted)
print(df_date_casted.schema)
```

Output:

```
--- Using String Dates with .cast(pl.Date) ---
shape: (3, 1)
┌────────────┐
│ event_date │
│ ---        │
│ date       │
╞════════════╡
│ 2024-06-01 │
│ 2024-02-15 │
│ 2024-12-25 │
└────────────┘
Schema({'event_date': Date})
```

The Time type represents only the time of day (without a date). You can use `pl.time()` to create a Time column in Polars, as follows:

```
import polars as pl

# Creating a DataFrame with a Time column
df_time = pl.DataFrame({
    "event_time": [pl.time("08:30:00"), pl.time("15:45:30"),
pl.time("23:59:59")]
})

print(df_time)
```

Output:

```
shape: (3, 1)
┌──────────────────────────────────┐
│ event_time                       │
│ ---                              │
│ object                           │
╞══════════════════════════════════╡
│ dyn int: 1970.dt.datetime([dyn… │
│ dyn int: 1970.dt.datetime([dyn… │
│ dyn int: 1970.dt.datetime([dyn… │
└──────────────────────────────────┘
```

The Duration type is used to represent the amount of time between two timestamps. You can create a Duration column using `pl.duration()`, as demonstrated in this example:

```
import polars as pl
from datetime import datetime
# Creating a DataFrame with a Date column
df_date = pl.DataFrame(
    {
        "event_date": [datetime(2024, 6, 1), datetime(2025, 12,
3),datetime(2025, 12, 3)],
        "delta": [1, 2,3],
    }
)
print("dataframe at begining")
print(df_date)
print("dates after adding duration")
print(df_date.select(
        (pl.col("event_date") + pl.duration(hours="delta")).
alias("hours_delta"),
    ))
```

Output:

```
dataframe at beginning
shape: (3, 2)
```

event_date --- datetime[μs]	delta --- i64
2024-06-01 00:00:00	1
2025-12-03 00:00:00	2
2025-12-03 00:00:00	3

```
dates after adding duration
shape: (3, 1)
```

hours_delta --- datetime[μs]
2024-06-01 01:00:00
2025-12-03 02:00:00
2025-12-03 03:00:00

The Datetime type combines both date and time. You can create a Datetime column using `pl.datetime()` or datetime, as shown here:

```
import polars as pl

# Creating a DataFrame with a Datetime column
df_datetime = pl.DataFrame({
    "event_datetime": [
            datetime(2024, 6, 11, 10, 10, 0),
            datetime(2025, 7, 12, 20, 7, 0),
            datetime(2026, 8, 10, 9, 8, 0),
        ]
})

print(df_datetime)
```

Output:

```
shape: (3, 1)
┌─────────────────────┐
│ event_datetime      │
│ ---                 │
│ datetime[μs]        │
╞═════════════════════╡
│ 2024-06-11 10:10:00 │
│ 2025-07-12 20:07:00 │
│ 2026-08-10 09:08:00 │
└─────────────────────┘
```

We will address how to work with temporal data types in the upcoming chapters.

Nested Data Types

In Polars, Nested Data Types refer to data structures that allow for complex, hierarchical data within a single column of a DataFrame. These data types enable more advanced data modeling by allowing columns to contain lists, structs, or even combinations of both. Nested data types are particularly useful when working with JSON-like data, hierarchical or nested records, and when dealing with data that has a natural structure of arrays or objects within each record.

Polars supports two primary forms of nested data types: List and Struct. These are explained as follows:

List Data Type

The List type allows a column to store an array of values. Each entry in the list can contain multiple elements, which enables the representation of sequences or collections of data. For example, a column could store lists of numbers, strings, or even other nested types. The list data type is highly beneficial when working with datasets where each record has a variable-length collection of values, such as transaction histories, event logs, or sensor readings over time.

Polars optimizes list operations, making it easy to apply transformations, perform aggregations, and filter data within nested lists. The flexibility of the List type allows for working with data that does not follow a strict tabular format, such as records containing multiple tags or attributes per entry.

Struct Data Type

The Struct type in Polars allows columns to hold complex objects consisting of multiple named fields. This is similar to a record or a dictionary in other languages, where each element is associated with a field name. A Struct type enables the representation of structured data within a single column, where each record is a combination of multiple attributes. For instance, a Struct column might contain a combination of a person's name, age, and address in one column, or it could represent a product with fields like price, quantity, and category.

The Struct type is particularly useful when dealing with semi-structured data, like JSON records, where each entry may contain a set of related attributes. With Polars, users can access and manipulate the fields within a struct, apply transformations to individual elements, and perform operations on the structured data directly.

Benefits and Use Cases

Nested data types in Polars offer a variety of benefits. First, they allow for more natural representation of real-world data that does not fit neatly into a traditional tabular structure. For example, a product catalog might have varying attributes across different product types, which can be efficiently modeled using Struct columns. Similarly, transactions may involve lists of items, and a List column can easily represent such variable-length data.

Moreover, these nested types are highly optimized for performance in Polars. Operations on List and Struct types are fast and memory-efficient, even for large datasets. This makes Polars an excellent choice for handling complex data structures, as it enables users to apply complex transformations, aggregations, and queries on hierarchical data without sacrificing performance.

Example:

```
import polars as pl

# Creating a DataFrame with List and Struct columns
df = pl.DataFrame({
```

```
    "names": [["Aarav", "Ishaan", "Raghav"], ["Saanvi", "Ananya"],
["Vivaan"]],
    "addresses": [
        {"street": "12 MG Road", "city": "Delhi", "zipcode": "110001",
"country": "India"},
        {"street": "22 Abbey Road", "city": "London", "zipcode": "W1A
1AA", "country": "UK"},
        {"street": "56 Park Avenue", "city": "New York", "zipcode":
"10016", "country": "USA"}
    ]
})

print(df)
```

Output:

```
shape: (3, 2)
```

names --- list[str]	addresses --- struct[4]
["Aarav", "Ishaan", "Raghav"]	{"12 MG Road","Delhi","110001"…
["Saanvi", "Ananya"]	{"22 Abbey Road","London","W1A…
["Vivaan"]	{"56 Park Avenue","New York","…

By supporting these complex nested structures, Polars provide the flexibility needed to handle a wide range of real-world data scenarios, including semi-structured data formats like JSON or nested logs, while maintaining performance and memory efficiency.

String Data Types

In Polars, String data types are used to represent sequences of characters, which makes them essential for working with textual data. The String type in Polars is highly optimized for both storage and performance, allowing for efficient manipulation, filtering, and transformation of text-based data. Strings in Polars are widely used in data analysis tasks such as text processing, cleaning, and extraction, as well as for tasks like pattern matching, aggregation, and transforming categorical variables.

Polars stores strings as UTF8 encoded data. This ensures compatibility with a wide range of text data, including special characters and multi-language content. The Utf8 format optimizes memory usage by employing variable-length encoding, which makes it efficient for storing strings of varying lengths. Additionally, Polars provides a set of built-in methods that allow for advanced string operations, including transformations, matching, splitting, and concatenation.

Key Features of String Data Types in Polars

- **Efficient Storage and Performance:** Polars utilize optimized memory layouts for storing and processing strings. The internal structure is designed to minimize memory overhead while ensuring fast processing speeds, especially when working with large datasets.
- **Rich Set of Operations**: Polars provide a wide array of string manipulation functions that include:
    - String matching (for example, str.contains() for pattern matching)
    - String transformations (for example, str.upper(), str.lower() for case conversion)
    - Splitting and joining strings (for example, str.split(), str.concat())
    - Replacing substrings (for example, str.replace())
- **Vectorized Operations**: All string operations in Polars are applied in a vectorized manner, which means that they can be executed on entire columns of data at once and offer substantial performance improvements over traditional loop-based approaches.
- **Handling Missing Values:** Polars handle missing string values (null) efficiently, which allows for proper handling of incomplete data in string-based columns.

In Polars, String, Categorical, and Enum data types provide flexibility in handling textual data, categorical variables, and predefined set of values, respectively. These types are integral for efficient data analysis, especially when working with large datasets or datasets with repetitive categorical information. Understanding when and how to use each of these data types is essential for optimizing performance and ensuring proper representation of data.

String Data Type

The String data type in Polars represents sequences of characters and is used for text-based data. It is highly efficient for operations involving words, sentences, or any other textual data, and supports a rich set of string manipulation methods such as case conversion, pattern matching, substring extraction, and replacement. The String type is encoded in Utf8 format, which allows for flexible handling of international text, symbols, and emojis.

Example: The following demonstrates working with the String data type, while performing some basic string transformations:

```
import polars as pl

# Creating a DataFrame with String column
df = pl.DataFrame({
```

```
    "names": ["Kane", "John", "Finlay", "David"]
})

# Converting the names to lowercase
df = df.with_columns(df["names"].str.to_lowercase().alias("lower_
names"))

# Filtering names that contain the letter "a"
filtered_df = df.filter(df["names"].str.contains("a"))

print(filtered_df)
```

Output:

```
shape: (3, 2)
┌────────┬─────────────┐
│ names  ┆ lower_names │
│ ---    ┆ ---         │
│ str    ┆ str         │
╞════════╪═════════════╡
│ Kane   ┆ kane        │
│ Finlay ┆ finlay      │
│ David  ┆ david       │
└────────┴─────────────┘
```

Categorical Data Type

The Categorical data type in Polars is used to represent variables that take on a limited, fixed number of possible values, typically used for categorical features like gender, status, or product categories. Unlike the String type, Categorical values are stored more efficiently, and use integer codes internally to represent the unique categories, which saves memory when working with large datasets. This optimization results in faster computations, especially when performing operations like groupby, joins, and aggregations.

Example: Using the Categorical data type for categorical variables looks like this:

```
import polars as pl

# Creating a DataFrame with a Categorical column
df = pl.DataFrame({
    "status": ["Active", "Inactive", "Active", "InProgress", "Closed"]
})

# Converting the "status" column to categorical type
df = df.with_columns(df["status"].cast(pl.Categorical).alias("status_cat"))

# Viewing the DataFrame
```

```
print(df)
```

Output:

```
shape: (5, 2)
┌────────────┬────────────┐
│ status     ┆ status_cat │
│ ---        ┆ ---        │
│ str        ┆ cat        │
╞════════════╪════════════╡
│ Active     ┆ Active     │
│ Inactive   ┆ Inactive   │
│ Active     ┆ Active     │
│ InProgress ┆ InProgress │
│ Closed     ┆ Closed     │
└────────────┴────────────┘
```

Enum Data Type

The Enum data type in Polars represents a fixed set of named values, typically used to represent a variable with a predefined set of choices. Unlike Categorical, which represents any arbitrary set of categories, Enum is designed to handle specific, predefined sets of values (similar to how enums are used in many programming languages). This data type is helpful when the set of possible values is known in advance and provides better type safety and code clarity.

Example: In this example, we will simulate an Enum type by using Categorical, assuming that the rating column has only a set of predefined values such as "Good", "Poor", and "Excellent.". It will look something like this:

```
import polars as pl

# Define an Enum-like structure (Polars Enum is not officially supported but you can simulate this with categorical)
df = pl.DataFrame({
    "rating": ["Good", "Poor", "Excellent", "Good", "PIP"]
})

# Simulating Enum by converting the "rating" column to Categorical
df = df.with_columns(df["rating"].cast(pl.Categorical).alias("rating_enum"))

# Viewing the DataFrame
print(df)
Output:
shape: (5, 2)
```

```
┌───────────┬─────────────┐
│ rating    ┆ rating_enum │
│ ---       ┆ ---         │
│ str       ┆ cat         │
╞═══════════╪═════════════╡
│ Good      ┆ Good        │
│ Poor      ┆ Poor        │
│ Excellent ┆ Excellent   │
│ Good      ┆ Good        │
│ PIP       ┆ PIP         │
```

Other Data Types

Polars provides a variety of data types beyond Numerical, String, Nested and Temporal to handle different kinds of data efficiently. These include Binary, Boolean, Null, Object, and Unknown data types. Each of these types serves a specific purpose and is designed to optimize memory and performance for particular use cases in data analysis and manipulation.

Binary Data Type

The Binary data type in Polars is used to represent raw byte sequences. It is useful when dealing with data that is not in a human-readable format, such as images, files, or encrypted data. The Binary type allows efficient handling of byte data in the form of fixed-size byte arrays, and it can be used in operations that involve raw data manipulation or data streaming tasks.

Example: The use of Binary data type is shown as follows:

```
import polars as pl

# Creating a DataFrame with Binary data
df = pl.DataFrame({
    "file_data": [b"xray1_data", b"xray2_data", b"xray_data"]
})

# Printing the DataFrame
print(df)
```

```
Output:
shape: (3, 1)
```

```
┌──────────────┐
│ file_data    │
│ ---          │
│ binary       │
╞══════════════╡
│ b"xray1_data"│
│ b"xray2_data"│
│ b"xray_data" │
└──────────────┘
```

In this example, we create a DataFrame with binary data representing file content. The binary type stores raw byte sequences, such as `b"xray1_data"`, which represent a file's byte content.

Boolean Data Type

The Boolean data type in Polars is used to represent True or False values, typically for logical operations. It is used extensively for filtering data, applying conditions, or representing binary states (such as success/failure, active/inactive). The Boolean type is highly optimized for performance and memory usage when dealing with large datasets.

Example: Using the Boolean data type looks like:

```
import polars as pl

# Creating a DataFrame with Boolean data
df = pl.DataFrame({
    "is_active": [True, False, True, False]
})

# Printing the DataFrame
print(df)
```

```
Output:
shape: (4, 1)
┌───────────┐
│ is_active │
│ ---       │
│ bool      │
╞═══════════╡
│ true      │
│ false     │
│ true      │
│ false     │
└───────────┘
```

In this example, the `is_active` column is a Boolean type, which represents whether a user or entity is active or not.

Null Data Type

The Null data type is used to represent missing or undefined values in Polars. It is an essential data type for handling incomplete or missing data and is often encountered in real-world datasets. The Null type ensures that the data is explicitly marked as missing, which makes it easier to handle during data cleaning, imputation, or transformation tasks.

Example: Using the Null data type looks like this:

```
import polars as pl

# Creating a DataFrame with Null values
df = pl.DataFrame({
    "age": [25, None, 30, None]
})

# Printing the DataFrame
print(df)
Output:
shape: (4, 1)
┌──────┐
│ age  │
│ ---  │
│ i64  │
╞══════╡
│ 25   │
│ null │
│ 30   │
│ null │
└──────┘
```

In this example, the age column contains None (which is interpreted as null in Polars). These Null values represent missing data in the dataset.

Object Data Type

The Object data type is a flexible data type that can hold any kind of Python object, including custom objects, lists, or dictionaries. While not as commonly used as other types, it is helpful when working with more complex or heterogeneous data that does not fit neatly into other data types. This type allows Polars to handle cases where you need to store various data structures that are not natively supported.

Example: Using the Object data type looks like:

```
import polars as pl

# Creating a DataFrame with Object data
```

```
df = pl.DataFrame({
    "user_info": [{"name": "Alice", "age": 25}, {"name": "Bob", "age":
30}]
})

# Printing the DataFrame
print(df)
```

```
Output:
shape: (2, 1)
┌──────────────┐
│ user_info    │
│ ---          │
│ struct[2]    │
╞══════════════╡
│ {"Alice",25} │
│ {"Bob",30}   │
└──────────────┘
```

In this example, the `user_info` column holds Python dictionary objects, each representing a user with a name and age. The Object type allows for more flexible and generic data storage.

Difference between Nested Data Type and Object Data Type in Polars

In Polars, Nested Data Types and Object Data Types are both used to handle complex or non-flat data structures, but they serve different purposes and are used in distinct scenarios. Let us explore their differences in more detail:

- Definition and Use Cases
    - **Nested Data Type:** A Nested Data Type refers to data that is structured hierarchically, where fields or values can be stored as multiple layers of data within a single column. This allows you to represent more complex structures like lists, dictionaries, or arrays. It is typically used when you need to store and manipulate structured data that involves multiple levels of relationships, such as a list of items or a dictionary within a column. Nested types are essential when dealing with data that can have varying lengths or types at each level, such as JSON or nested records.
    - **Object Data Type:** The Object Data Type is a more general-purpose data type used for storing any arbitrary Python object, such as a custom Python object, list, or dictionary. Unlike Nested data types, which typically follow a defined schema (like a list of items or a struct of records), Object data types are essentially "catch-all" containers. They

are useful when the data cannot be strictly categorized into a specific structure or when the data is heterogeneous and may contain arbitrary objects like user-defined classes or complex data structures.

Unknown Data Type

The Unknown data type is used when the type of data in a column is not immediately identifiable. This type is mostly used internally by Polars for scenarios where the data type is uncertain, such as when reading data from external sources or performing certain transformations where the type is inferred rather than explicitly defined. It acts as a placeholder until a more specific type can be determined.

Example: Using the Unknown data type looks like:

```
import polars as pl

# Creating a DataFrame with Unknown type
df = pl.DataFrame({
    "unknown_type": ["apple", 25, 30.5]
},strict=False)

# Printing the DataFrame

print(df)
```

output:

shape: (3, 1)

```
┌──────────────┐
│ unknown_type │
│ ---          │
│ str          │
╞══════════════╡
│ apple        │
│ 25           │
│ 30.5         │
└──────────────┘
```

Conclusion

We explored the various data types available in Polars and focused on their specific use cases and how they contribute to efficient data manipulation and analysis. We began with an introduction to Series and DataFrames, which are the foundational structures in Polars, and how they interact with different data types. We discussed Numeric, Temporal, Nested, String, Categorical, Object, and other specialized data types such as Boolean and Binary, while emphasizing their role in handling diverse datasets.

We also delved into the practical aspects of working with these data types and provided examples of how to use them effectively, and discussed strategies for choosing the appropriate data type for specific scenarios, whether we are optimizing for memory or precision. From using Integer and Float columns for numerical operations, to utilizing Nested and Object types for hierarchical or complex data structures, we saw how Polars offers flexibility and performance for large-scale data analysis.

By understanding these data types and their optimal usage, you can ensure more efficient data processing and transformation, which make Polars a powerful tool for handling diverse and large datasets with ease. In the next chapter, we will cover how to configure Polars for different requirements.

Key Takeaways

- **Polars Data Types Offer Flexibility**: Polars provides a wide range of data types, including numeric, temporal, nested, and object types. This allows users to handle diverse datasets with ease and efficiency.
- **Optimized Memory Usage:** Choosing the appropriate data type (for example, using smaller bit-width types like Int8 or UInt8 for data with smaller ranges) helps optimize memory usage and improve performance, especially for large datasets.
- **Efficient Data Handling**: Polars' support for structured data types such as Nested (for example, Lists, Structs) enables the efficient representation of complex, hierarchical data, which is useful for working with JSON or similar formats.
- **Versatility of Series:** Series serve as the building blocks of DataFrames, and their ability to hold various data types, such as integers, floats, and strings, makes them versatile for both intermediate calculations and final data storage.
- **Strong Temporal Support:** Polars offers robust support for Temporal Data Types (such as Date, Time, Duration, and Datetime), which enables precise handling and manipulation of date and time-related data.

Exercises

1. Exercise: Creating and Manipulating Numeric Data Types
    - Objective: Create a DataFrame with columns of different numeric types (integer, float), and perform basic arithmetic operations on them.
    - Instructions:
        1. Create a DataFrame with two columns:

      a. Prices: A column of type Float64 representing prices of products (for example, 29.99, 45.50, 18.75, 22.30).

      b. Quantities: A column of type Int32 representing quantities of products (for example, 10, 20, 5, 12).

   2. Add a new column, total, which calculates the total price for each product (prices * quantities).

   3. Print the resulting DataFrame with the new column.

2. Exercise: Working with Temporal Data Types

   - Objective: Create a DataFrame using Polars' temporal data types and perform operations related to dates and times.

   - Instructions:

     1. Create a DataFrame with the following columns:

        a. start_date: A column of type Date containing a list of dates (for example, "2023-01-01", "2023-02-15", "2023-03-20")

        b. end_date: A column of type Date containing a list of dates (for example, "2023-01-10", "2023-02-20", "2023-03-25")

     2. Add a new column duration which calculates the difference between end_date and start_date using the Duration type.

     3. Print the DataFrame and observe the computed durations.

3. Exercise: Nested Data Types - Lists and Structs

   - Objective: Explore how nested data types (Lists and Structs) can be used in Polars for hierarchical data.

   - Instructions:

     1. Create a DataFrame with a column of type List that contains lists of strings representing names (for example, ["Alice", "Bob"], ["Charlie", "David"], and so on).

     2. Create another column of type Struct containing two fields: city (string) and postal_code (integer).

     3. Access the individual elements within the list and the fields within the struct by using Polars' expressions or column selections.

     4. Print the resulting DataFrame showing the nested structures and the data contained within.

CHAPTER 3
Polars Configuration

"Software design is a balancing act between flexibility and usability. The more configurable it is, the more likely it is to meet diverse needs."

Martin Fowler

Introduction

Polars is a state-of-the-art DataFrame library in Python, which is designed to deliver unmatched speed and efficiency in data manipulation. Its versatility extends beyond performance and offers extensive configuration options that allow users to tailor the library's behavior to suit their unique analytical needs. Whether working on lightweight tasks or processing massive multi-gigabyte datasets, Polars provides the tools necessary to optimize workflows, manage resources effectively, and achieve unparalleled results.

The configurability in Polars makes it adaptable to diverse data formats and workflows. By understanding and utilizing these configuration features, users can unlock the full potential of Polars, which makes it a cornerstone tool in high-performance data analysis.

Structure

In this chapter, we will discuss the following topics:

- Importance of Configuration in Software
- Need of Configurations in DataFrame Processing
- Polars Configuration

    - Table Display Configuration
    - Formatting and Precision Configuration
    - Data Structuring and Streaming Configuration
    - Debugging
    - Config State Management
- Configuring Context Scope and Multiple Instances

Importance of Configuration in Software

The need for configurable software arises from modern industries' ever-changing demands and diverse workflows. In today's dynamic environment, businesses require solutions that adapt to shifting requirements, without incurring costly and time-consuming re-engineering. Configurability enables software systems to cater to varied use cases, user preferences, and operational needs, while ensuring that they remain relevant and efficient over time. This adaptability is crucial for organizations striving to stay competitive and responsive in rapidly evolving markets.

One significant advantage of configurable software is its ability to optimize performance and resource usage. By offering adjustable settings for memory allocation, execution modes, or user-defined parameters, software can be fine-tuned to perform optimally on different hardware or within specific constraints. For instance, a data processing tool can be configured to use fewer threads on low-power machines or allocate additional resources when working with large datasets on high-performance systems. This flexibility ensures efficiency and scalability, regardless of the context in which the software is deployed.

A real-world example of the importance of configurability is the rise of cloud-based platforms like AWS and Microsoft Azure. These platforms offer highly configurable services, which allow users to adjust computing power, storage, and network settings to fit their needs. Businesses can scale their resources up during peak usage periods and scale them down during quieter times to save costs and maintain performance. This level of configurability not only enhances the user experience but also aligns the software with an organization's strategic goals.

In addition to performance and cost benefits, configurable software simplifies compliance with industry regulations and unique organizational standards. Configurable systems can meet the stringent requirements of industries like finance, healthcare, and manufacturing by allowing users to modify behavior, access control, and reporting formats. This ability to customize software without extensive redevelopment makes configurability a cornerstone of modern software design. It also offers longevity, usability, and value across varied scenarios.

Need of Configurations in DataFrame Processing

The need for configuration in DataFrame libraries stems from the diverse requirements of data analysis tasks across industries. Data analysts, scientists, and engineers work with datasets that vary significantly in size, complexity, and format. Configurability allows DataFrame libraries to adapt to these differences and provides options to optimize performance, manage memory usage, and customize processing behavior. For instance, users working with small datasets may prioritize interactive performance, while those handling massive datasets require efficient resource management and scalability. By offering configurable settings, DataFrame libraries enable users to tailor their workflows to achieve maximum efficiency and accuracy.

An essential area where configurability proves invaluable is in data ingestion and preprocessing. Different datasets come in various formats, such as CSV, Parquet, or JSON, and may include inconsistencies like missing values or schema mismatches. Configurable DataFrame libraries allow users to specify how data should be parsed, cleaned, and transformed during ingestion. For example, users can configure how missing data is handled and whether they should fill missing values with defaults, drop rows, or raise errors. Such flexibility ensures that the data processing pipeline aligns with the specific needs of a project, which reduces manual intervention and improves overall productivity.

Consider the example of Pandas, which is one of the most widely used DataFrame libraries. It offers several configuration options through its 'pandas.set_option()' function, which enables users to adjust display settings, precision of numerical outputs, and memory usage. For instance, users can configure how many rows or columns are displayed when viewing a DataFrame. This makes it easier to explore large datasets interactively. Additionally, Pandas provides flexibility in handling missing data with functions like fillna() and dropna(), which allow users to tailor the treatment of incomplete data to suit their analysis. This configurability ensures that Pandas can support a wide range of use cases, from small-scale exploratory analysis to more complex, production-grade workflows.

Polars Configuration

Polars offer a robust configuration system that allows users to fine-tune their data processing workflows for optimal performance and display.

Let us explore Polars configuration options in more detail.

Table Display Configuration

Polars provide a comprehensive set of configuration options for fine-tuning the display of tables. This allows users to control various aspects of table formatting, alignment, and visibility. These options can be grouped into several categories based on their functionality, while ensuring that users can tailor the table display to their specific needs.

Table Formatting and Alignment

Polars offer various configuration options to control the alignment and formatting of tables. For instance, the `Config.set_ascii_tables([active])` option enables the use of ASCII characters to display table outlines and makes it easier to view tables in environments that do not support graphical characters. Users can also control the alignment of cells using `Config.set_tbl_cell_alignment(format)` for general cell alignment and `Config.set_tbl_cell_numeric_alignment(format)` for numeric columns, while ensuring that data is presented in a clean, readable format.

Visibility and Display Control

When dealing with large datasets, it is often essential to control which parts of the table are visible. The `Config.set_tbl_cols(n)` option allows users to set the number of columns visible in the table, while preventing the display from becoming overwhelmed when working with wide DataFrames. Similarly, `Config.set_tbl_rows(n)` limits the number of rows displayed, ensuring that tables remain manageable. For cases where the table is particularly wide, the `Config.set_tbl_width_chars(width)` option can be used to set the maximum width of the table and avoid horizontal scrolling.

Data Detail and Column Information

Polars gives users the ability to adjust the level of detail shown for each table. With `Config.set_tbl_column_data_type_inline([active])`, users can display the data type next to the column name, providing a quick reference for the type of data in each column. To further simplify the table, users can hide column names with `Config.set_tbl_hide_column_names([active])` or hide column data types using `Config.set_tbl_hide_column_data_types([active])`. For a more streamlined view, `Config.set_tbl_hide_dataframe_shape([active])` and `Config.set_tbl_hide_dtype_separator([active])` allow users to remove the shape information or the separator between column names and data types.

Table Summary and Formatting Style

Besides controlling the content and appearance of tables, Polars allow users to set the overall formatting style. The `Config.set_tbl_formatting([format, ...])` option provides the flexibility to choose different formatting styles, such as "MARKDOWN" or "CSV", depending on the intended use case. For those who need a summary of the DataFrame, the `Config.set_tbl_dataframe_shape_below([active])` option enables users to print the DataFrame's shape information below the table and offers a quick summary of the structure without cluttering the display.

These configuration options ensure that users can fully customize the way data is presented. This makes it easier to work with large datasets ensuring that the table display aligns with the specific requirements of their project.

Example:

```
import polars as pl

# Creating a sample DataFrame
data = {
    "Name": ["Alice", "Bob", "Charlie"],
    "Age": [25, 30, 35],
    "Salary": [50000.0, 60000.0, 70000.0]
}

df = pl.DataFrame(data)

# Display the DataFrame without any custom configurations
print("DataFrame without custom configurations:")
print(df)
```

```
Output :

DataFrame without custom configurations:
shape: (3, 3)
```

Name --- str	Age --- i64	Salary --- f64
Alice	25	50000.0
Bob	30	60000.0
Charlie	35	70000.0

```
# Configuring Polars to display the DataFrame with custom settings
pl.Config.set_ascii_tables(True)  # Use ASCII characters for table
outlines

pl.Config.set_tbl_cols(2)  # Display only two columns
pl.Config.set_tbl_rows(2)  # Display only two rows
pl.Config.set_tbl_formatting("MARKDOWN")  # Use Markdown formatting
pl.Config.set_tbl_column_data_type_inline(True)  # Display data type
inline

# Display the DataFrame with custom configurations
print("\nDataFrame with custom configurations:")
print(df)
```

```
Output :

DataFrame with custom configurations:
shape: (3, 3)
| Name (str) | … | Salary (f64) |
|------------|---|--------------|
| Alice      | … | 50000.0      |
| …          | … | …            |
| Charlie    | … | 70000.0      |
```

We can clearly see that the changes in display format have been made as per the config set by us.

Formatting and Precision Configuration

Polars offer a variety of configuration options that help users control the formatting and precision of numerical and string data displayed within DataFrames. These options can be particularly useful when working with datasets that require specific formatting for consistency, readability, or presentation.

Decimal and Floating-Point Precision

One of the key configurations for numerical precision is `Config.set_decimal_separator([separator])`. This setting allows users to specify the character used to separate the integer and fractional parts of decimal values, such as a period (.) or comma (,). This is especially helpful for users working in locales where different separators are used. Similarly, `Config.set_float_precision([precision])` controls the number of decimal places displayed for floating-point values and ensures that numerical outputs meet the desired level of precision. If users prefer a more customized display format for floating-point numbers, they can use `Config.set_fmt_float([fmt])` to define how the floating-point values are presented (for example, scientific notation, fixed-point, and so on).

String and List Formatting

In addition to numerical values, Polars allow users to control how string and list data are displayed. The `Config.set_fmt_str_lengths(n)` option specifies the number of characters used to display string values, which can be useful for formatting long strings in a more compact and readable manner. For lists, `Config.set_fmt_table_cell_list_len(n)` limits the number of elements displayed in a list within a table cell. This ensures that only a concise summary of list data is shown, without overwhelming the table layout.

Thousands Separator and Trim Decimal Zeros

For numerical readability, Polars provides the `Config.set_thousands_separator([separator])` option, which allows users to define a character to be used as a thousands grouping separator, such as a comma (,) or space. This is particularly helpful when dealing with large numbers to improve clarity and make the data easier to read. Additionally, `Config.set_trim_decimal_zeros([active])` allows users to strip trailing zeros from decimal values, which is useful when working with financial or scientific data where exact precision is needed, without encountering redundant zeros in the output.

Together, these formatting and precision configurations give users fine-grained control over how their data is displayed in Polars. These configurations ensure that both numerical and string values are formatted in a way that aligns with their specific requirements.

Example:

```
import polars as pl

# Creating a sample DataFrame with different data types
df = pl.DataFrame({
    "Amount": [12345.6789, 23456.7890, 34567.8901],
    "Description": ["Payment for services", "Refund", "Salary"],
    "Date": [pl.date(2024,1,1), pl.date(2024,1,2), pl.date(2024,1,3)],
   "Items": [["apple", "banana"], ["orange", "grape"], ["mango", "kiwi"]]
})

# Display the DataFrame without any custom configurations
print("DataFrame without custom configurations:")
print(df)
```

```
Output :
DataFrame without custom configurations:
shape: (3, 4)
┌────────────┬──────────────────────┬──────────────────────────────────┬
───────────────────┐
│ Amount     ┆ Description          ┆ Date                             ┆
Items             │
│ ---        ┆ ---                  ┆ ---                              ┆
---               │
│ f64        ┆ str                  ┆ object                           ┆
list[str]         │
╞════════════╪══════════════════════╪══════════════════════════════════╪
═══════════════════╡
│ 12345.6789 ┆ Payment for services ┆ 2024-01-01 00:00:00.alias("dat… ┆
["apple", "banana"] │
│ 23456.789  ┆ Refund               ┆ 2024-01-02 00:00:00.alias("dat… ┆
["orange", "grape"] │
│ 34567.8901 ┆ Salary               ┆ 2024-01-03 00:00:00.alias("dat… ┆
["mango", "kiwi"]   │
└────────────┴──────────────────────┴──────────────────────────────────┴
───────────────────┘
```

```
pl.Config.set_decimal_separator(",") # Use comma as the decimal separator
pl.Config.set_float_precision(1) # Display two decimal places for floating-
point values
pl.Config.set_fmt_str_lengths(10)  # Limit string display length to 15
characters
pl.Config.set_thousands_separator("_")  # Use comma as the thousands
separator
pl.Config.set_trim_decimal_zeros(True)  # Remove trailing zeros from
decimals

# Display the DataFrame with formatting applied
print("\nDataFrame with custom configurations:")
print(df)
```

```
DataFrame with custom configurations:
shape: (3, 4)
```

Amount --- f64	Descriptio… --- str	Date --- object	Items --- list[str]
12_345,7	Payment fo…	2024-01-01…	["apple", …
23_456,8	Refund	2024-01-02…	["orange",…
34_567,9	Salary	2024-01-03…	["mango", …

These configuration changes allow for greater control over how the data is displayed, especially when working with different locales or specific formatting requirements.

Data Structuring and Streaming Configuration

Polars provide important configuration options for structuring data and managing large-scale data streaming. These configurations ensure that users can efficiently work with complex expressions and control memory usage, particularly when dealing with large datasets. By utilizing the `Config.set_auto_structify()` and `Config.set_streaming_chunk_size()` options, users can optimize how data is processed and displayed.

Automatic Structification of Multi-Output Expressions

The configuration `Config.set_auto_structify([active])` allows Polars to automatically convert multi-output expressions into structs. This is particularly useful when dealing with expressions that result in multiple columns, as it ensures that the outputs are grouped together as a single unit in the form of a `Struct`. When enabled, Polars will handle complex multi-output expressions more intuitively, which simplifies the user experience while working with grouped data. By default, multi-output expressions may return separate columns, but enabling auto structify will automatically bundle them into a structured format.

Example Without Configuration: Without the auto structify configuration, multi-output expressions are returned as individual columns. For example, consider a DataFrame where we return two columns from a dataframe. By default, these would be returned as separate columns, as shown here:

```
import polars as pl
# Sample DataFrame
df_without = pl.DataFrame({
    "Values": [1, 2, 3, 4, 5],
    "Values2": [1, 2, 3, 4, 5]
})
# Multi-output expressions without auto structify
df_without = df_without.select(pl.all())
print("Without Auto Structify:")
print(df_without)
Output :
Without Auto Structify:
shape: (5, 2)
```

Values --- i64	Values2 --- i64
1	1
2	2
3	3
4	4
5	5

Example With Configuration: When `Config.set_auto_structify(True)` is enabled, the same multi-output expression will return the results as a single `Struct` and group the two values together. This is especially helpful for complex expressions where it makes sense to bundle related outputs in a more organized manner.

```
import polars as pl
# Enable auto structify
pl.Config.set_auto_structify(True)
# Sample DataFrame
# Multi-output expressions with auto structify
```

```
df_with = df_without.select(pl.all())
print("\nWith Auto Structify:")
print(df_with)
Output :
With Auto Structify:
shape: (5, 1)
┌────────────┐
│ Values     │
│ ---        │
│ struct[2]  │
╞════════════╡
│ {1,1}      │
│ {2,2}      │
│ {3,3}      │
│ {4,4}      │
│ {5,5}      │
└────────────┘
```

Debugging

Polars provide a valuable configuration option for enabling verbose logging, which is useful for debugging and monitoring the internal operations of the library. The `Config.set_verbose([active])` setting controls whether additional logging information is displayed during data processing, helping users understand what is happening under the hood. This feature can be particularly helpful when troubleshooting issues or analyzing the performance of complex operations. By enabling verbose logging, users gain insights into the execution flow, including any optimizations and potential bottlenecks.

When verbose logging is turned on, Polars will output more detailed information about its operations, such as the query execution steps, intermediate results, and performance metrics. By default, verbose logging is disabled, but it can be enabled with a simple configuration call.

Config State Management

Polars offer robust functionality for saving, loading, and managing configuration settings, which is particularly helpful in scenarios where users need to persist settings across sessions or share configurations between different environments. The `Config.load(cfg)` method allows users to load previously saved configuration options from a JSON string, which makes it easy to apply a set of predefined settings to a new session. Similarly, `Config.load_from_file(file)` enables users to load settings from a file and ensures that the configuration state is consistent every time the application is restarted or deployed to a different environment.

On the other hand, the `Config.save(*[, if_set])` and `Config.save_to_file(file)` methods provide a way to store the current configuration settings, either as a JSON string or in a file. This allows users to save their custom configurations and easily reload them later. The `Config.state(*[, if_set, env_only])` method is useful for checking the current configuration state, as it provides a dictionary representation of all active settings. Additionally, Polars offers the `Config.restore_defaults()` method to reset all configuration options back to their default values. This is useful when users want to revert to the original settings, either after testing or due to a misconfiguration. For more granular control, individual options can be reset to `None`, such as when resetting the number of rows to display with `Config.set_tbl_rows(None)`.

Configuring Context Scope and Multiple Instances

Using Config as a Decorator in Polars

Polars provide an elegant way to manage configuration settings by using a Config instance as a function decorator. This allows you to temporarily apply configuration options for the duration of a function call, without affecting other parts of your code. By setting the configuration inside the decorator, the options are automatically applied when the function is called and are reverted back when the function exits. This is particularly useful in scenarios where you need to apply specific settings for a particular operation, such as controlling table formatting for displaying data frames in a markdown format.

For example, in a healthcare application, you might want to display patient data in a specific table format for generating reports. You can use a Polars Config instance to apply the required table formatting only for the report generation function. By using the decorator pattern, you ensure that the settings are applied only for the duration of the function. This makes the code cleaner and more manageable. The following is an example demonstrating how to use the Config decorator for formatting a patient data frame in markdown format:

```
import polars as pl
import sys

# Define a Config instance for markdown formatting
cfg_markdown = pl.Config(tbl_formatting="MARKDOWN", apply_on_context_
enter=True)

# Example function to display patient data in markdown format
@cfg_markdown
def display_patient_report(df: pl.DataFrame) -> None:
    sys.stdout.write(str(df))

# Sample healthcare data
```

```
patient_data = pl.DataFrame({
    "Patient ID": [101, 102, 103],
    "Name": ["John Doe", "Jane Smith", "Jim Brown"],
    "Age": [45, 50, 60],
    "Diagnosis": ["Hypertension", "Diabetes", "Asthma"]
})

# Call the function with the applied markdown formatting
display_patient_report(patient_data)
```

In this example, the `display_patient_report` function formats the patient data as a markdown table, thanks to the `Config` decorator. This ensures that the markdown formatting is applied only within the scope of the function, without impacting other areas of the program that may require different configurations such as standard table formatting for internal data analysis.

Managing Multiple Config Instances

In scenarios where different parts of your code require different configurations, Polars offers the ability to create multiple `Config` instances. Each instance can hold a separate bundle of configuration options. These can be applied individually in specific parts of your code using decorators or context managers. This approach allows for greater flexibility and modularity, as you can update and modify configuration options centrally and apply them as needed throughout your codebase. This is particularly useful when working with different datasets or operations that require distinct configurations such as verbose logging for debugging or specific table formatting for reporting.

For example, in a healthcare analytics application, you might need to manage patient data with verbose logging for error tracking, while generating reports with a specific table formatting style. You can create separate `Config` instances for verbose logging and markdown formatting, besides applying them individually to the relevant functions. This ensures that each function has the appropriate configuration settings without interfering with others. Here is an example:

```
# Define Config instances for verbose logging and markdown formatting
cfg_verbose = pl.Config(verbose=True, apply_on_context_enter=True)
cfg_markdown = pl.Config(tbl_formatting="MARKDOWN", apply_on_context_
enter=True)

# Example function for detailed data processing with verbose logging
@cfg_verbose
def process_patient_data(df: pl.DataFrame) -> None:
    # Simulate processing the patient data with verbose logging
    df.select(pl.col("Age").sum())
    print("Processed patient data")

# Example function for displaying patient report with markdown formatting
@cfg_markdown
```

```
def generate_patient_report(df: pl.DataFrame) -> None:
    sys.stdout.write(str(df))

# Sample healthcare data
patient_data = pl.DataFrame({
    "Patient ID": [101, 102, 103],
    "Name": ["John Doe", "Jane Smith", "Jim Brown"],
    "Age": [45, 50, 60],
    "Diagnosis": ["Hypertension", "Diabetes", "Asthma"]
})

# Call the functions with appropriate configurations
process_patient_data(patient_data)
generate_patient_report(patient_data)
```

Conclusion

Polars provide a powerful and flexible configuration system that allows users to fine-tune various aspects of data manipulation, display, and performance optimization. Through configurable options for table formatting, precision control, verbose logging, and even the ability to manage settings within specific function scopes via decorators, Polars ensures that data processing tasks can be tailored to meet specific needs. Whether you are working with large healthcare datasets, generating reports, or debugging complex workflows, Polars' configuration options enable you to maintain both efficiency and clarity in your code. By leveraging these capabilities, you can optimize your data analysis pipeline and make it adaptable to diverse scenarios while ensuring that your code is maintainable and clean.

The next chapter will cover different I/O operations using Polars and rudimentary data manipulation methods.

Key Takeaways

- Polars offer highly customizable configuration options to optimize data handling and performance.
- Configuration settings can be applied temporarily using context managers or decorators, as they enhance flexibility.
- Table formatting, precision, and verbose logging can be tailored to suit specific use cases.
- Multiple Config instances allow for managing different settings for different tasks within the same codebase.
- The ability to load, save, and restore configurations makes Polars ideal for consistent and repeatable data workflows.

CHAPTER 4
I/O Operations and Basic Data Manipulation

"Every input file is a potential treasure chest of insights."

Unknown

Introduction

Efficient data handling is at the heart of any successful data analysis workflow. To simplify and accelerate it, we can use a powerful library like Polars. In this chapter, we will explore how Polars handles diverse data formats and equips you with robust tools for efficient data manipulation. Whether you are working with structured data in CSV files, hierarchical data in JSON, or columnar storage formats like Parquet, Polars provides seamless integration and exceptional performance.

We will begin by understanding how to read and write data across multiple formats, including JSON, Parquet, CSV, and Excel files. From there, the chapter will dive into essential data manipulation techniques such as selecting, renaming, filtering, sorting, and modifying columns. These foundational skills form the basis for creating clean, structured datasets ready for analysis.

Next, we will discuss advanced operations like calculating new columns, deriving summary statistics, and addressing missing values. You will learn how to clean and transform your data by removing duplicates, standardizing column names, and processing string data effectively. These techniques not only ensure consistency and accuracy in your datasets but also streamline workflows for complex analyses.

Thus, by the end of this chapter, you will have a comprehensive understanding of Polars' capabilities for efficient data handling

Structure

In this chapter, we will discuss the following topics:

- Reading and Writing Data
    - Supported file formats and Why They Matter (JSON, Parquet, CSV, Excel)
    - Working with File Formats
- Selecting and Manipulating Data
    - Selecting Columns: Accessing Specific Columns for Analysis
    - Renaming Columns: Techniques for Renaming Columns Efficiently
    - Modifying Columns: Adding or Replacing Columns with New Values
    - Filtering Rows: Applying Conditions to Extract Subsets of Data
    - Sorting Data: Sorting by One or More Columns with Ascending/Descending Options
- Transforming Data
    - Calculating New Columns
    - Summary Statistics
    - Handling Missing Values
- Data Cleaning
    - Removing Duplicates
    - Standardizing Column Names
    - Cleaning String Data

Reading and Writing Data

Files play a critical role in data archival and analytics and serve as fundamental units of storage and portability in data workflows. In modern analytics, data files are ubiquitous across industries. They act as snapshots of data at specific points in time. Formats such as JSON, Parquet, and CSV are widely used due to their flexibility, simplicity, and ability to be shared seamlessly between systems. Files are often used for long-term archival, where data is stored for compliance, reference, or historical analysis. This ensures that valuable information can be preserved independently of the databases or systems used at the time of collection.

Despite the rise of robust database systems, analytics workflows often continue to include files, as they provide advantages that databases cannot always match. For instance, files are platform-agnostic. This means that they can be easily transferred and accessed across different environments without requiring database infrastructure or specific software dependencies. In scenarios like machine learning (ML), files allow researchers and analysts to store and share datasets in standardized formats (like Parquet or CSV), which are universally compatible with tools and frameworks. Furthermore, files can be processed locally or on distributed systems without the need for a live database connection, which makes them ideal for offline workflows.

One example where storing data in a file makes more sense than a database table is when dealing with large, immutable datasets intended for batch analysis. Consider a scenario where a data engineering team processes IoT sensor data collected over a year. The raw data, stored in hourly JSON files, is analyzed monthly to generate aggregated insights. Since the data does not require frequent updates or real-time querying, storing it in files like Parquet or Iceberg ensures faster read times for batch operations and reduces the overhead of maintaining a database. Additionally, these files can be compressed efficiently, which results in reduced storage costs while maintaining query performance during analysis.

Files remain a cornerstone of data workflows, offering a lightweight, cost-effective, and flexible approach for handling large-scale or historical data. With Polars, reading and writing files becomes streamlined, which allows data professionals to unlock the full potential of these versatile storage formats, while ensuring high performance and compatibility in analytics pipelines.

Supported File Formats and Reasons They Matter

We will now cover different data file formats, their advantages and use cases.

JSON

JSON (JavaScript Object Notation) is a lightweight data-interchange format that represents data as nested key-value pairs. It is highly readable and easy to generate and parse, which makes it ideal for APIs and data sharing between systems. Its primary advantage is its human-readable structure and flexibility in representing complex, hierarchical data. However, JSON is not optimized for large datasets due to its verbose nature and lack of compression. It is best suited for scenarios like configuration files, web APIs, or when dealing with semi-structured data.

Parquet

Parquet is a columnar storage file format optimized for large-scale data analytics. It offers excellent performance for read-heavy workloads by enabling selective column retrieval and efficient compression. Its primary advantage lies in its ability to handle large datasets with minimal storage overhead and faster query performance. However, its columnar structure makes it less suitable for write-heavy applications or when data is accessed sequentially. Parquet is widely used in big data environments, such as distributed processing frameworks like Apache Spark, for storing and querying massive datasets efficiently.

CSV

CSV (Comma-Separated Values) is a simple and widely used file format for tabular data. It stores data as plain text, which makes it highly compatible with most programming languages and tools. The primary advantage of CSV is its simplicity and universal adoption. However, it lacks support for metadata, complex data structures, and efficient compression. Therefore, it is less suitable for large datasets or advanced analytics. CSV files are primarily used for data exchange between systems, quick data storage, and as an input/output format for many data processing tasks.

Excel

Excel is a spreadsheet-based file format designed for manual data entry, visualization, and lightweight data analysis. It is user-friendly and comes with a graphical interface that allows users to interact with data without programming knowledge. The primary advantage of Excel lies in its accessibility and ability to perform basic analytics and visualizations. However, it is not well-suited for handling large datasets due to memory limitations and performance bottlenecks. Excel files are primarily used in small-scale data analysis, reporting, and collaborative work environments.

Working with Files: Read Operations

Now that we have explored the basic characteristics, advantages, and use cases of various file formats, it is time to dive into how Polars handles these formats. In the following sections, we will guide you through the process of reading data from different file types such as JSON, Parquet, CSV, Iceberg, and Excel, using Polars.

JSON

Polars provides robust support for both JSON and NDJSON file formats and enables efficient data processing for a wide range of use cases. When working with JSON, Polars can load data from a single JSON object or array, which makes it easy to handle structured and nested data. This makes JSON ideal for smaller datasets or scenarios where data is exchanged between systems in a human-readable format. On the other hand, Polars excel in handling NDJSON (Newline Delimited JSON) files, which store data as individual JSON objects on separate lines. NDJSON is particularly useful for large-scale data processing and streaming applications, as it allows for line-by-line reading and processing. Therefore, it significantly reduces memory overhead. Whether you are working with small, complex datasets in JSON or large, incremental data in NDJSON, Polars ensures high performance and scalability with both formats.

Now, let us create a traditional JSON file and DataFrame using Polars:

```
import json
import random
# Function to create a random record
def create_record(trade_number):
    return {
        "trade_number": trade_number,
        "trade_price": round(random.uniform(100, 1000), 2),  # Random
price between 100 and 1000
        "trade_size": random.randint(1, 1000)  # Random size between 1
and 1000
    }
# Generate 1000 records
records = [create_record(i) for i in range(1, 1001)]
# Write records to a JSON file
with open('trades.json', 'w') as json_file:
    json.dump(records, json_file, indent=4)
JSON Structure :
[
    {
        "trade_number": 1,
        "trade_price": 727.46,
        "trade_size": 142
    },
    {
        "trade_number": 2,
        "trade_price": 154.7,
        "trade_size": 262
    },
    {
        "trade_number": 3,
        "trade_price": 163.13,
        "trade_size": 793
    },
    {
        "trade_number": 4,
        "trade_price": 947.73,
        "trade_size": 925
    },...
]
```

Now, we will try to create a DataFrame using the same JSON file:

```
import polars as pl
# Read the JSON file into a Polars DataFrame
df = pl.read_json('trades.json')
# Show the first few rows of the DataFrame
print(df.head())

Output:
shape: (5, 3)
```

trade_number --- i64	trade_price --- f64	trade_size --- i64
1	727.46	142
2	154.7	262
3	163.13	793
4	947.73	925
5	909.59	741

Additionally, we can pass on the schema information with data type detail to override inferred data types.

```
import polars as pl
# Define the schema for the columns
schema = {
    "trade_number": pl.Float64,
    "trade_price": pl.Float64,
    "trade_size": pl.Float64,
}
# Read the JSON file into a Polars DataFrame with the specified schema
df = pl.read_json('trades.json', schema=schema)
# Show the first few rows of the DataFrame
print(df.head())


Output:
shape: (5, 3)
```

trade_number --- f64	trade_price --- f64	trade_size --- f64
1.0	727.46	142.0
2.0	154.7	262.0
3.0	163.13	793.0
4.0	947.73	925.0
5.0	909.59	741.0

NDJSON

Now, we will create an NDJSON file using the following code snippet and read it using Polars:

```
import json
import random

# Function to create a random record
def create_record(trade_number):
    return {
        "trade_number": trade_number,
        "trade_price": round(random.uniform(100, 1000), 2),  # Random
price between 100 and 1000
        "trade_size": random.randint(1, 1000)  # Random size between 1
and 1000
    }

# Generate 1000 records
records = [create_record(i) for i in range(1, 1001)]

# Write records to an NDJSON file
with open('tradesnd.json', 'w') as ndjson_file:
    for record in records:
        ndjson_file.write(json.dumps(record) + '\n')

NDJSON Structure :
{"trade_number": 1, "trade_price": 569.87, "trade_size": 824}
{"trade_number": 2, "trade_price": 363.76, "trade_size": 107}
{"trade_number": 3, "trade_price": 659.97, "trade_size": 137}
{"trade_number": 4, "trade_price": 284.83, "trade_size": 224}
```

Now, let us create a dataframe using the same file. We have different methods in Polars to achieve it.

```
import polars as pl

# Read the NDJSON file into a Polars DataFrame
df = pl.read_ndjson('tradesnd.json')

# Show the first few rows of the DataFrame
print(df.head())
```

```
Output :
shape: (5, 3)
```

trade_number --- i64	trade_price --- f64	trade_size --- i64
1	569.87	824
2	363.76	107
3	659.97	137
4	284.83	224
5	993.05	17

Parquet

Parquet is a columnar storage file format optimized for efficient data processing, especially for large datasets. It stores data in a binary format and enables faster read and write operations compared to row-based formats like CSV. Parquet files support complex nested data structures, are highly compressed, and are well-suited for distributed data processing.

In Polars, reading Parquet files is straightforward using the pl.read_parquet() function. This method loads the file into a Polars DataFrame, which allows for efficient data manipulation and analysis. Here is an example:

```
import polars as pl
import os

# File path
file_path = 'credit_card_transactions.parquet'

# Read the Parquet file into a Polars DataFrame
df = pl.read_parquet(file_path)

# Get the file size
file_size = os.path.getsize(file_path)

# Print the DataFrame and file size
print(df.head())
```

```
print(df.height)
print(f"File size: {file_size / (1024 * 1024):.2f} MB")
```

Output:

```
shape: (5, 19)
┌──────────────┬──────────────┬──────────────┬──────────────┬─────┬──────────
──────┬─────────┬─────────┬─────────┐
│ transaction_ ┆ transaction_ ┆ merchant_id ┆ merchant_cat ┆ … ┆
transaction_ ┆ fraudulent ┆ account_bal ┆ reward_poin │
│ id ┆ date ┆ --- ┆ egory ┆ ┆ fee
│ --- ┆ ance ┆ ts │
│ --- ┆ --- ┆ i64 ┆ --- ┆ ┆ ---
│ bool ┆ --- ┆ --- │
│ i64 ┆ str ┆ ┆ str ┆ ┆ f64
│ ┆ f64 ┆ i64 │
╞══════════════╪══════════════╪══════════════╪══════════════╪═════╪══════════
══════╪═════════╪═════════╪═════════╡
│ 1 ┆ 2024-11-23 ┆ 1024 ┆ Retail ┆ … ┆ 12.96
│ true ┆ 9534.19 ┆ 264 │
│ 2 ┆ 2024-07-26 ┆ 4452 ┆ Retail ┆ … ┆ 1.09
│ true ┆ 892.54 ┆ 394 │
│ 3 ┆ 2024-10-23 ┆ 7972 ┆ Food & ┆ … ┆ 10.76
│ false ┆ 1602.18 ┆ 208 │
│ ┆ ┆ ┆ Beverage ┆ ┆
│ ┆ ┆ │
│ 4 ┆ 2024-06-23 ┆ 3064 ┆ Food & ┆ … ┆ 13.02
│ true ┆ 2790.63 ┆ 56 │
│ ┆ ┆ ┆ Beverage ┆ ┆
│ ┆ ┆ │
│ 5 ┆ 2024-10-08 ┆ 7302 ┆ Retail ┆ … ┆ 1.81
│ false ┆ 4043.73 ┆ 325 │
└──────────────┴──────────────┴──────────────┴──────────────┴─────┴──────────
──────┴─────────┴─────────┴─────────┘
row count is =  1000000
File size: 28.45 MB
```

We have stored 1 million rows in a Parquet file with 19 columns. It consumed only 28.45 MB of storage space.

CSV

CSV (Comma-Separated Values) files are a widely used text format for storing tabular data, where each row represents a record and each column is separated by a delimiter, which is often a comma or pipe (|). In Polars, we can efficiently read CSV files using the `pl.read_csv()` function. Here is an example:

```
import polars as pl
# File path for the CSV file
file_path = 'credit_card_transactions.csv'

# Read the CSV file into a Polars DataFrame
df = pl.read_csv(file_path, separator='|', skip_rows=4)

# Show the first few rows of the DataFrame
print(df.head())
```

```
Output:
shape: (5, 19)
┌──────┬────────────┬──────┬────────────────┬─────┬───────┬───────┬────────────
──┬──────┐
│ 4    ┆ 2024-05-31 ┆ 4479 ┆ Food & Beverage ┆ … ┆ 11.16 ┆ True  ┆
5670.21 ┆ 14 │
│ ---  ┆ ---        ┆ ---  ┆ ---            ┆     ┆ ---   ┆ ---   ┆ ---
┆ ---  │
│ i64  ┆ str        ┆ i64  ┆ str            ┆     ┆ f64   ┆ bool  ┆ f64
┆ i64  │
╞══════╪════════════╪══════╪════════════════╪═════╪═══════╪═══════╪════════════
══╪══════╡
│ 5    ┆ 2024-09-10 ┆ 9965 ┆ Entertainment  ┆ … ┆ 12.44 ┆ false ┆ 4303.5
┆ 324  │
│ 6    ┆ 2024-09-16 ┆ 5217 ┆ Retail         ┆ … ┆ 5.18  ┆ false ┆
2811.86 ┆ 120 │
│ 7    ┆ 2024-10-26 ┆ 1678 ┆ Online         ┆ … ┆ 13.71 ┆ false ┆
5720.12 ┆ 402 │
│ 8    ┆ 2024-12-21 ┆ 2620 ┆ Food & Beverage ┆ … ┆ 9.36  ┆ true  ┆
1144.61 ┆ 398 │
│ 9    ┆ 2024-12-28 ┆ 3988 ┆ Entertainment  ┆ … ┆ 14.68 ┆ true  ┆
4061.88 ┆ 190 │
└──────┴────────────┴──────┴────────────────┴─────┴───────┴───────┴────────────
──┴──────┘
```

Excel

Microsoft Excel, first released in 1985, has evolved into one of the most widely used spreadsheet applications globally. Originally intended for financial analysis and data management, Excel revolutionized how individuals and organizations handle data by providing an intuitive interface for performing calculations, creating tables, and generating visualizations. Its flexibility and ease of use have made it a cornerstone for professionals across various domains. In data science and analytics, Excel serves as an accessible tool for exploratory data analysis (EDA), data cleaning, and creating quick, insightful visualizations through charts and pivot tables. Analysts frequently use Excel to handle small to medium-sized datasets and prepare reports. In data engineering, it acts as a lightweight copysolution for testing data pipelines, mapping schemas, and storing configuration details. Despite the emergence of more advanced tools and programming languages, Excel remains integral to many workflows due to its ubiquity, simplicity, and compatibility with other systems.

Polars does not include a native Excel reader but relies on external libraries, that are referred to as "engines," to parse Excel files into a format compatible with Polars. The available engines include fastexcel, xlsx2csv, and openpyxl. Among these, fastexcel is the fastest, as it leverages the Rust-based Calamine crate to parse .xlsx files into an Apache Arrow in-memory representation. This allows Polars to read the data efficiently without requiring a data copy. The xlsx2csv engine converts .xlsx files into in-memory CSVs, which Polars then reads using its highly optimized CSV reader. On the other hand, openpyxl, while slower, offers greater flexibility for handling complex or unconventional Excel files.

To use any of these engines, you must install the corresponding Python packages as additional dependencies. For instance, the following command installs all the three engines:

```
pip install fastexcel xlsx2csv openpyxl
```

By default, Polars employs the fastexcel engine for reading .xlsx files, while ensuring efficient data parsing and minimizing memory overhead. The other engines serve as fallbacks or alternatives for cases that require advanced parsing capabilities or handling tricky Excel files. Here is an example of reading an Excel file using Polars, where we are trying to read an Excel file which has pillar measurements:

```
import polars as pl
df = pl.read_excel(r"C:\Users\khila\Downloads\Excel Pillar Data.xlsx",
sheet_name="Sheet1")
print(df.head())
Output:
shape: (5, 4)
```

A --- f64	B --- f64	C --- f64	D --- f64
0.87139	0.614969	0.650503	0.695612
0.096167	0.98015	0.462977	0.03551
0.156749	0.308499	0.304978	0.31578
0.888987	0.777063	0.467058	0.51262
0.322345	0.631882	0.369446	0.554432

Reading Multiple Files

Polars can efficiently handle multiple files, which allow users to manage large datasets with varying memory demands. To create context, one can generate multiple CSV files by writing the same DataFrame to different files. When it comes to reading these files, Polars makes it easy to load them into a single DataFrame using globbing patterns. This method allows you to read multiple files at once and automatically combines the data into one cohesive structure. The ability to use patterns like `*.csv` ensures that even if the files are scattered across directories or numbered sequentially, Polars can efficiently process them and merge the content, while providing a unified view of the dataset.

We will create 10 files of loan data with the following snippet:

```
import polars as pl
import random

# Function to generate random loan data
def generate_loan_data(rows):
    data = {
        "Loan ID": [f"LN{str(i).zfill(5)}" for i in range(rows)],
        "Customer ID": [f"CUST{random.randint(1000, 9999)}" for _ in
range(rows)],
        "Loan Amount": [random.randint(5000, 50000) for _ in
range(rows)],
        "Interest Rate": [round(random.uniform(3.0, 15.0), 2) for _ in
range(rows)],
        "Loan Term (Years)": [random.choice([5, 10, 15, 20]) for _ in
range(rows)],
        "Status": [random.choice(["Approved", "Pending", "Rejected"])
for _ in range(rows)],
    }
    return pl.DataFrame(data)

# Directory to save the files
output_dir = "loan_data/"
os.makedirs(output_dir, exist_ok=True)

# Create 10 CSV files with 10 rows each.
for i in range(1, 11):
    file_name = f"{output_dir}loan_data_part_{i}.csv"
    df = generate_loan_data(10)
    df.write_csv(file_name)
```

Now, we will load the same files using a single Polars line.

```
df = pl.read_csv("loan_data/loan_data_part_*.csv")
print(df.shape)
```

```
Output:
(100, 6)
```

Working with Files: Write Operations

Polars provides a convenient way to write data to multiple files, which can be useful for managing large datasets or splitting data across different storage locations. By using a loop, you can write the same DataFrame to several CSV files and ensure that each file contains a portion of the data. This approach is beneficial when dealing with memory limitations or when you want to distribute the data into smaller, manageable files. With Polars, you can easily control how your data is written across multiple files, which allows for better scalability and data organization.

First, we will create a DataFrame and then export it to different file formats.

```
import polars as pl
import random
from datetime import datetime, timedelta

# Function to generate random traffic data
def generate_traffic_data(rows):
    vehicle_types = ["Car", "Bus", "Motorbike", "Truck", "Auto"]
    road_conditions = ["Clear", "Congested", "Accident", "Construction", 
"Heavy Rain"]

    # Generate random data.
    data = {
        "Timestamp": [datetime.now() - timedelta(minutes=random.
randint(1, 1000)) for _ in range(rows)],
        "Traffic Volume": [random.randint(50, 3000) for _ in range(rows)], 
# Vehicles per hour
        "Road Condition": [random.choice(road_conditions) for _ in 
range(rows)],
        "Speed Limit": [random.choice([40, 50, 60, 70, 80]) for _ in 
range(rows)],  # km/h
        "Vehicle Type": [random.choice(vehicle_types) for _ in 
range(rows)],
    }

    return pl.DataFrame(data)

# Create the DataFrame with 100 rows.
df = generate_traffic_data(100)
print(df.head())
```

Output:

```
shape: (5, 5)
┌─────────────────────────────────────┬─────────────────┬──────────────────┬───────────
──────┬──────────────┐
│ Timestamp                           ┆ Traffic Volume ┆ Road Condition ┆ Speed
Limit ┆ Vehicle Type │
│ ---                                 ┆ ---            ┆ ---            ┆ ---
┆ ---          │
│ datetime[μs]                        ┆ i64            ┆ str            ┆ i64
┆ str          │
╞═════════════════════════════════════╪═════════════════╪══════════════════╪═══════════
══════╪══════════════╡
│ 2025-01-14 08:18:07.701815 ┆ 1431           ┆ Construction   ┆ 60
┆ Truck        │
│ 2025-01-14 07:31:07.701831 ┆ 523            ┆ Clear          ┆ 50
┆ Bus          │
│ 2025-01-14 14:02:07.701836 ┆ 375            ┆ Heavy Rain     ┆ 70
┆ Auto         │
│ 2025-01-14 14:57:07.701839 ┆ 309            ┆ Accident       ┆ 80
┆ Truck        │
│ 2025-01-14 17:19:07.701842 ┆ 557            ┆ Accident       ┆ 60
┆ Motorbike    │
└─────────────────────────────────────┴─────────────────┴──────────────────┴───────────
──────┴──────────────┘
```

Now, we will export these into multiple formats.

```
df.write_csv("bangalore_traffic_data.csv")
df.write_json("bangalore_traffic_data.json")
df.write_ndjson("bangalore_traffic_data.ndjson")
```

We need the xlswriter library installed as an additional dependency to write to Excel files. After installing it, we can export the dataframe to Excel.

```
df.write_excel("bangalore_traffic_data.xlsx")
```

Selecting and Manipulating Data

Let us create a DataFrame of a sales data collected from an electronic store, we will perform all our operation on this DataFrame:

```
import polars as pl
import random
from datetime import datetime

# Create a sample DataFrame for electronic store sales data.
data = {
```

```
    "Transaction ID": [f"TXN{str(i).zfill(5)}" for i in range(1, 11)],
    "Product": ["Laptop", "Phone", "Tablet", "Laptop", "Headphones",
"Phone", "Tablet", "Laptop", "Phone", "Headphones"],
    "Quantity": [random.randint(1, 5) for _ in range(10)],
    "Price per Unit": [random.randint(500, 1500) for _ in range(10)],
    "Date of Sale": [datetime.now().strftime("%Y-%m-%d") for _ in range(10)],
    "Store Location": ["Bangalore", "Chennai", "Mumbai", "Bangalore",
"Delhi", "Chennai", "Mumbai", "Bangalore", "Delhi", "Chennai"]
}

df = pl.DataFrame(data)
print("Original DataFrame:")
print(df)
output :
Original DataFrame:
shape: (10, 6)
```

Transaction ID Store Location	Product	Quantity	Price per Unit	Date of Sale
--- ---	---	---	---	---
str str	str	i64	i64	str
TXN00001 Bangalore	Laptop	5	1466	2025-01-14
TXN00002 Chennai	Phone	4	859	2025-01-14
TXN00003 Mumbai	Tablet	4	1219	2025-01-14
TXN00004 Bangalore	Laptop	5	1076	2025-01-14
TXN00005 Delhi	Headphones	1	661	2025-01-14
TXN00006 Chennai	Phone	2	518	2025-01-14
TXN00007 Mumbai	Tablet	3	1346	2025-01-14
TXN00008 Bangalore	Laptop	1	780	2025-01-14
TXN00009 Delhi	Phone	5	676	2025-01-14
TXN00010 Chennai	Headphones	5	1063	2025-01-14

Selecting Columns

To select specific columns, you can simply use the column names in square brackets or use `.select()` for multiple columns.

```
# Selecting a single column (Price per Unit)
price_column = df["Price per Unit"]
print("Selected 'Price per Unit' column:")
print(price_column)

# Selecting multiple columns (Product, Quantity, Price per Unit)
selected_columns = df.select(["Product", "Quantity", "Price per Unit"])
print("Selected multiple columns (Product, Quantity, Price per Unit):")
print(selected_columns)
output :
Selected 'Price per Unit' column:
shape: (10,)
Series: 'Price per Unit' [i64]
[
	1466
	859
	1219
	1076
	661
	518
	1346
	780
	676
	1063
]
Selected multiple columns (Product, Quantity, Price per Unit):
shape: (10, 3)
```

Product --- str	Quantity --- i64	Price per Unit --- i64
Laptop	5	1466
Phone	4	859
Tablet	4	1219
Laptop	5	1076
Headphones	1	661
Phone	2	518
Tablet	3	1346
Laptop	1	780
Phone	5	676
Headphones	5	1063

Selecting columns allows you to focus on the data relevant to the analysis, such as extracting the price or quantity for a cost-based analysis.

Renaming Columns

You can rename columns using the `.rename()` method by providing a dictionary of old column names to new ones.

```
# Renaming columns
df_renamed = df.rename({"Transaction ID": "TransactionID", "Price per
Unit": "Unit Price"})
print("DataFrame with renamed columns:")
print(df_renamed)
output :
DataFrame with renamed columns:
shape: (10, 6)
┌───────────────┬────────────┬──────────┬────────────┬──────────────┬────────
───────────────┐
│ TransactionID ┆ Product    ┆ Quantity ┆ Unit Price ┆ Date of Sale ┆
Store Location │
│ ---           ┆ ---        ┆ ---      ┆ ---        ┆ ---          ┆
---            │
│ str           ┆ str        ┆ i64      ┆ i64        ┆ str          ┆
str            │
╞═══════════════╪════════════╪══════════╪════════════╪══════════════╪════════
═══════════════╡
│ TXN00001      ┆ Laptop     ┆ 5        ┆ 1466       ┆ 2025-01-14   ┆
Bangalore      │
│ TXN00002      ┆ Phone      ┆ 4        ┆ 859        ┆ 2025-01-14   ┆
Chennai        │
│ TXN00003      ┆ Tablet     ┆ 4        ┆ 1219       ┆ 2025-01-14   ┆
Mumbai         │
│ TXN00004      ┆ Laptop     ┆ 5        ┆ 1076       ┆ 2025-01-14   ┆
Bangalore      │
│ TXN00005      ┆ Headphones ┆ 1        ┆ 661        ┆ 2025-01-14   ┆
Delhi          │
│ TXN00006      ┆ Phone      ┆ 2        ┆ 518        ┆ 2025-01-14   ┆
Chennai        │
│ TXN00007      ┆ Tablet     ┆ 3        ┆ 1346       ┆ 2025-01-14   ┆
Mumbai         │
│ TXN00008      ┆ Laptop     ┆ 1        ┆ 780        ┆ 2025-01-14   ┆
Bangalore      │
│ TXN00009      ┆ Phone      ┆ 5        ┆ 676        ┆ 2025-01-14   ┆
Delhi          │
│ TXN00010      ┆ Headphones ┆ 5        ┆ 1063       ┆ 2025-01-14   ┆
Chennai        │
└───────────────┴────────────┴──────────┴────────────┴──────────────┴────────
───────────────┘
```

Renaming columns is useful when the original column names are not descriptive enough or need to be standardized for better readability and consistency.

Modifying Columns

You can add new columns or modify existing ones by assigning new values.

```
# Adding a new column for total sales (Quantity * Price per Unit)
df_with_total = df.with_columns((df["Quantity"] * df["Price per Unit"]).
alias("Total Sales"))
print("DataFrame with 'Total Sales' column:")
print(df_with_total)
output :
DataFrame with 'Total Sales' column:
shape: (10, 7)
```

Transaction ID	Product	Quantity	Price per Unit	Date of Sale	Store Location	Total Sales
---	---	---	---	---	---	---
str	str	i64	i64	str	str	i64
TXN00001	Laptop	5	1466	2025-01-14	Bangalore	7330
TXN00002	Phone	4	859	2025-01-14	Chennai	3436
TXN00003	Tablet	4	1219	2025-01-14	Mumbai	4876
TXN00004	Laptop	5	1076	2025-01-14	Bangalore	5380
TXN00005	Headphones	1	661	2025-01-14	Delhi	661
TXN00006	Phone	2	518	2025-01-14	Chennai	1036
TXN00007	Tablet	3	1346	2025-01-14	Mumbai	4038
TXN00008	Laptop	1	780	2025-01-14	Bangalore	780
TXN00009	Phone	5	676	2025-01-14	Delhi	3380
TXN00010	Headphones	5	1063	2025-01-14	Chennai	5315

Modifying columns allows you to derive new information (like the total sales for each transaction) by performing operations on existing columns.

Filtering Rows

To filter rows, you can apply conditions using logical expressions, as shown here:

```
# Filtering rows where the quantity sold is greater than 2
filtered_df = df.filter(df["Quantity"] > 2)
print("Filtered DataFrame where Quantity > 2:")
print(filtered_df)
output :
Filtered DataFrame where Quantity > 2:
shape: (7, 6)
```

Transaction ID Store Location	Product	Quantity	Price per Unit	Date of Sale
--- ---	---	---	---	---
str str	str	i64	i64	str
TXN00001 Bangalore	Laptop	5	1466	2025-01-14
TXN00002 Chennai	Phone	4	859	2025-01-14
TXN00003 Mumbai	Tablet	4	1219	2025-01-14
TXN00004 Bangalore	Laptop	5	1076	2025-01-14
TXN00007 Mumbai	Tablet	3	1346	2025-01-14
TXN00009 Delhi	Phone	5	676	2025-01-14
TXN00010 Chennai	Headphones	5	1063	2025-01-14

Filtering rows helps you focus on specific subsets of data based on business logic or analysis requirements, such as identifying high-volume transactions.

Sorting Data with Ascending/Descending Options

You can sort data by one or more columns in ascending or descending order using the `.sort()` method.

```
# Sorting by 'Quantity' in descending order
sorted_df_desc = df.sort("Quantity", reverse=True)
print("DataFrame sorted by 'Quantity' in descending order:")
print(sorted_df_desc)

# Sorting by 'Product' and 'Quantity' (first by product, then by
quantity)
sorted_df_multiple = df.sort(["Product", "Quantity"])
print("DataFrame sorted by 'Product' and 'Quantity':")
print(sorted_df_multiple)
output :
DataFrame sorted by 'Quantity' in descending order:
shape: (10, 6)
```

Transaction ID Store Location	Product	Quantity	Price per Unit	Date of Sale
--- ---	---	---	---	---
str str	str	i64	i64	str
TXN00005 Delhi	Headphones	1	661	2025-01-14
TXN00008 Bangalore	Laptop	1	780	2025-01-14
TXN00006 Chennai	Phone	2	518	2025-01-14
TXN00007 Mumbai	Tablet	3	1346	2025-01-14
TXN00002 Chennai	Phone	4	859	2025-01-14
TXN00003 Mumbai	Tablet	4	1219	2025-01-14
TXN00001 Bangalore	Laptop	5	1466	2025-01-14
TXN00004	Laptop	5	1076	2025-01-14

```
│ Bangalore      │            │          │                │            │
│ TXN00009       │ Phone      │ 5        │ 676            │ 2025-01-14 │
│ Delhi          │            │          │                │            │
│ TXN00010       │ Headphones │ 5        │ 1063           │ 2025-01-14 │
│ Chennai        │            │          │                │            │
└────────────────┴────────────┴──────────┴────────────────┴────────────┴
───────────────┘

DataFrame sorted by 'Product' and 'Quantity':
shape: (10, 6)
┌────────────────┬────────────┬──────────┬────────────────┬────────────┬
───────────────┐
│ Transaction ID │ Product    │ Quantity │ Price per Unit │ Date of Sale
│ Store Location │            │          │                │            │
│ ---            │ ---        │ ---      │ ---            │ ---        │
│ ---            │            │          │                │            │
│ str            │ str        │ i64      │ i64            │ str        │
│ str            │            │          │                │            │
╞════════════════╪════════════╪══════════╪════════════════╪════════════╪
═══════════════╡
│ TXN00005       │ Headphones │ 1        │ 661            │ 2025-01-14 │
│ Delhi          │            │          │                │            │
│ TXN00010       │ Headphones │ 5        │ 1063           │ 2025-01-14 │
│ Chennai        │            │          │                │            │
│ TXN00008       │ Laptop     │ 1        │ 780            │ 2025-01-14 │
│ Bangalore      │            │          │                │            │
│ TXN00001       │ Laptop     │ 5        │ 1466           │ 2025-01-14 │
│ Bangalore      │            │          │                │            │
│ TXN00004       │ Laptop     │ 5        │ 1076           │ 2025-01-14 │
│ Bangalore      │            │          │                │            │
│ TXN00006       │ Phone      │ 2        │ 518            │ 2025-01-14 │
│ Chennai        │            │          │                │            │
│ TXN00002       │ Phone      │ 4        │ 859            │ 2025-01-14 │
│ Chennai        │            │          │                │            │
│ TXN00009       │ Phone      │ 5        │ 676            │ 2025-01-14 │
│ Delhi          │            │          │                │            │
│ TXN00007       │ Tablet     │ 3        │ 1346           │ 2025-01-14 │
│ Mumbai         │            │          │                │            │
│ TXN00003       │ Tablet     │ 4        │ 1219           │ 2025-01-14 │
│ Mumbai         │            │          │                │            │
└────────────────┴────────────┴──────────┴────────────────┴────────────┴
───────────────┘
```

Sorting data helps you organize the data in a way that is easy to analyze, such as sorting by quantity to find which products sold the most, or sorting by product type to group sales by category.

Transforming Data

Data transformation is needed to clean and standardize raw data, while ensuring consistency and accuracy. It helps in converting data into a suitable format for analysis, improving efficiency and insights. Transformation enables integration from multiple sources, which makes the data comparable and meaningful. It enhances data quality, reduces redundancy, and supports better decision-making in businesses.

We will cover some common data transformation operations.

Calculating New Columns

To calculate new columns, you can use existing columns and apply arithmetic or logical operations to generate derived fields.

```
# Adding a new column for Total Sales (Quantity * Price per Unit)
df_with_total_sales = df.with_columns((df["Quantity"] * df["Price per Unit"]).alias("Total Sales"))
print(df_with_total_sales)

# Adding a column that categorizes products into 'High Value' or 'Low Value' based on a threshold
df_with_value_category = df_with_total_sales.with_columns(
    (pl.col("Total Sales") > 3000).alias("High Value")
)
print(df_with_value_category)
output :
shape: (10, 7)
```

```
┌─────────────────┬──────────────┬──────────┬────────────────┬─────────────
┬─────────────────┬──────────────┐
│ Transaction ID  ┆ Product      ┆ Quantity ┆ Price per Unit ┆ Date of Sale
┆ Store Location  ┆ Total Sales  │
│ ---             ┆ ---          ┆ ---      ┆ ---            ┆ ---
┆ ---             ┆ ---          │
│ str             ┆ str          ┆ i64      ┆ i64            ┆ str
┆ str             ┆ i64          │
╞═════════════════╪══════════════╪══════════╪════════════════╪═════════════
╪═════════════════╪══════════════╡
│ TXN00001        ┆ Laptop       ┆ 5        ┆ 1466           ┆ 2025-01-14
┆ Bangalore       ┆ 7330         │
│ TXN00002        ┆ Phone        ┆ 4        ┆ 859            ┆ 2025-01-14
┆ Chennai         ┆ 3436         │
│ TXN00003        ┆ Tablet       ┆ 4        ┆ 1219           ┆ 2025-01-14
┆ Mumbai          ┆ 4876         │
│ TXN00004        ┆ Laptop       ┆ 5        ┆ 1076           ┆ 2025-01-14
┆ Bangalore       ┆ 5380         │
```

```
│ TXN00005       │ Headphones ┆ 1        ┆ 661            ┆ 2025-01-14
│ Delhi          ┆ 661        │
│ TXN00006       ┆ Phone      ┆ 2        ┆ 518            ┆ 2025-01-14
│ Chennai        ┆ 1036       │
│ TXN00007       ┆ Tablet     ┆ 3        ┆ 1346           ┆ 2025-01-14
│ Mumbai         ┆ 4038       │
│ TXN00008       ┆ Laptop     ┆ 1        ┆ 780            ┆ 2025-01-14
│ Bangalore      ┆ 780        │
│ TXN00009       ┆ Phone      ┆ 5        ┆ 676            ┆ 2025-01-14
│ Delhi          ┆ 3380       │
│ TXN00010       ┆ Headphones ┆ 5        ┆ 1063           ┆ 2025-01-14
│ Chennai        ┆ 5315       │
└────────────────┴────────────┴──────────┴────────────────┴───────────
─┴───────────────┴────────────┘

shape: (10, 8)
┌────────────────┬────────────┬──────────┬────────────────┬───────────
─┬───────────────┬────────────┬──────────┐
│ Transaction ID ┆ Product    ┆ Quantity ┆ Price per Unit ┆ Date of Sale
┆ Store Location ┆ Total Sales ┆ High Value │
│ ---            ┆ ---        ┆ ---      ┆ ---            ┆ ---
┆ ---            ┆ ---        ┆ ---      │
│ str            ┆ str        ┆ i64      ┆ i64            ┆ str
┆ str            ┆ i64        ┆ bool     │
╞════════════════╪════════════╪══════════╪════════════════╪═══════════
═╪═══════════════╪════════════╪══════════╡
│ TXN00001       ┆ Laptop     ┆ 5        ┆ 1466           ┆ 2025-01-14
┆ Bangalore      ┆ 7330       ┆ true     │
│ TXN00002       ┆ Phone      ┆ 4        ┆ 859            ┆ 2025-01-14
┆ Chennai        ┆ 3436       ┆ true     │
│ TXN00003       ┆ Tablet     ┆ 4        ┆ 1219           ┆ 2025-01-14
┆ Mumbai         ┆ 4876       ┆ true     │
│ TXN00004       ┆ Laptop     ┆ 5        ┆ 1076           ┆ 2025-01-14
┆ Bangalore      ┆ 5380       ┆ true     │
│ TXN00005       ┆ Headphones ┆ 1        ┆ 661            ┆ 2025-01-14
┆ Delhi          ┆ 661        ┆ false    │
│ TXN00006       ┆ Phone      ┆ 2        ┆ 518            ┆ 2025-01-14
┆ Chennai        ┆ 1036       ┆ false    │
│ TXN00007       ┆ Tablet     ┆ 3        ┆ 1346           ┆ 2025-01-14
┆ Mumbai         ┆ 4038       ┆ true     │
│ TXN00008       ┆ Laptop     ┆ 1        ┆ 780            ┆ 2025-01-14
┆ Bangalore      ┆ 780        ┆ false    │
│ TXN00009       ┆ Phone      ┆ 5        ┆ 676            ┆ 2025-01-14
┆ Delhi          ┆ 3380       ┆ true     │
│ TXN00010       ┆ Headphones ┆ 5        ┆ 1063           ┆ 2025-01-14
┆ Chennai        ┆ 5315       ┆ true     │
└────────────────┴────────────┴──────────┴────────────────┴───────────
─┴───────────────┴────────────┴──────────┘
```

Adding Calculated Columns: The first operation adds a new column called Total Sales, which is computed by multiplying the Quantity by the Price per Unit. The second operation creates a new Boolean column called High Value, which categorizes transactions based on whether the total sales are greater than 3000.

Summary Statistics

You can calculate summary statistics such as mean, median, count, and more for numerical columns. Polars also allow group-wise aggregation for more detailed insights.

```
# Descriptive statistics for numerical columns
summary = df.describe()
print(summary)
output :
shape: (9, 7)
┌──────────────┬────────────────┬────────────┬──────────┬───────────────┐
┌──────────────┬────────────────┐
│ statistic    ┆ Transaction ID ┆ Product    ┆ Quantity ┆ Price per Unit ┆
Date of Sale   ┆ Store Location │
│ ---          ┆ ---            ┆ ---        ┆ ---      ┆ ---            ┆
---            ┆ ---            │
│ str          ┆ str            │ str        ┆ f64      ┆ f64            ┆
str            ┆ str            │
╞══════════════╪════════════════╪════════════╪══════════╪═══════════════╡
╞══════════════╪════════════════╡
│ count        ┆ 10             │ 10         ┆ 10.0     ┆ 10.0           ┆
10             ┆ 10             │
│ null_count   ┆ 0              │ 0          ┆ 0.0      ┆ 0.0            ┆
0              ┆ 0              │
│ mean         ┆ null           │ null       ┆ 3.5      ┆ 966.4          ┆
null           ┆ null           │
│ std          ┆ null           │ null       ┆ 1.649916 ┆ 316.892972     ┆
null           ┆ null           │
│ min          ┆ TXN00001       │ Headphones ┆ 1.0      ┆ 518.0          ┆
2025-01-14     ┆ Bangalore      │
│ 25%          ┆ null           │ null       ┆ 2.0      ┆ 676.0          ┆
null           ┆ null           │
│ 50%          ┆ null           │ null       ┆ 4.0      ┆ 1063.0         ┆
null           ┆ null           │
│ 75%          ┆ null           │ null       ┆ 5.0      ┆ 1219.0         ┆
null           ┆ null           │
│ max          ┆ TXN00010       │ Tablet     ┆ 5.0      ┆ 1466.0         ┆
2025-01-14     ┆ Mumbai         │
└──────────────┴────────────────┴────────────┴──────────┴───────────────┘
└──────────────┴────────────────┘
```

Summary Statistics: The `describe()` method calculates standard statistics such as mean, median, and count for all numerical columns. This helps understand the overall distribution of data.

Handling Missing Values

Polars provide a range of methods to handle missing values, including filling, dropping, or identifying them.

```
null_row = pl.DataFrame({
    "Transaction ID": [None],
    "Product": [None],
    "Quantity": [None],
    "Price per Unit": [None],
    "Date of Sale": [None],
    "Store Location": [None]
})

# Append the null row to the existing dataframe.
df = df.vstack(null_row)
print(df)
# Identifying missing data: Check for missing values in the 'Quantity'
column
missing_quantity = df.filter(pl.col("Quantity").is_null())
print(missing_quantity)

# Handling missing values: Replace missing values with a default value
(for example, fill with 0 for 'Quantity' and 1000 for 'Price per Unit').
df_filled = df.fill_null(3)
print(df_filled)

# Drop rows with missing values (optional).
df_dropped = df.drop_nulls()
print(df_dropped)

Output :
shape: (11, 6)
┌─────────────────┬──────────┬──────────┬────────────────┬──────────────
┬────────────────┐
│ Transaction ID  ┆ Product  ┆ Quantity ┆ Price per Unit ┆ Date of Sale
│ Store Location  ┆
│ ---             ┆ ---      ┆ ---      ┆ ---            ┆ ---
│ ---             ┆
│ str             ┆ str      ┆ i64      ┆ i64            ┆ str
│ str             ┆
```

```
╞═══════════════════════╪════════════╪════════╪════════════════╪══════════════
═══════════════════════╡
│ TXN00001             ┆ Laptop     ┆ 3      ┆ 745            ┆ 2025-01-14
Bangalore
│ TXN00002             ┆ Phone      ┆ 2      ┆ 729            ┆ 2025-01-14
Chennai
│ TXN00003             ┆ Tablet     ┆ 1      ┆ 523            ┆ 2025-01-14
Mumbai
│ TXN00004             ┆ Laptop     ┆ 2      ┆ 1063           ┆ 2025-01-14
Bangalore
│ TXN00005             ┆ Headphones ┆ 5      ┆ 1441           ┆ 2025-01-14
Delhi
│ …                    ┆ …          ┆ …      ┆ …              ┆ …
…
│ TXN00007             ┆ Tablet     ┆ 5      ┆ 1316           ┆ 2025-01-14
Mumbai
│ TXN00008             ┆ Laptop     ┆ 1      ┆ 1496           ┆ 2025-01-14
Bangalore
│ TXN00009             ┆ Phone      ┆ 3      ┆ 966            ┆ 2025-01-14
Delhi
│ TXN00010             ┆ Headphones ┆ 1      ┆ 1225           ┆ 2025-01-14
Chennai
│ null                 ┆ null       ┆ null   ┆ null           ┆ null
null
└──────────────────────┴────────────┴────────┴────────────────┴──────────────
────────────────────┘
shape: (1, 6)
┌────────────────┬─────────┬──────────┬────────────────┬──────────────┬
────────────────┐
│ Transaction ID ┆ Product ┆ Quantity ┆ Price per Unit ┆ Date of Sale ┆
Store Location │
│ ---            ┆ ---     ┆ ---      ┆ ---            ┆ ---          ┆
---            │
│ str            ┆ str     ┆ i64      ┆ i64            ┆ str          ┆
str            │
╞════════════════╪═════════╪══════════╪════════════════╪══════════════╪
════════════════╡
│ null           ┆ null    ┆ null     ┆ null           ┆ null         ┆
null           │
└────────────────┴─────────┴──────────┴────────────────┴──────────────┴
────────────────┘
shape: (11, 6)
┌──────────────────────┬────────────┬──────────┬────────────────┬─────────────
──────────────────────┐
│ Transaction ID       ┆ Product    ┆ Quantity ┆ Price per Unit ┆ Date of Sale
Store Location
│ ---                  ┆ ---        ┆ ---      ┆ ---            ┆ ---
```

```
│ ---              │
│ str              │ str        ┆ i64      ┆ i64            ┆ str
│ str              │
╞══════════════════╪════════════╪══════════╪════════════════╪═══════════════
═╪═══════════════════╡
│ TXN00001         ┆ Laptop     ┆ 3        ┆ 745            ┆ 2025-01-14
│ Bangalore        │
│ TXN00002         ┆ Phone      ┆ 2        ┆ 729            ┆ 2025-01-14
│ Chennai          │
│ TXN00003         ┆ Tablet     ┆ 1        ┆ 523            ┆ 2025-01-14
│ Mumbai           │
│ TXN00004         ┆ Laptop     ┆ 2        ┆ 1063           ┆ 2025-01-14
│ Bangalore        │
│ TXN00005         ┆ Headphones ┆ 5        ┆ 1441           ┆ 2025-01-14
│ Delhi            │
│ …                ┆ …          ┆ …        ┆ …              ┆ …
│ …                │
│ TXN00007         ┆ Tablet     ┆ 5        ┆ 1316           ┆ 2025-01-14
│ Mumbai           │
│ TXN00008         ┆ Laptop     ┆ 1        ┆ 1496           ┆ 2025-01-14
│ Bangalore        │
│ TXN00009         ┆ Phone      ┆ 3        ┆ 966            ┆ 2025-01-14
│ Delhi            │
│ TXN00010         ┆ Headphones ┆ 1        ┆ 1225           ┆ 2025-01-14
│ Chennai          │
│ null             ┆ null       ┆ 0        ┆ 0              ┆ null
│ null             │
└──────────────────┴────────────┴──────────┴────────────────┴───────────────
─┴───────────────────┘
shape: (10, 6)
┌──────────────────┬────────────┬──────────┬────────────────┬───────────────
─┬───────────────────┐
│ Transaction ID   ┆ Product    ┆ Quantity ┆ Price per Unit ┆ Date of Sale
│ Store Location   │
│ ---              ┆ ---        ┆ ---      ┆ ---            ┆ ---
│ ---              │
│ str              ┆ str        ┆ i64      ┆ i64            ┆ str
│ str              │
╞══════════════════╪════════════╪══════════╪════════════════╪═══════════════
═╪═══════════════════╡
│ TXN00001         ┆ Laptop     ┆ 3        ┆ 745            ┆ 2025-01-14
│ Bangalore        │
│ TXN00002         ┆ Phone      ┆ 2        ┆ 729            ┆ 2025-01-14
│ Chennai          │
│ TXN00003         ┆ Tablet     ┆ 1        ┆ 523            ┆ 2025-01-14
│ Mumbai           │
│ TXN00004         ┆ Laptop     ┆ 2        ┆ 1063           ┆ 2025-01-14
```

```
│ Bangalore     │
│ TXN00005      ┆ Headphones ┆ 5         ┆ 1441         ┆ 2025-01-14
│ Delhi         │
│ TXN00006      ┆ Phone      ┆ 3         ┆ 1059         ┆ 2025-01-14
│ Chennai       │
│ TXN00007      ┆ Tablet     ┆ 5         ┆ 1316         ┆ 2025-01-14
│ Mumbai        │
│ TXN00008      ┆ Laptop     ┆ 1         ┆ 1496         ┆ 2025-01-14
│ Bangalore     │
│ TXN00009      ┆ Phone      ┆ 3         ┆ 966          ┆ 2025-01-14
│ Delhi         │
│ TXN00010      ┆ Headphones ┆ 1         ┆ 1225         ┆ 2025-01-14
│ Chennai       │
└───────────────┴────────────┴───────────┴──────────────┴──────────────
─┘─────────────────┘
```

Identifying Missing Data: The `is_null()` function identifies rows where values are missing (None or NaN). In this case, we filter the rows where the quantity column has null values.

Filling Missing Values: The `fill_none()` method allows you to fill missing values with default values, such as 0 for quantity and 1000 for price per unit. This is useful when you want to maintain consistency in the dataset.

Dropping Missing Values: The `drop_nulls()` method removes rows containing any missing values. This is a common step when dealing with datasets that require complete data for further analysis.

Data Cleaning

Data cleaning removes errors, inconsistencies, and missing values, while ensuring data accuracy and reliability. It improves data quality, leading to better analysis, decision-making, and performance in applications. Polars, with its fast, memory-efficient processing, can quickly filter, de-duplicate, and handle missing data. Let us look at some rudimentary data cleaning tasks.

Removing Duplicates

In Polars, you can remove duplicate rows from a DataFrame using the `unique()` method or by specifying certain columns to identify duplicates.

```
# Remove duplicate rows based on all columns.
df_no_duplicates = df.unique()
print("unique rows with one column for selection")
print(df_no_duplicates)
```

```
# Remove duplicate rows based on specific columns (for example, 'Product'
and 'Store Location').
df_no_duplicates_specific = df.unique(subset=["Product", "Store Location"])
print("unique rows with two columns for selection")
print(df_no_duplicates_specific)
```

```
output :
unique rows with one column for selection
shape: (10, 6)
```

Transaction ID	Product	Quantity	Price per Unit	Date of Sale	Store Location
---	---	---	---	---	---
str	str	i64	i64	str	str
TXN00007	Tablet	1	597	2025-01-14	Mumbai
TXN00010	Headphones	3	1384	2025-01-14	Chennai
TXN00006	Phone	3	792	2025-01-14	Chennai
TXN00005	Headphones	1	1174	2025-01-14	Delhi
TXN00004	Laptop	4	598	2025-01-14	Bangalore
TXN00001	Laptop	2	1139	2025-01-14	Bangalore
TXN00008	Laptop	4	953	2025-01-14	Bangalore
TXN00002	Phone	5	1296	2025-01-14	Chennai
TXN00009	Phone	2	1198	2025-01-14	Delhi
TXN00003	Tablet	4	1014	2025-01-14	Mumbai

```
unique rows with two columns for selection
shape: (6, 6)
```

Transaction ID	Product	Quantity	Price per Unit	Date of Sale	Store Location
---	---	---	---	---	---
str	str	i64	i64	str	str
TXN00002	Phone	5	1296	2025-01-14	Chennai
TXN00010	Headphones	3	1384	2025-01-14	Chennai
TXN00003	Tablet	4	1014	2025-01-14	Mumbai
TXN00001	Laptop	2	1139	2025-01-14	Bangalore
TXN00009	Phone	2	1198	2025-01-14	Delhi
TXN00005	Headphones	1	1174	2025-01-14	Delhi

`unique()`: This method removes duplicate rows based on all columns by default. You can also specify certain columns to check for duplicates by using the subset parameter.

The first example removes duplicates across all columns, while the second example removes duplicates based on the combination of Product and Store Location.

Standardizing Column Names

Column names might not always follow consistent conventions, so you can standardize them by converting to lower case, removing spaces, or replacing special characters.

```
# Standardize column names: Convert to lower case and replace spaces
with underscores.
df_standardized_columns = df.rename({col: col.lower().replace(" ", "_")
for col in df.columns})
print(df_standardized_columns)
output :

shape: (10, 6)
```

```
┌────────────────┬─────────────┬──────────┬────────────────┬─────────────
─┬────────────────┐
│ transaction_id ┆ product     ┆ quantity ┆ price_per_unit ┆ date_of_sale
┆ store_location │
│ ---            ┆ ---         ┆ ---      ┆ ---            ┆ ---          ┆
---            │
│ str            ┆ str         ┆ i64      ┆ i64            ┆ str          ┆
str            │
╞════════════════╪═════════════╪══════════╪════════════════╪═════════════
═╪════════════════╡
│ TXN00001       ┆ Laptop      ┆ 2        ┆ 1139           ┆ 2025-01-14
┆ Bangalore      │
│ TXN00002       ┆ Phone       ┆ 5        ┆ 1296           ┆ 2025-01-14
┆ Chennai        │
│ TXN00003       ┆ Tablet      ┆ 4        ┆ 1014           ┆ 2025-01-14
┆ Mumbai         │
│ TXN00004       ┆ Laptop      ┆ 4        ┆ 598            ┆ 2025-01-14
┆ Bangalore      │
│ TXN00005       ┆ Headphones  ┆ 1        ┆ 1174           ┆ 2025-01-14
┆ Delhi          │
│ TXN00006       ┆ Phone       ┆ 3        ┆ 792            ┆ 2025-01-14
┆ Chennai        │
│ TXN00007       ┆ Tablet      ┆ 1        ┆ 597            ┆ 2025-01-14
┆ Mumbai         │
│ TXN00008       ┆ Laptop      ┆ 4        ┆ 953            ┆ 2025-01-14
┆ Bangalore      │
│ TXN00009       ┆ Phone       ┆ 2        ┆ 1198           ┆ 2025-01-14
┆ Delhi          │
│ TXN00010       ┆ Headphones  ┆ 3        ┆ 1384           ┆ 2025-01-14
┆ Chennai        │
└────────────────┴─────────────┴──────────┴────────────────┴─────────────
─┴────────────────┘
```

`rename()`: The `rename()` method is used to rename columns based on a dictionary. In this case, we use a dictionary comprehension to convert all column names to lowercase and replace spaces with underscores.

This ensures consistent and clean column names, which is a common practice in data engineering and analysis.

Cleaning String Data through String Operations

Polars provide a wide range of string operations to clean and transform string data, including handling case sensitivity, trimming whitespace, and using regex. This is demonstrated as follows:

```
# Clean strings: Convert to lowercase, trim leading/trailing whitespace,
and remove any extra spaces between words.
df_cleaned_strings = df.with_columns([
    pl.col("Product")
    .str.strip_chars()  # Trim whitespace
    .str.to_lowercase()  # Convert to lowercase
   .str.replace_all(r"\s+", " ")  # Replace multiple spaces with a single
space
    .alias("Cleaned Product")
])
print("cleaned column")
print(df_cleaned_strings)

# Explode a string column into a list of words (split by spaces).
df_exploded = df.with_columns([
    pl.col("Product").str.split(" ").alias("Exploded Product")
])
print("exploded column")
print(df_exploded)

# Extract a substring using regular expressions (for example, extract the
first char).
df_regex_extracted = df.with_columns([
    pl.col("Product").str.extract(r"(\w)", 1).alias("First Word")
])
print("Regex Extraction")
print(df_regex_extracted)

output :

cleaned column
shape: (10, 7)
┌─────────────────┬─────────────┬──────────┬────────────────┬─────────────
─┬────────────────┬─────────────────┐
│ Transaction ID ┆ Product     ┆ Quantity ┆ Price per Unit ┆ Date of Sale
┆ Store Location ┆ Cleaned Product │
│ ---            ┆ ---         ┆ ---      ┆ ---            ┆ ---          ┆
---            ┆ ---             │
│ str            ┆ str         ┆ i64      ┆ i64            ┆ str          ┆
str            ┆ str             │
╞═════════════════╪═════════════╪══════════╪════════════════╪═════════════
═╪════════════════╪═════════════════╡
│ TXN00001       ┆ Laptop      ┆ 2        ┆ 1139           ┆ 2025-01-14   ┆
Bangalore      ┆ laptop          │
│ TXN00002       ┆ Phone       ┆ 5        ┆ 1296           ┆ 2025-01-14   ┆
```

```
Chennai         ┆ phone         │
│ TXN00003      ┆ Tablet     ┆ 4        ┆ 1014           ┆ 2025-01-14   ┆
Mumbai          ┆ tablet        │
│ TXN00004      ┆ Laptop     ┆ 4        ┆ 598            ┆ 2025-01-14   ┆
Bangalore       ┆ laptop        │
│ TXN00005      ┆ Headphones ┆ 1        ┆ 1174           ┆ 2025-01-14   ┆
Delhi           ┆ headphones    │
│ TXN00006      ┆ Phone      ┆ 3        ┆ 792            ┆ 2025-01-14   ┆
Chennai         ┆ phone         │
│ TXN00007      ┆ Tablet     ┆ 1        ┆ 597            ┆ 2025-01-14   ┆
Mumbai          ┆ tablet        │
│ TXN00008      ┆ Laptop     ┆ 4        ┆ 953            ┆ 2025-01-14   ┆
Bangalore       ┆ laptop        │
│ TXN00009      ┆ Phone      ┆ 2        ┆ 1198           ┆ 2025-01-14   ┆
Delhi           ┆ phone         │
│ TXN00010      ┆ Headphones ┆ 3        ┆ 1384           ┆ 2025-01-14   ┆
Chennai         ┆ headphones    │
└───────────────┴────────────┴──────────┴────────────────┴──────────────
──┴───────────────┴────────────────┘

exploded column
shape: (10, 7)
┌───────────────┬────────────┬──────────┬────────────────┬──────────────
──┬───────────────┬────────────────┐
│ Transaction ID ┆ Product    ┆ Quantity ┆ Price per Unit ┆ Date of Sale
┆ Store Location ┆ Exploded Product │
│ ---           ┆ ---        ┆ ---      ┆ ---            ┆ ---          ┆
---             ┆ ---           │
│ str           ┆ str        ┆ i64      ┆ i64            ┆ str          ┆
str             ┆ list[str]     │
╞═══════════════╪════════════╪══════════╪════════════════╪══════════════
══╪═══════════════╪════════════════╡
│ TXN00001      ┆ Laptop     ┆ 2        ┆ 1139           ┆ 2025-01-14   ┆
Bangalore       ┆ ["Laptop"]      │
│ TXN00002      ┆ Phone      ┆ 5        ┆ 1296           ┆ 2025-01-14   ┆
Chennai         ┆ ["Phone"]       │
│ TXN00003      ┆ Tablet     ┆ 4        ┆ 1014           ┆ 2025-01-14   ┆
Mumbai          ┆ ["Tablet"]      │
│ TXN00004      ┆ Laptop     ┆ 4        ┆ 598            ┆ 2025-01-14   ┆
Bangalore       ┆ ["Laptop"]      │
│ TXN00005      ┆ Headphones ┆ 1        ┆ 1174           ┆ 2025-01-14   ┆
Delhi           ┆ ["Headphones"]  │
│ TXN00006      ┆ Phone      ┆ 3        ┆ 792            ┆ 2025-01-14   ┆
Chennai         ┆ ["Phone"]       │
│ TXN00007      ┆ Tablet     ┆ 1        ┆ 597            ┆ 2025-01-14   ┆
Mumbai          ┆ ["Tablet"]      │
│ TXN00008      ┆ Laptop     ┆ 4        ┆ 953            ┆ 2025-01-14   ┆
```

```
Bangalore        ┆ ["Laptop"]      │
│ TXN00009        ┆ Phone      ┆ 2          ┆ 1198            ┆ 2025-01-14    ┆
Delhi            ┆ ["Phone"]       │
│ TXN00010        ┆ Headphones ┆ 3          ┆ 1384            ┆ 2025-01-14    ┆
Chennai          ┆ ["Headphones"]  │
└─────────────────┴────────────┴────────────┴─────────────────┴───────────────
─┴────────────────┴───────────────┘

Regex Extraction
shape: (10, 7)
┌─────────────────┬────────────┬────────────┬─────────────────┬───────────────
─┬────────────────┬───────────────┐
│ Transaction ID  ┆ Product    ┆ Quantity   ┆ Price per Unit  ┆ Date of Sale
┆ Store Location  ┆ First Word │
│ ---             ┆ ---        ┆ ---        ┆ ---             ┆ ---           ┆
---              ┆ ---        │
│ str             ┆ str        ┆ i64        ┆ i64             ┆ str           ┆
str              ┆ str        │
╞═════════════════╪════════════╪════════════╪═════════════════╪═══════════════
═╪════════════════╪═══════════╡
│ TXN00001        ┆ Laptop     ┆ 2          ┆ 1139            ┆ 2025-01-14    ┆
Bangalore        ┆ L          │
│ TXN00002        ┆ Phone      ┆ 5          ┆ 1296            ┆ 2025-01-14    ┆
Chennai          ┆ P          │
│ TXN00003        ┆ Tablet     ┆ 4          ┆ 1014            ┆ 2025-01-14    ┆
Mumbai           ┆ T          │
│ TXN00004        ┆ Laptop     ┆ 4          ┆ 598             ┆ 2025-01-14    ┆
Bangalore        ┆ L          │
│ TXN00005        ┆ Headphones ┆ 1          ┆ 1174            ┆ 2025-01-14    ┆
Delhi            ┆ H          │
│ TXN00006        ┆ Phone      ┆ 3          ┆ 792             ┆ 2025-01-14    ┆
Chennai          ┆ P          │
│ TXN00007        ┆ Tablet     ┆ 1          ┆ 597             ┆ 2025-01-14    ┆
Mumbai           ┆ T          │
│ TXN00008        ┆ Laptop     ┆ 4          ┆ 953             ┆ 2025-01-14    ┆
Bangalore        ┆ L          │
│ TXN00009        ┆ Phone      ┆ 2          ┆ 1198            ┆ 2025-01-14    ┆
Delhi            ┆ P          │
│ TXN00010        ┆ Headphones ┆ 3          ┆ 1384            ┆ 2025-01-14    ┆
Chennai          ┆ H          │
└─────────────────┴────────────┴────────────┴─────────────────┴───────────────
─┴────────────────┴───────────┘
```

String Cleaning:

- The `str.strip()` method is used to remove leading and trailing whitespace from the Product column.

- `str.to_lowercase()` converts the strings to lowercase, while ensuring case insensitivity.
- `str.replace_all(r"\s+", " ")` replaces multiple spaces with a single space.

Exploding a Column: The `str.split()` method splits the Product string into a list of words (based on spaces). This is useful for further analysis.

Regex Extraction: The `str.extract()` method is used to extract the first word (using the regex pattern (\w+)). This can be helpful when extracting structured data from unstructured text.

Conclusion

In this chapter, we covered a comprehensive range of techniques for efficiently working with data using Polars. By learning how to read and write various file formats, such as JSON, Parquet, CSV, and Excel, you have gained the flexibility to handle datasets across different storage systems. The ability to select, manipulate, and filter data allows for refined analysis and customized workflows, which enables you to focus on the most relevant information.

Furthermore, the methods for transforming and cleaning data, such as creating calculated columns, generating summary statistics, handling missing values, and standardizing data, ensure that you can prepare datasets that are both clean and insightful. Removing duplicates and managing string data effectively are also essential skills for maintaining high-quality datasets.

By mastering these operations, you are now equipped to handle real-world data engineering and analysis tasks with confidence. The techniques covered in this chapter will serve as the foundation for more advanced data manipulation and provide a strong base for any future data projects.

In the next chapter, we will cover more complex data transformation with practical examples.

Exercises

Exercise 1: Reading and Writing Data

Task: Write the steps to read a Parquet file and write the data into a CSV file using Polars.

Exercise 2: File Format Understanding

Task: In your own words, explain the differences between Parquet and CSV file formats. In which scenarios would you choose one over the other for analysis?

Exercise 3: Selecting and Manipulating Data

Task: Describe the steps to select only the product and price columns from a dataset and filter rows where the quantity is greater than 10 using Polars.

Exercise 4: Renaming Columns

Task: Describe the steps to rename the column Price to Unit_Price in the dataset using Polars.

Exercise 5: Modifying Columns

Task: Explain how to create a new column Total_Cost by multiplying the Quantity and Price columns in a Polars DataFrame.

Exercise 6: Sorting Data

Task: Describe how to sort a DataFrame by the Date column in descending order using Polars.

Exercise 7: Calculating New Columns

Task: Explain how to calculate a new column Total_Amount by adding Sales and the tax (calculated from Tax_Rate) in the dataset.

Exercise 8: Summary Statistics

Task: Describe the steps to calculate the mean, median, and standard deviation for the Price column using Polars.

Exercise 9: Handling Missing Values

Task: Explain how to replace missing values in the Product column with a placeholder value 'Unknown' in a Polars DataFrame.

Exercise 10: Data Cleaning

Task: Describe the steps to clean the Product_Name column by converting all the text to lowercase and removing any leading/trailing spaces.

CHAPTER 5
Complex Data Transformation with Polars

"The key to unlocking value in data lies in its transformation—turning noise into knowledge."

Pieter den Hamer

Introduction

As data grows in volume and complexity, advanced techniques become essential to extract meaningful insights efficiently. This chapter will delve into powerful data manipulation methods that allow analysts to transform, reshape, and refine datasets for deeper analysis. From grouping and aggregating data to performing complex joins and merges, we will explore techniques that streamline data integration and enhance analytical workflows. These methods are crucial for preparing raw data into structured formats that support effective decision-making.

Beyond basic transformations, this chapter will also cover more advanced reshaping techniques such as concatenation, pivoting, and unpivoting (melting), which enable analysts to restructure datasets based on specific analytical needs. We will further examine resampling methods to modify data frequency, as well as mapping and transformation techniques that facilitate value conversions. By mastering these tools, analysts can optimize data processing and ensure consistency while dealing with dynamic datasets.

Additionally, we will address challenges related to data integrity and quality, including handling outliers, parsing date and time values, and managing inconsistencies. Techniques such as numerical bucketing and normalization will be discussed to improve data distribution and comparability. Lastly, we will explore working with nested data structures, which are becoming increasingly common in modern data storage formats. By the end of this chapter, readers will be equipped with a robust set of skills to manipulate and analyze complex datasets with confidence.

Structure

In this chapter, we will discuss the following topics:

- Grouping and Aggregations
- Joining and Merging Datasets
- Concatenating DataFrames
- Pivoting and Unpivoting (Melt)
- Reshaping and Resampling Data
- Mapping and Transforming Data Values
    - Applying Functions to Transform Values
    - Efficient Data Mapping Techniques
    - Handling Categorical Data Transformations
- Window Functions
    - Types of Window Functions (Rolling, Expanding, Cumulative)
    - Practical Applications in Trend Analysis
- Handling Inconsistent Data
    - Identifying Outliers Using Statistical Methods
- Handling Outliers
    - Identifying Outliers Using Statistical Methods
    - Techniques for Treating and Managing Outliers
    - Impact of Outliers on Analytical Models
- Parsing Dates and Times
    - Extracting and Manipulating Date-time Data
    - Handling Time Zones and Date Formats
    - Common Challenges in Working with Temporal Data
- Bucketing Numerical Data
    - Binning and Categorizing Numerical Values
    - Use Cases of Bucketing in Segmentation and Classification
    - Choosing Appropriate Bin Sizes for Analysis

- Normalizing Numerical Data
  - Standardization vs. Normalization: Key Differences
  - Scaling Techniques for Numerical Attributes
  - Impact of Normalization on Machine Learning Models
- Working with Nested Data
  - Understanding Hierarchical and Nested Structures
  - Flattening and Extracting Meaningful Information

Grouping and Aggregations

Grouping and aggregation are fundamental techniques in data analysis that allow us to summarize and extract meaningful insights from large datasets. Grouping involves dividing data into subsets based on one or more criteria, while aggregation applies statistical operations such as sum, mean, count, or maximum to each subset. These operations help identify trends, patterns, and anomalies in data, which make them invaluable in real-world analytics.

For example, consider a dataset that tracks electricity consumption in different cities. Each row represents a daily electricity usage record with columns for City, Date, and Consumption (kWh). To analyze the total electricity consumption per city over a month, we can use grouping and aggregation. By grouping the data by the City column and applying the sum() function to the Consumption column, we obtain the total consumption for each city. Similarly, using mean(), we can calculate the average daily electricity usage per city.

In the background, when a 'groupby' operation is executed, the data is first sorted based on the grouping column(s). Internally, the dataset is split into separate chunks, with each chunk containing rows that share the same group key. Then, the specified aggregation function is applied to each group independently. The results are then combined into a new dataset, where each unique group key is associated with its aggregated value. This process is optimized using hash-based and tree-based algorithms, ensuring efficiency even for large datasets.

Now, let us explore how we can perform groupby using Polars.

Our Data looks like this:

City --- str	Date --- str	Consumption (kWh) --- i64	Temperature (°C) --- f64	Peak Hours Usage (kWh) --- f64
New York	2024-01-01	437	10.9	165.0
New York	2024-01-02	469	29.3	229.4
New York	2024-01-03	559	31.3	229.8
New York	2024-01-04	414	11.6	173.1
New York	2024-01-05	563	-0.5	244.7
New York	2024-01-06	436	23.3	167.8
New York	2024-01-07	685	34.8	313.0
New York	2024-01-08	677	31.3	243.0
New York	2024-01-09	607	7.0	220.2
New York	2024-01-10	646	28.6	294.9

***Figure 5.1**: Electricity Consumption Data*

Let us calculate the average consumption of electricity for a city using Polars.

```
import polars as pl
# Load the dataset
df = pl.read_csv("electricity_consumption.csv", try_parse_dates=True)
# Calculate the average consumption per city
average_consumption = df.group_by("City").agg(pl.col("Consumption
(kWh)").mean().alias("Avg Consumption (kWh)"))
# Display the result
print(average_consumption)
```

```
Output :
shape: (5, 2)
```

City --- str	Avg Consumption (kWh) --- f64
Los Angeles	557.6
Houston	526.066667
Chicago	545.266667
New York	537.466667
San Francisco	599.566667

Now, if we had to calculate max peak hour usage for capacity planning of the grid, we can do so by adding another aggregation.

```
import polars as pl

# Load the dataset
```

```
df = pl.read_csv("electricity_consumption.csv", try_parse_dates=True)

# Group by City and calculate required metrics
city_stats = df.group_by("City").agg([
    pl.col("Consumption (kWh)").mean().alias("Avg Consumption (kWh)"),
    pl.col("Peak Hours Usage (kWh)").max().alias("Max Peak Hour Usage
(kWh)")
])

# Display the result
print(city_stats)
```

Output:
shape: (5, 3)

City --- str	Avg Consumption (kWh) --- f64	Max Peak Hour Usage (kWh) --- f64
Los Angeles	557.6	315.9
Chicago	545.266667	333.9
New York	537.466667	315.3
Houston	526.066667	306.0
San Francisco	599.566667	316.9

We have successfully calculated max peak hour usage using Polars. Now, we will also cover a scenario where we need to calculate two measurements against the same column. Then, we will calculate the minimum and maximum temperatures.

```
import polars as pl

# Load the dataset
df = pl.read_csv("electricity_consumption.csv", try_parse_dates=True)

# Group by City and calculate required metrics
city_stats = df.group_by("City").agg([
    pl.col("Consumption (kWh)").mean().alias("Avg Consumption (kWh)"),
    pl.col("Peak Hours Usage (kWh)").max().alias("Max Peak Hour Usage
(kWh)"),
    pl.col("Temperature (°C)").min().alias("Min Temperature (°C)"),
    pl.col("Temperature (°C)").max().alias("Max Temperature (°C)")
])

# Display the result
print(city_stats)
```

Output:
shape: (5, 5)

City	Avg Consumption (kWh)	Max Peak Hour Usage (kWh)	Min Temperature (°C)	Max Temperature (°C)
---	---	---	---	---
str	f64	f64	f64	f64
New York	537.466667	315.3	-4.7	34.8
Los Angeles	557.6	315.9	-3.5	34.9
San Francisco	599.566667	316.9	-2.7	34.6
Houston	526.066667	306.0	-2.9	31.3
Chicago	545.266667	333.9	-4.4	35.0

Now, we will calculate peak hour load factor using custom function and apply it to groups.

Peak Hour Load Factor = (Total Consumption (kWh)) / (Number of Days × Max Peak Hours Usage (kWh))

```
import polars as pl

# Load dataset
df = pl.read_csv("electricity_consumption.csv", try_parse_dates=True)

# Define a custom function to calculate Peak Hour Load Factor
def calculate_peak_hour_load_factor(df):
    total_consumption = df["Consumption (kWh)"].sum()
    max_peak_hour_usage = df["Peak Hours Usage (kWh)"].max()
    num_days = df["Date"].n_unique()  # Count unique days in the data
    peak_hour_load_factor = total_consumption / (num_days * max_peak_
hour_usage) if max_peak_hour_usage > 0 else None
    return pl.DataFrame({"Peak Hour Load Factor": [peak_hour_load_
factor]})

# Apply custom function using groupby_map
city_stats = df.group_by("City").map_groups(calculate_peak_hour_load_
factor)

# Display results
```

```
print(city_stats)
```

```
Output :
shape: (5, 1)
```

Peak Hour Load Factor --- f64
1.891974
1.70462
1.633024
1.719172
1.765116

Here, we have created a custom function to calculate peak hour load factor and applied to the groups using `map_groups`. One thing to note is the custom functions(UDF) will be slower with respect to execution speed.

Multi-Level Grouping

Multi-level grouping, also known as hierarchical grouping, allows us to group data based on multiple columns instead of just one. In Polars, this is done using .groupby(["Column1", "Column2"]) for more granular aggregations. For example, in an electricity consumption dataset, we might group by both City and Week to analyze Weekly electricity usage per city. When `groupby` is applied at multiple levels, Polars first sorts data by the first column (City), then further groups within each city by the second column (Week). This hierarchical grouping ensures that computations such as sum(), mean(), or max() are applied within each sub-group. This provides deeper insights into trends across different dimensions. Multi-level grouping is particularly useful when analyzing time-series data, regional trends, or categorical segmentations.

```
import polars as pl

# Load the dataset
df = pl.read_csv("electricity_consumption.csv", try_parse_dates=True).
with_columns(pl.col("Date").dt.week().alias("Week_Number"))

# Group by City and calculate required metrics
city_stats = df.group_by("City","Week_Number").agg([
    pl.col("Consumption (kWh)").mean().alias("Avg Consumption (kWh)"),
    pl.col("Peak Hours Usage (kWh)").max().alias("Max Peak Hour Usage 
(kWh)")
])

# Display the result
```

```
print(city_stats)
```

Output:

shape: (25, 4)

City	Week_Number	Avg Consumption (kWh)	Max Peak Hour Usage (kWh)
---	---	---	---
str	i8	f64	f64
Chicago	3	523.857143	304.7
Houston	4	565.714286	306.0
Chicago	2	548.0	270.0
New York	5	631.0	291.0
Houston	2	488.571429	274.2
…	…	…	…
New York	1	509.0	313.0
San Francisco	2	589.428571	316.9
Houston	5	489.5	239.0
San Francisco	3	593.0	301.1
Chicago	5	588.0	276.5

Joining Datasets

In real-world data analysis, information is often spread across multiple datasets. To gain meaningful insights, we need to combine these datasets effectively. Merging and joining allow us to integrate data from different sources based on shared columns (keys). This is particularly useful when working with large, relational datasets where relevant details are stored separately to maintain data integrity and avoid redundancy.

In Polars, joining of datasets is performed using `.join()` with different types of joins, which is similar to SQL joins:

- **Inner Join:** Keeps only matching records from both datasets
- **Left Join:** Retains all records from the left dataset and matches available data from the right
- **Right Join:** Similar to left join but keeps all records from the right dataset
- **Outer Join:** Includes all records from both datasets, filling missing values where necessary

Merging is the process of combining multiple datasets by stacking them either vertically (adding rows) or horizontally (adding columns). This is useful when appending new records to an existing dataset (for example, merging monthly electricity consumption reports) or when integrating different datasets with related but distinct columns. In Polars, concatenation is performed using the `.concat()` function, which efficiently merges multiple DataFrames. For vertical stacking, we pass a list of DataFrames to `pl.concat()` to ensure they have the same columns. For horizontal concatenation, we use `.hstack()`, provided that both DataFrames have the same number of rows. Additionally, `.extend()` can be used to append rows directly to an existing DataFrame without creating a new copy, optimizing memory usage. These methods allow efficient dataset combination, which makes them essential for large-scale data processing and analytics.

To demonstrate join functionality, we will add a state column from City-State mapping stored in another DataFrame.

```
import polars as pl
states = pl.DataFrame({
    "City": [
        "New York", "Los Angeles", "Chicago", "Houston", "Phoenix",
        "Philadelphia", "San Antonio", "San Diego", "Dallas", "San Jose"
    ],
    "State": [
        "New York", "California", "Illinois", "Texas", "Arizona",
        "Pennsylvania", "Texas", "California", "Texas", "California"
    ]
})
df = pl.read_csv("electricity_consumption.csv", try_parse_dates=True)

# Perform a INNER OUTER JOIN on "City"
merged_df = df.join(states, on="City", how="inner")

# Display the result
print(merged_df)

output :
shape: (120, 6)
```

City	Date	Consumption (kWh)	Temperature (°C)	Peak Hours Usage (kWh)	State
---	---	---	---	---	---
str	date	i64	f64	f64	str
New York	2024-01-01	437	10.9	165.0	New York
New York	2024-01-02	469	29.3	229.4	New York
New York	2024-01-03	559	31.3	229.8	New York
New York	2024-01-04	414	11.6	173.1	New York
New York	2024-01-05	563	-0.5	244.7	New York
…	…	…	…	…	…
Houston	2024-01-26	639	-0.4	223.7	Texas
Houston	2024-01-27	614	5.1	246.8	Texas
Houston	2024-01-28	661	12.1	306.0	Texas
Houston	2024-01-29	551	27.6	239.0	Texas
Houston	2024-01-30	428	7.9	205.8	Texas

We performed an inner join between the electricity_consumption dataset and the states DataFrame using the "City" column as the key. An inner join only keeps records where a match exists in both datasets. This ensures that we retain only cities that appear in both the electricity consumption data and the states dataset, while removing any unmatched entries. This approach is useful when we only want to analyze electricity consumption for cities with a known state mapping, filtering out irrelevant or missing locations. In case of duplicate columns, we can use the "suffix" argument to identify from which DataFrame columns have been mapped.

We can also merge multiple DataFrames using method chaining as illustrated in the following code snippet.

```
import polars as pl
```

```
# Example DataFrames
df1 = pl.DataFrame({
    "City": ["New York", "Los Angeles", "Chicago"],
    "Consumption": [5000, 4500, 6000]
})
df2 = pl.DataFrame({
    "City": ["New York", "Los Angeles", "Chicago"],
    "Temperature": [30, 28, 25]
})
df3 = pl.DataFrame({
    "City": ["New York", "Los Angeles", "Chicago"],
    "Peak Hours Usage": [2500, 2200, 2800]
})
# Merge the DataFrames
merged_df = df1.join(df2, on="City", how="inner") \
               .join(df3, on="City", how="inner")

# Display the merged DataFrame
print(merged_df)
```

```
shape: (3, 4)
```

City --- str	Consumption --- i64	Temperature --- i64	Peak Hours Usage --- i64
New York	5000	30	2500
Los Angeles	4500	28	2200
Chicago	6000	25	2800

Concatenation/Merging

When concatenating two datasets (**electricity_consumption_2025.csv** and **electricity_consumption.csv**) using Polars, we will load the two CSV files into Polars DataFrames (**df_2025** and **df_previous**). We then print the row counts of both datasets to check how many records are in each. The function **df_2025.shape[0]** and **df_previous.shape[0]** give the number of rows (or records) in the 2025 and 2024 datasets, respectively. After that, we concatenate the two datasets vertically using `pl.concat()`, which stacks the rows from the two DataFrames into a new one, **concatenated_df**. Finally, we print the row count of the concatenated DataFrame to verify that the two datasets have been successfully combined. This approach allows us to combine data from two different time periods (January 2024 and 2025) into a single unified dataset for further analysis.

```
import polars as pl

# Load the two CSV files
df_2025 = pl.read_csv("electricity_consumption_2025.csv")
print("2025 dataset row count" , df_2025.shape[0])
df_previous = pl.read_csv("electricity_consumption.csv")
print("2024 dataset row count" , df_previous.shape[0])

# Concatenate the DataFrames vertically (stacking rows)
concatenated_df = pl.concat([df_2025, df_previous])

# Display the first few rows of the concatenated DataFrame
print("concatenated df row count" , concatenated_df.shape[0])

output :
2025 dataset row count 150
2024 dataset row count 150
concatenated df row count 300
```

Please note that the concatenated DataFrame has all the rows from both the DataFrames and the number of columns remain the same as we vertically merged the DataFrames. To merge DataFrames horizontally, we can use **hstack**. The following is an example of vertical merging of DataFrames:

```
import polars as pl

# Create first DataFrame (First 5 Days)
df1 = pl.DataFrame({
    "City": ["New York", "Los Angeles", "Chicago"],
    "2025-01-01": [500, 450, 600],
    "2025-01-02": [520, 460, 620],
    "2025-01-03": [530, 470, 630],
    "2025-01-04": [540, 480, 640],
    "2025-01-05": [550, 490, 650],
})

# Create second DataFrame (Next 5 Days)
df2 = pl.DataFrame({
    "City": ["New York", "Los Angeles", "Chicago"],
    "2025-01-06": [560, 500, 660],
    "2025-01-07": [570, 510, 670],
    "2025-01-08": [580, 520, 680],
    "2025-01-09": [590, 530, 690],
    "2025-01-10": [600, 540, 700],
})

# Horizontally stack the two DataFrames
```

```
hstacked_df = df1.hstack(df2.drop("City"))

# Display the result
print(hstacked_df)

Output :

shape: (3, 11)
┌─────────────┬────────────┬────────────┬────────────┬─────┬────────────┬
────────────┬────────────┬────────────┐
│ City        ┆ 2025-01-01 ┆ 2025-01-02 ┆ 2025-01-03 ┆ … ┆ 2025-01-07 ┆
2025-01-08 ┆ 2025-01-09 ┆ 2025-01-10 │
│ ---         ┆ ---        ┆ ---        ┆ ---        ┆   ┆ ---        ┆
---        ┆ ---        ┆ ---        │
│ str         ┆ i64        ┆ i64        ┆ i64        ┆   ┆ i64        ┆
i64        ┆ i64        ┆ i64        │
╞═════════════╪════════════╪════════════╪════════════╪═════╪════════════╪
════════════╪════════════╪════════════╡
│ New York    ┆ 500        ┆ 520        ┆ 530        ┆ … ┆ 570        ┆
580        ┆ 590        ┆ 600        │
│ Los Angeles ┆ 450        ┆ 460        ┆ 470        ┆ … ┆ 510        ┆
520        ┆ 530        ┆ 540        │
│ Chicago     ┆ 600        ┆ 620        ┆ 630        ┆ … ┆ 670        ┆
680        ┆ 690        ┆ 700        │
└─────────────┴────────────┴────────────┴────────────┴─────┴────────────┴
────────────┴────────────┴────────────┘
```

Pivoting and Unpivoting (Melt)

Data transformation is a crucial step in any data analysis workflow. The two fundamental techniques used for restructuring data are pivoting and unpivoting (melting). These techniques allow analysts to reshape datasets to suit different analytical needs. This makes datasets more readable and easier to process. Pivoting is the process of converting long-format data into a wider format by turning unique values from a column into separate columns. This is particularly useful when summarizing large datasets, such as aggregating daily electricity consumption per city into a table where each date becomes a column. On the other hand, unpivoting (melting) is the reverse operation where wide-format data is converted back into a long format. This makes data more suitable for statistical analysis and visualization.

Pivoting helps in cases where analysts want to compare multiple attributes side by side or perform calculations across columns. For example, in electricity consumption data, a dataset where each row represents a city's daily power usage can be pivoted to transform the "Date" column into multiple columns, each holding consumption values for that specific day. This makes it easier to track trends over time. Conversely, unpivoting (melting) is useful when working with ML models or databases that require a tidy structure, where each observation is recorded in a single row. For example, instead of storing each date as a separate column, we might store three columns: City, Date, and Consumption (kWh).

Let us pivot our original DataFrame, where city is an index and dates are columns.

```
import polars as pl

# Load the dataset
df = pl.read_csv("electricity_consumption.csv", try_parse_dates=True)

# Pivot the data: City as index, Dates as columns, and Consumption as values
pivot_df = df.pivot(
    index="City",
    on="Date",
    values="Consumption (kWh)"
)

# Display the pivoted DataFrame
print(pivot_df)
```

shape: (5, 31)

City	2024-01-01	2024-01-02	2024-01-03	…	2024-01-27	2024-01-28	2024-01-29	2024-01-30
str	i64	i64	i64		i64	i64	i64	i64
New York	437	469	559	…	450	604	609	653
Los Angeles	442	695	578	…	447	585	617	419
Chicago	533	581	680	…	674	404	690	486
Houston	685	455	474	…	614	661	551	428
San Francisco	655	693	533	…	487	685	690	668

We can also apply aggregations just like groupby to the pivot tables via aggregate_function.

We can unpivot this dataframe through the unpivot method in Polars.

```
# Unpivot the data: Convert multiple date columns into "Date" and
"Consumption (kWh)"
melted_df = pivot_df.unpivot(
    index=["City"],          # Columns to keep unchanged
    on=pivot_df.columns[1:],  # Columns to unpivot (all date columns)
    variable_name="Date",          # New column for dates
    value_name="Consumption (kWh)"  # New column for consumption values
)

# Display the unpivoted DataFrame
print(melted_df)
```

```
Output :
shape: (150, 3)
```

City --- str	Date --- str	Consumption (kWh) --- i64
New York	2024-01-01	437
Los Angeles	2024-01-01	442
Chicago	2024-01-01	533
Houston	2024-01-01	685
San Francisco	2024-01-01	655
…	…	…
New York	2024-01-30	653
Los Angeles	2024-01-30	419
Chicago	2024-01-30	486
Houston	2024-01-30	428
San Francisco	2024-01-30	668

The given Polars code performs an unpivot (melt) operation on a pivoted DataFrame (pivot_df) to transform wide-format data back into a long-format structure. The unpivot() function is used to achieve this by keeping the "City" column unchanged while converting all other columns (which represent different dates) into two new columns: "Date" and "Consumption (kWh)". The on parameter selects all date columns for unpivoting, and variable_name="Date" assigns these column names (dates) to a new "Date" column. Similarly, value_name="Consumption (kWh)" stores the corresponding electricity consumption values in a single column. This transformation makes the dataset more suitable for time-series analysis, filtering, and visualization. This is because row now represents a unique combination of city, date, and electricity consumption, instead of a wider and less flexible format.

Resampling Techniques for Time-Series Data

Resampling is the process of changing the frequency of time-series data to either increase (upsampling) or decrease (downsampling) its resolution. Time-series data often comes in a high-frequency format (for example, minute-wise power consumption readings), but for many analyses, aggregating this data to a lower frequency (for example, daily, weekly, or monthly averages) is more insightful. Conversely, when dealing with missing timestamps or irregularly spaced data points, upsampling helps create a continuous time series, as it fills in missing values appropriately.

Polars provides efficient time-based resampling using `groupby_dynamic()`, which allows users to group data dynamically based on a time interval. This method is especially useful for financial data, energy consumption analysis, and IoT sensor data, where analyzing trends over specific time windows is critical. Consider an example where we want to convert daily electricity consumption data into weekly totals:

```
import polars as pl

# Load the dataset and parse dates
df = pl.read_csv("electricity_consumption.csv", try_parse_dates=True)

# Sort the DataFrame by Date before resampling
df_sorted = df.sort("Date")

# Convert daily consumption data into weekly totals
weekly_consumption = df_sorted.group_by_dynamic("Date", every="1w").
agg(pl.col("Consumption (kWh)").sum())

# Display the weekly aggregated consumption
print(weekly_consumption)
```

```
Output:
shape: (5, 2)
```

Date --- date	Consumption (kWh) --- i64
2024-01-01	19470
2024-01-08	19296
2024-01-15	18762
2024-01-22	19640
2024-01-29	5811

Sorting ensures that when Polars applies `group_by_dynamic()`, the time-based grouping occurs sequentially and avoids inconsistencies in time-based aggregations. This is particularly useful when handling real-world time-series data where timestamps may not always be in order.

On the other hand, upsampling increases the frequency of time-series data by adding missing timestamps and filling in estimated values. This is necessary when data has gaps or when high-frequency interpolations are required for forecasting or simulations. For example, if electricity consumption data is available only on a weekly basis but we need daily estimates, we can upsample and interpolate missing values.

```
import polars as pl
import numpy as np

# Load the dataset and parse dates
df = pl.read_csv("electricity_consumption.csv", try_parse_dates=True)
print("original dataframe", df.shape)

# Sort the DataFrame by Date before any operation
df_sorted = df.sort("Date")

# Delete random rows before performing interpolation
random_indices = np.random.choice(df_sorted.height, 50, replace=False)
df_without_random_dates    =    df_sorted.filter(~pl.col("Date").is_in(df_
sorted["Date"][random_indices]))

print("modified dataframe with random samples removed",df_without_random_
dates)
# Perform interpolation on the remaining data
df_upsampled           =           df_without_random_dates.upsample(time_
column="Date",every="1d",group_by          ="City",maintain_order=True).
select(pl.all().forward_fill())

# Display the upsampled data
print("upsampled dataframe" , df_upsampled)
```

```
Output:

original dataframe (150, 5)
modified dataframe with random samples removed shape: (15, 5)
┌───────────────┬────────────┬───────────────────┬──────────────────┬─────
──────────────────────┐
│ City          ┆ Date       ┆ Consumption (kWh) ┆ Temperature (°C) ┆ Peak
Hours Usage (kWh) │
│ ---           ┆ ---        ┆ ---               ┆ ---              ┆
---                   │
│ str           ┆ date       ┆ i64               ┆ f64              ┆
f64                   │
```

```
╞═══════════════╪════════════╪══════════════════════════╪════════════════════════╪═════
═══════════════════════╡
│ New York      ┆ 2024-01-22 ┆ 556                      ┆ 5.2                    ┆
270.7                   │
│ Los Angeles   ┆ 2024-01-22 ┆ 537                      ┆ 4.2                    ┆
193.1                   │
│ Chicago       ┆ 2024-01-22 ┆ 678                      ┆ 18.0                   ┆
333.9                   │
│ Houston       ┆ 2024-01-22 ┆ 410                      ┆ 13.1                   ┆
149.2                   │
│ San Francisco ┆ 2024-01-22 ┆ 537                      ┆ 8.9                    ┆
214.5                   │
│ …             ┆ …          ┆ …                        ┆ …                      ┆
…                       │
│ New York      ┆ 2024-01-30 ┆ 653                      ┆ 26.2                   ┆
291.0                   │
│ Los Angeles   ┆ 2024-01-30 ┆ 419                      ┆ 10.7                   ┆
128.5                   │
│ Chicago       ┆ 2024-01-30 ┆ 486                      ┆ 7.7                    ┆
228.0                   │
│ Houston       ┆ 2024-01-30 ┆ 428                      ┆ 7.9                    ┆
205.8                   │
│ San Francisco ┆ 2024-01-30 ┆ 668                      ┆ 28.5                   ┆
305.6                   │
└───────────────┴────────────┴──────────────────────────┴────────────────────────┴─────
───────────────────────┘
upsampled dataframe shape: (45, 5)
┌────────────┬───────────────┬──────────────────────────┬────────────────────────┬─────
───────────────────────┐
│ Date       ┆ City          ┆ Consumption (kWh) ┆ Temperature (°C) ┆ Peak
Hours Usage (kWh) │
│ ---        ┆ ---           ┆ ---                      ┆ ---                    ┆
---                     │
│ date       ┆ str           ┆ i64                      ┆ f64                    ┆
f64                     │
╞════════════╪═══════════════╪══════════════════════════╪════════════════════════╪═════
═══════════════════════╡
│ 2024-01-22 ┆ New York      ┆ 556                      ┆ 5.2                    ┆
270.7                   │
│ 2024-01-23 ┆ New York      ┆ 556                      ┆ 5.2                    ┆
270.7                   │
│ 2024-01-24 ┆ New York      ┆ 556                      ┆ 5.2                    ┆
270.7                   │
│ 2024-01-25 ┆ New York      ┆ 556                      ┆ 5.2                    ┆
270.7                   │
```

```
│ 2024-01-26 ┆ New York      ┆ 556               ┆ 5.2              ┆
270.7        │
│ …          ┆ …             ┆ …                 ┆ …                ┆
…            │
│ 2024-01-26 ┆ San Francisco ┆ 537               ┆ 8.9              ┆
214.5        │
│ 2024-01-27 ┆ San Francisco ┆ 487               ┆ 8.9              ┆
208.5        │
│ 2024-01-28 ┆ San Francisco ┆ 487               ┆ 8.9              ┆
208.5        │
│ 2024-01-29 ┆ San Francisco ┆ 487               ┆ 8.9              ┆
208.5        │
│ 2024-01-30 ┆ San Francisco ┆ 668               ┆ 28.5             ┆
305.6        │
└────────────┴───────────────┴───────────────────┴──────────────────┴──
─────────────┘
```

The provided code demonstrates how to load and manipulate a dataset containing electricity consumption data using Polars. Initially, the dataset (`electricity_consumption.csv`) is read into a Polars DataFrame with dates parsed properly. The data is then sorted by the Date column to ensure chronological consistency. Next, the code generates 50 random indices and removes the corresponding rows to simulate missing data, while mimicking real-world scenarios where some entries might be absent. After this, the data is upsampled to a daily frequency using the upsample method, which groups the data by the City column and fills in the missing dates. The forward_fill() method is applied to the upsampled data. This action ensures that any newly created missing values are filled with the last available value for that city. Finally, the resulting upsampled dataset is displayed, showing daily electricity consumption data with missing values filled. This process is useful for handling time-series data, particularly when resampling and filling missing entries are necessary for further analysis or modeling.

Mapping and Transforming Data Values

Polars provides efficient ways to handle data transformations, mapping, and categorical data processing. Functions can be applied to transform column values using vectorized operations, which enable quick calculations such as mathematical or custom transformations on large datasets. For data mapping, Polars allows easy and efficient mapping of values across columns using dictionaries or functions. This makes transformations both fast and memory efficient. Additionally, it provides robust tools for handling categorical data, such as converting columns to categorical types and applying techniques such as one-hot encoding, optimizing memory usage and preparing data for ML tasks. These capabilities make Polars an excellent choice for managing and transforming large, complex datasets in data analysis workflows.

Applying Functions to Transform Values

In Polars, transforming values in a dataset can be done efficiently using expressions, which provide high-performance alternatives to Python-based row-wise operations. A common example of applying a function is calculating the logarithm of a numeric column. Polars facilitates this transformation using its built-in `apply` or through vectorized operations for improved performance. For instance, you might want to scale the `Consumption` column by applying a custom function. The following is an example of applying a mathematical operation to transform values using Polars:

```
import polars as pl
import numpy as np

# Create a sample DataFrame
df = pl.DataFrame({
    "City": ["New York", "Los Angeles", "Chicago", "Houston"],
    "Consumption (kWh)": [450, 600, 350, 500]
})

# Apply a transformation: Scaling the consumption values by 1.2
df_transformed = df.with_columns(
    (pl.col("Consumption (kWh)") * 1.2).alias("Scaled Consumption")
)

print(df_transformed)

Output:
shape: (4, 3)
```

City --- str	Consumption (kWh) --- i64	Scaled Consumption --- f64
New York	450	540.0
Los Angeles	600	720.0
Chicago	350	420.0
Houston	500	600.0

This code scales the consumption values in the Consumption (kWh) column by a factor of 1.2 and stores it in a new column 'Scaled Consumption'. Using vectorized operations in Polars ensures that this transformation is efficient even with large datasets.

Efficient Data Mapping Techniques

Efficient data mapping allows you to modify column values or map them to new values based on predefined rules. For instance, mapping city names to corresponding state codes is a common operation. Polars makes this operation efficient through its expressions, which apply transformations across entire columns rather than row-by-row. Here is an example where we map city names to state codes:

```
# Create a sample DataFrame
df = pl.DataFrame({
    "City": ["New York", "Los Angeles", "Chicago", "Houston"]
})

# Define a dictionary for mapping cities to state codes
city_to_state = {
    "New York": "NY",
    "Los Angeles": "CA",
    "Chicago": "IL",
    "Houston": "TX"
}

# Map the cities to state codes using the apply method
df_with_states = df.with_columns(
    pl.col("City").map_elements(lambda x: city_to_state.get(x,
"Unknown"),return_dtype=pl.Utf8).alias("State")
)

print(df_with_states)

output :
shape: (4, 2)
```

City --- str	State --- str
New York	NY
Los Angeles	CA
Chicago	IL
Houston	TX

The code creates a sample Polars DataFrame with a column of city names. It then defines a dictionary mapping each city to its corresponding state code. Using the `map_elements()` function, the city names are mapped to state codes based on the dictionary, with a fallback value of "Unknown" for cities not in the dictionary. The transformed column is added to the DataFrame as a new column called "State" and the result is printed.

Handling Categorical Data Transformations

Polars provides efficient tools for working with categorical data, especially when transforming or encoding categorical columns. One common operation is converting a column of string-based categories into numeric representations or one-hot encoding. For example, you can convert city names into categorical variables for more efficient processing or apply one-hot encoding to prepare data for ML models. Here is how you can perform these transformations:

```
# Create a sample DataFrame
df = pl.DataFrame({
    "City": ["New York", "Los Angeles", "Chicago", "Houston"]
})
print(df.dtypes," <--- default data types")

# Convert the 'City' column to a categorical type
df_categorized = df.with_columns(pl.col("City").cast(pl.Categorical).
alias("City Categorical"))

print(df_categorized.dtypes," <--- Categorical data types")

# One-hot encode the categorical column
df_one_hot = df_categorized.to_dummies()

print(df_one_hot)
Output:
[String]  <--- default data types
[String, Categorical(ordering='physical')]  <--- Categorical data types
shape: (4, 8)
┌──────────────────┬─────────────────┬──────────────┬───────────┬─────────────────┐
┌──────────────┬──────────────┬──────────────┐
| City_Chicago    ┆ City_Houston   ┆ City_Los ┆ City_New ┆ City Categori ┆
City Categori ┆ City Categori ┆ City Categori |
| ---             ┆ ---            ┆ Angeles  ┆ York     ┆ cal_Chicago   ┆
cal_Houston    ┆ cal_Los        ┆ cal_New York |
| u8              ┆ u8             ┆ ---      ┆ ---      ┆ ---           ┆
---            ┆ Angeles        ┆ ---          |
|                 ┆                ┆ u8       ┆ u8       ┆ u8            ┆
u8             ┆ ---            ┆ u8           |
|                 ┆                ┆          ┆          ┆               ┆
  u8            ┆                |
╞══════════════════╪═════════════════╪══════════════╪═══════════╪═════════════════╪
══════════════╪══════════════╪══════════════╡
| 0               ┆ 0              ┆ 0        ┆ 1        ┆ 0             ┆
0              ┆ 0              ┆ 1            |
| 0               ┆ 0              ┆ 1        ┆ 0        ┆ 0             ┆
```

```
0                 ¦ 1                  ¦ 0                  │
│ 1                 ¦ 0                  ¦ 0            ¦ 0            ¦ 1                    ¦
0                 ¦ 0                  ¦ 0                  │
│ 0                 ¦ 1                  ¦ 0            ¦ 0            ¦ 0                    ¦
1                 ¦ 0                  ¦ 0                  │
└─────────────────────┴────────────────────┴─────────────┴─────────────┴──────────────────────┘
──────────────────┴───────────────────┴────────────────────┘
```

Window Functions

Window operations are an essential concept in data processing, allowing calculations over a subset or "window" of data rather than the entire dataset. These operations are particularly useful in time-series analysis and scenarios where trends, moving averages, or cumulative values need to be computed dynamically over a sliding window of observations. Unlike standard aggregation functions that operate on an entire column, window functions maintain the original row-level granularity while computing metrics within a defined window. This makes them powerful for performing contextual calculations, such as smoothing out fluctuations, detecting anomalies, or identifying long-term patterns in data.

In Polars, window operations work efficiently on large datasets due to its optimized execution engine. These functions can be applied over grouped data, where computations are performed within specific categories rather than across the entire dataset. For example, in electricity consumption analysis, window operations can help analyze the moving average of daily consumption for each city. This allows energy providers to detect demand surges or seasonal variations. The flexibility and performance of window operations make them indispensable in various domains, including finance, healthcare, and business analytics.

Types of Window Functions (Rolling, Expanding, Cumulative)

Window functions can be broadly categorized into rolling, expanding, and cumulative operations, each serving a distinct analytical purpose.

- **Rolling Window Functions:** These functions operate on a fixed-size window that moves across the data, while recalculating the metric for each step. A common example is a rolling average, where each row contains the average of the last N observations. This is particularly useful for smoothing time-series data, such as monitoring fluctuations in daily electricity consumption.
- **Expanding Window Functions:** Unlike rolling functions, expanding windows start from the first observation and progressively include more data points, while recalculating the metric as the dataset grows. This is useful for tracking

cumulative trends, such as the total energy consumption since the beginning of the year for each city.

- **Cumulative Window Functions:** These functions compute running totals, minimums, maximums, or other statistics for each row based on all previous data points up to that row. For example, a cumulative sum can track the total power consumption over time, while giving insights into long-term trends.

Each of these functions plays a crucial role in data processing, allowing analysts to extract meaningful patterns and also allows for maintaining flexibility in analyzing data across different time spans.

Rolling Average of Stock Prices (Rolling Window Function)

In financial markets, moving averages help track stock price trends by smoothing out short-term fluctuations.

```
import polars as pl

# Sample dataset: Daily stock prices
df = pl.DataFrame({
      "Date": ["2024-01-01", "2024-01-02", "2024-01-03", "2024-01-04",
"2024-01-05",
                "2024-01-06", "2024-01-07", "2024-01-08", "2024-01-09",
"2024-01-10"],
    "Stock_Price": [100, 102, 98, 105, 110, 108, 112, 115, 118, 120]
},schema={"Date": pl.Date, "Stock_Price": pl.Int32})

# Compute a 5-day rolling mean using expr.rolling_mean()
df = df.with_columns(
      pl.mean("Stock_Price").rolling(index_column="Date", period="3d").
alias("Rolling_Avg_3d")
)

print(df)
```

Output:

shape: (10, 3)

Date --- date	Stock_Price --- i32	Rolling_Avg_3d --- f64
2024-01-01	100	100.0

2024-01-02	102	101.0
2024-01-03	98	100.0
2024-01-04	105	101.666667
2024-01-05	110	104.333333
2024-01-06	108	107.666667
2024-01-07	112	110.0
2024-01-08	115	111.666667
2024-01-09	118	115.0
2024-01-10	120	117.666667

This computes a 3-day rolling average of stock prices, which will help traders and analysts identify trends while smoothing out daily fluctuations.

Cumulative Sum of Cars Produced (Cumulative Window Function)

In the automobile industry, tracking the total number of cars produced over time can help manufacturers measure production efficiency.

```
import polars as pl

# Create a sample dataset for car production
df = pl.DataFrame({
    "Date": [
          "2024-01-01", "2024-01-03", "2024-01-05", "2024-01-06", "2024-
01-08",
          "2024-01-10", "2024-01-12", "2024-01-15", "2024-01-17", "2024-
01-20"
    ],
    "Cars_Produced": [200, 250, 180, 300, 320, 400, 350, 370, 390, 420]
})

# Compute cumulative sum of cars produced
df = df.with_columns(
    pl.col("Cars_Produced").cum_sum().alias("Total_Cars_Produced")
)

print(df)
```

Output:

shape: (10, 3)

Date ---	Cars_Produced ---	Total_Cars_Produced ---

str	i64	i64
2024-01-01	200	200
2024-01-03	250	450
2024-01-05	180	630
2024-01-06	300	930
2024-01-08	320	1250
2024-01-10	400	1650
2024-01-12	350	2000
2024-01-15	370	2370
2024-01-17	390	2760
2024-01-20	420	3180

This tracks the total number of cars produced over time, which helps manufacturing teams measure productivity and optimize production schedules.

We can write SQL style window function in Polars, which provides granular control over the output. `polars.Expr.over()` is a powerful window function that allows computations over specific groups of data, much like SQL window functions. It works by grouping data based on one or more columns (partition_by), then applying functions such as sum, mean, or rank within each group. Additionally, an order_by parameter can be used to define the sequence of calculations, such as cumulative sums or rankings. This helps in performing calculations within a subset of data while maintaining the original structure. It is unlike traditional aggregations that collapse data into a single summary row per group.

This function also provides different strategies for handling grouped data. The default strategy, group_to_rows, ensures that computed values align with the original DataFrame structure. The join option returns grouped results as lists, which may increase memory usage, while explode transforms grouped values into new rows and changes the dataset's row count. These options offer flexibility depending on the type of analysis needed, which makes Expr.over() useful for tasks like ranking sales by region, tracking rolling averages, or identifying trends across time-series data.

Example:

```
import polars as pl

# Sample patient visit data
df = pl.DataFrame({
    "Hospital": ["H1", "H1", "H1", "H2", "H2", "H2"],
    "Patient_ID": [101, 102, 103, 201, 202, 203],
     "Visit_Date": ["2024-02-01", "2024-02-03", "2024-02-05", "2024-02-
02", "2024-02-04", "2024-02-06"]
}).with_columns(pl.col("Visit_Date").str.to_date())
```

```
# Rank patients based on visit order within each hospital
df = df.with_columns(
    pl.col("Visit_Date").rank().over("Hospital", order_by="Visit_Date").
alias("Visit_Rank")
)

print(df)
```

Output:

```
shape: (6, 4)
```

Hospital --- str	Patient_ID --- i64	Visit_Date --- date	Visit_Rank --- f64
H1	101	2024-02-01	1.0
H1	102	2024-02-03	2.0
H1	103	2024-02-05	3.0
H2	201	2024-02-02	1.0
H2	202	2024-02-04	2.0
H2	203	2024-02-06	3.0

The code creates a Polars DataFrame that represents patient visits to hospitals and assigns a ranking based on the visit order within each hospital.

1. **Creating the DataFrame:** The dataset includes columns for Hospital, Patient_ID, and Visit_Date. The Visit_Date column, initially a string, is converted to an actual date format using str.to_date().

2. **Ranking Visits:** Using Expr.over(), the Visit_Date column is ranked within each hospital group. The ranking is applied using rank().over("Hospital", order_by="Visit_Date"), which means that patients who visited earlier receive a lower rank.

3. **Final Output:** The DataFrame now includes an additional column, Visit_Rank, which shows the order in which patients visited each hospital. This is useful for analyzing patient flow and visit patterns per hospital.

Another example can be the following:

```
import polars as pl

# Sample electricity consumption data
df = pl.DataFrame({
    "City": ["NY", "NY", "NY", "LA", "LA", "LA"],
      "Date": ["2024-03-01", "2024-03-01", "2024-03-01", "2024-03-01",
"2024-03-01", "2024-03-01"],
```

```
    "Hour": [1, 2, 3, 1, 2, 3],
    "Power_Usage": [500, 600, 550, 700, 750, 720]
}).with_columns(pl.col("Date").str.to_date())

# Compute max hourly power usage per city per day
df = df.with_columns(
        pl.col("Power_Usage").max().over(["City",  "Date"]).alias("Peak_
Hourly_Usage")
)

print(df)
```

```
Output:
shape: (6, 5)
```

City --- str	Date --- date	Hour --- i64	Power_Usage --- i64	Peak_Hourly_Usage --- i64
NY	2024-03-01	1	500	600
NY	2024-03-01	2	600	600
NY	2024-03-01	3	550	600
LA	2024-03-01	1	700	750
LA	2024-03-01	2	750	750
LA	2024-03-01	3	720	750

The given code is designed to calculate the maximum hourly power usage for each city on a particular day based on electricity consumption data.

1. **Creating the DataFrame:** The code starts by creating a sample DataFrame that includes electricity consumption data for two cities, "NY" and "LA". Each row represents a particular city's power usage at a specific hour of the day (given by the Hour column) on a particular Date. The Power_Usage column holds the power consumption values for each hour. The Date column is initially in string format, but it is converted to a proper date format using str.to_date().
2. **Calculating Maximum Power Usage:** The key part of this code is using the max().over() function to compute the maximum power usage per city (City) and day (Date). Here, over(["City", "Date"]) groups the data by both City and Date to make sure the calculation considers the maximum power usage for each city on each specific day. For each group, the max() function finds the highest value in the Power_Usage column, which is then labeled as Peak_Hourly_Usage. This is done for each group of city and date.
3. **Final Output:** After applying the max() function, the DataFrame now includes a new column Peak_Hourly_Usage that shows the maximum power usage per

city per day. The result is a DataFrame where, for each row, the Peak_Hourly_Usage is the same for all hours of the same city on the same date, representing the maximum consumption within that city on that specific day.

Handling Inconsistent Data

Inconsistent data, such as missing values, duplicate records, incorrect formats, and outliers, can significantly impact data analysis and decision-making. Ensuring data consistency is crucial for deriving meaningful insights and maintaining data integrity. Polars thus offers a comprehensive set of tools to clean, transform, and standardize inconsistent data. Its ability to process large datasets efficiently makes it an excellent choice for handling data quality issues at scale.

One of the most common data inconsistencies is missing values, which can lead to inaccurate analyses and skewed results. Polars provides methods such as .fill_null() to replace missing values with a default value, mean, median, or mode, depending on the context. If missing data is significant and cannot be reliably filled, .drop_nulls() can be used to remove incomplete rows. These functions ensure that the data remains structured and meaningful.

Duplicate records are another challenge that can introduce redundancy and distort statistical analysis. Polars make it easy to identify and remove duplicates using the .unique() method, which retains distinct values based on specified columns. For more control, .drop_duplicates() allows users to specify which columns should be considered when removing duplicate rows, while ensuring that the dataset remains clean without any unnecessary repetition.

Incorrect data formats, such as inconsistent date representations, variations in text capitalization, or improperly stored numerical values, can lead to processing errors. Polars offers built-in string manipulation functions such as .str.strip_chars(), .str.to_lowercase(), and .str.replace() to standardize text-based data. The .cast() function ensures that numerical and categorical columns are correctly formatted and reduces errors in data analysis workflows.

Outliers and extreme values can also introduce inconsistencies in datasets, which affects statistical accuracy. Polars provides functions like .quantile(), .describe(), and .filter() to identify and remove outliers based on statistical thresholds. By applying filtering techniques, analysts can ensure that extreme values do not distort patterns and trends in the data. This leads to more reliable insights.

Handling Outliers

Outliers are data points that significantly differ from other observations in a dataset. Identifying these outliers is crucial because they can distort statistical analysis and skew model results.

Outliers can have a significant impact on the performance and accuracy of analytical models. In traditional statistical models such as linear regression, the model's coefficients are highly sensitive to extreme values. Since linear regression minimizes the sum of squared errors, large errors caused by outliers can disproportionately affect the estimated parameters, which leads to a poor fit of the model. In addition, outliers can distort performance metrics such as mean squared error (MSE) and inflate the error. This can mislead analysts into thinking that the model is underperforming, when, in fact, the issues are caused by the extreme data points.

Identifying Outliers Using Statistical Methods

One of the most common methods for detecting outliers is through statistical measures such as the z-score and Interquartile Range (IQR). The z-score represents how many standard deviations a data point is away from the mean. A z-score greater than 3 or less than -3 typically indicates an outlier. The IQR method, on the other hand, involves calculating the 1st quartile (Q1) and the 3rd quartile (Q3) of a dataset. The IQR is the difference between Q3 and Q1, and any data point outside of 1.5 times the IQR above Q3 or below Q1 is considered an outlier. These statistical methods offer simple, interpretable ways to flag data points for further analysis or removal.

Another approach for identifying outliers is through boxplots, which graphically display the distribution of data. In a boxplot, data points outside the whiskers (which represent 1.5 times the IQR) are potential outliers. For multivariate data, Mahalanobis distance is a popular method that accounts for correlations between variables. This distance measure identifies how far away a data point is from the mean, while considering the covariance of the variables. Advanced ML models such as isolation forests and one-class SVMs are also used to detect outliers, especially in high-dimensional datasets where traditional methods might fall short. These methods automatically flag anomalies based on learned patterns from the data, which is especially useful for large, complex datasets.

Techniques for Treating and Managing Outliers

Once outliers are identified, the next challenge is determining how to handle them. The treatment of outliers depends on the domain, the type of data, and the impact the outliers have on the analysis. One common approach is removal, where the outlier data points are excluded from the dataset. This technique is particularly effective when the outliers are errors or when they represent rare occurrences that do not contribute meaningfully to the analysis. However, removal must be done cautiously, as removing too many data points can lead to biased results or loss of valuable information.

In cases where the outliers carry important information but need to be scaled down, transformation techniques can be applied. Logarithmic transformations or winsorization (where extreme values are capped at a certain percentile) are common techniques used to reduce the influence of extreme values. Imputation is another technique, where missing or outlying values are replaced with estimates, such as the mean, median, or a model-based estimate. This method is particularly useful when dealing with missing data or when the outlier is not erroneous but rather a rare event that should be included in the dataset. Lastly, if outliers reflect natural variability and are essential for analysis, a robust statistical model that is less sensitive to outliers can be chosen, such as using median-based methods, instead of mean-based methods for central tendency or applying robust regression techniques.

Impact of Outliers on Analytical Models

In ML models such as decision trees and random forests, outliers can lead to overfitting. These models may assign undue importance to outliers, resulting in overly complex models that do not generalize well to unseen data. For clustering algorithms such as K-means, outliers can distort the mean of clusters, which can cause the algorithm to misclassify data points. Similarly, in support vector machines (SVMs), outliers can affect the placement of the optimal hyperplane, leading to suboptimal classification performance. In neural networks, outliers can lead to slow convergence during training or cause the model to overfit to these extreme values. This results in poor generalization.

While outliers can degrade the performance of many analytical models, there are some models that are inherently more resistant to the effects of outliers. For example, tree-based models such as random forests and gradient boosting machines tend to be more robust to outliers, as they split data into smaller subsets, while reducing the influence of extreme values on the overall decision-making process. Robust regression techniques, which use methods such as Huber loss or quantile regression, are designed to mitigate the impact of outliers on model training. In these cases, outliers are either downweighted or handled in a way that reduces their effect without needing to remove them entirely.

Overall, managing outliers is a crucial step in the data preprocessing pipeline, as they can distort model parameters, reduce predictive accuracy, and impact the robustness of the model. Proper identification, treatment, and understanding of outliers allow analysts to improve model performance and ensure more reliable and generalizable results.

The following is an example of outlier detection using IQR with Polars , The IQR method detects outliers by calculating the range between the 25th and 75th percentiles (Q1 and Q3) and flags values outside the range of Q1 - 1.5 * IQR to Q3 + 1.5 * IQR.

```
import polars as pl
import numpy as np

# Generate a larger sample size (50 cities with random power usage values)
np.random.seed(42)  # For reproducibility
cities = [f"City_{i}" for i in range(1, 51)]  # 50 cities
power_usage = np.random.randint(100, 1500, size=50)  # Random power usage
between 100 and 1500

# Add one extreme value to simulate an outlier
power_usage[-1] = 15000  # Set last value as an outlier

# Create the DataFrame
df = pl.DataFrame({
    "City": cities,
    "Power_Usage": power_usage
})

# Calculate Q1, Q3, and IQR
Q1 = df["Power_Usage"].quantile(0.25)
Q3 = df["Power_Usage"].quantile(0.75)
IQR = Q3 - Q1

# Determine outlier thresholds
lower_bound = Q1 - 1.5 * IQR
upper_bound = Q3 + 1.5 * IQR

# Flag outliers (values outside the threshold range)
df = df.with_columns(
    pl.when(pl.col("Power_Usage") < lower_bound)
    .then(True)
     .otherwise(pl.when(pl.col("Power_Usage") > upper_bound).then(True).
otherwise(False))
    .alias("Is_Outlier")
)

print(df)
```

Output:

shape: (50, 3)

City --- str	Power_Usage --- i32	Is_Outlier --- bool
City_1	1226	false
City_2	960	false

```
│ City_3  ┆ 1394          ┆ false    │
│ City_4  ┆ 1230          ┆ false    │
│ City_5  ┆ 1195          ┆ false    │
│ …       ┆ …             ┆ …        │
│ City_46 ┆ 940           ┆ false    │
│ City_47 ┆ 266           ┆ false    │
│ City_48 ┆ 1397          ┆ false    │
│ City_49 ┆ 487           ┆ false    │
│ City_50 ┆ 15000         ┆ true     │
└─────────┴───────────────┴──────────┘
```

In this example:

- We calculate the first quartile (Q1), third quartile (Q3), and the interquartile range (IQR).
- We determine the lower and upper bounds for normal values by subtracting and adding 1.5 times the IQR from Q1 and Q3, respectively.
- We then flag outliers as those values that fall outside the lower and upper bounds.

Parsing Dates and Times

Working with date-time data is a fundamental aspect of data analysis in many domains, as it helps in identifying trends, patterns, and time-based relationships. Extracting date-time data typically involves converting string representations into datetime objects or specific formats that are more manageable for analysis. Common operations include extracting parts of the date, such as year, month, day, hour, or minute, to break down the temporal data into more granular components. This enables further aggregation and comparisons over different time periods. Additionally, manipulating date-time data allows for adjustments such as calculating the difference between two dates, performing time shifts, or resampling data at different frequencies (for example, daily, monthly, or yearly).

Polars provide an efficient way to extract and manipulate date-time data using its datetime module and various date functions such as `str.strptime`, `dt.year`, `dt.month`, and `dt.day`. The following example demonstrates how to extract specific parts of a datetime column and manipulate date-time data:

```
import polars as pl

# Create a DataFrame with date-time data
df = pl.DataFrame({
    "Timestamp": ["2024-01-01 12:30:00", "2024-01-02 14:45:00", "2024-
01-03 16:15:00"]
}).with_columns(pl.col("Timestamp").str.strptime(pl.Datetime).alias("Date"))
```

```
# Extracting year, month, day, and hour
df = df.with_columns([
    pl.col("Date").dt.year().alias("Year"),
    pl.col("Date").dt.month().alias("Month"),
    pl.col("Date").dt.day().alias("Day"),
    pl.col("Date").dt.hour().alias("Hour")
])

print(df)

Output:
shape: (3, 6)
```

Timestamp --- str	Date --- datetime[μs]	Year --- i32	Month --- i8	Day --- i8	Hour --- i8
2024-01-01 12:30:00	2024-01-01 12:30:00	2024	1	1	12
2024-01-02 14:45:00	2024-01-02 14:45:00	2024	1	2	14
2024-01-03 16:15:00	2024-01-03 16:15:00	2024	1	3	16

Time zone management is a common challenge when working with temporal data. Different time zones can lead to inconsistencies when aggregating or comparing date-time values across regions. In data processing, it is crucial to standardize the time zone or convert dates and times to a common reference (usually UTC) before performing further analysis. Polars offers functionality to convert between time zones and adjust dates to local time or UTC using dt.convert_time_zone. Another challenge arises from dealing with inconsistent date formats in datasets, where dates might be recorded in various formats (for example, MM-DD-YYYY, DD-MM-YYYY, or YYYY-MM-DD). Standardizing these formats ensures consistency in data processing and analysis.

Polars support date parsing in multiple formats, and you can easily handle time zone conversion and date formatting as follows:

```
import polars as pl

# Create a DataFrame with time-zone-aware data
```

```
df = pl.DataFrame({
    "Timestamp": ["2024-01-01 12:30:00+05:30", "2024-01-02
14:45:00+05:30", "2024-01-03 16:15:00+05:30"]
}).with_columns(pl.col("Timestamp").str.strptime(pl.Datetime, "%Y-%m-%d
%H:%M:%S%z").alias("Date"))

# Convert timestamps to UTC
df = df.with_columns(pl.col("Date").dt.convert_time_zone("UTC").
alias("Date_UTC"))

print(df)
Output:
shape: (3, 3)
┌───────────────────────────┬─────────────────────────┬─────────────────
─────────┐
│ Timestamp                 ┆ Date                    ┆ Date_UTC
│
│ ---                       ┆ ---                     ┆ ---
│
│ str                       ┆ datetime[μs, UTC]       ┆ datetime[μs,
UTC]     │
╞═══════════════════════════╪═════════════════════════╪═════════════════
═════════╡
│ 2024-01-01 12:30:00+05:30 ┆ 2024-01-01 07:00:00 UTC ┆ 2024-01-01
07:00:00 UTC │
│ 2024-01-02 14:45:00+05:30 ┆ 2024-01-02 09:15:00 UTC ┆ 2024-01-02
09:15:00 UTC │
│ 2024-01-03 16:15:00+05:30 ┆ 2024-01-03 10:45:00 UTC ┆ 2024-01-03
10:45:00 UTC │
└───────────────────────────┴─────────────────────────┴─────────────────
─────────┘
```

Common Challenges in Working with Temporal Data

Working with temporal data presents several challenges. One of the main difficulties is dealing with inconsistent or missing timestamps, which can occur when data is recorded irregularly or there are errors in the data collection process. Missing dates can lead to incorrect conclusions if not handled properly. Another challenge is time-zone mismatches, as different systems or regions may record data in varying time zones. Additionally, issues such as daylight saving time changes, leap years, and leap seconds can introduce complexity when performing date arithmetic. Furthermore, handling high-frequency data, such as stock prices or sensor data, may require advanced techniques such as resampling or time-windowing to aggregate data to a specific time resolution.

Bucketing Numerical Data

Bucketing (also known as binning) is a technique used to group continuous numerical data into discrete intervals or categories, which make the data easier to analyze. This technique is especially useful when dealing with large datasets, as it reduces the complexity of the data by converting continuous variables into categorical ones. Bucketing allows for simplifying data analysis and enhances the interpretability of the results, especially when the data spans a wide range of values. In data analysis, bucketing can be employed to categorize ages into age groups, incomes into income ranges, or scores into rating bands. The primary goal is to assign similar values to the same group to facilitate easier processing and comparison.

In Polars, bucketing can be easily accomplished using the `cut` function, which divides a numerical column into bins. You can specify the number of bins or the bin edges (intervals), and Polars will assign each value to a corresponding bin. Here is an example of bucketing numerical data into specific ranges:

```
import polars as pl

# Sample data with numerical values
df = pl.DataFrame({
    "Age": [18, 25, 40, 55, 60, 72, 85, 90, 32, 41]
})

# Define bin edges (age ranges)
bins = [0, 20, 40, 60, 80, 100]

# Create a new column "Age_Bucket" by binning the "Age" column
df = df.with_columns(
    pl.col("Age").cut(bins).alias("Age_Bucket")
)
print(df)
Output:
shape: (10, 2)
```

Age --- i64	Age_Bucket --- cat
18	(0, 20]
25	(20, 40]
40	(20, 40]
55	(40, 60]
60	(40, 60]
72	(60, 80]
85	(80, 100]

```
│ 90     ┆ (80, 100] │
│ 32     ┆ (20, 40]  │
│ 41     ┆ (40, 60]  │
└────────┴───────────┘
```

Binning and Categorizing Numerical Values

Binning is the process of transforming continuous numerical values into a set of discrete categories. When working with large datasets, this can make statistical analysis more manageable and the relationships between variables clearer. For instance, income data can be binned into low, medium, and high categories to segment populations into different economic groups. The decision of how many bins to create is essential, as too many bins can lead to overfitting, while too few can result in the loss of important variations. In addition, binning also improves the computational efficiency of analysis by reducing the granularity of the data.

Polars provide the `cut` function for creating bins from numerical columns, which allows you to categorize the data into a limited set of predefined intervals. The following example demonstrates binning salary data into categories of "Low", "Medium", and "High":

```
df = pl.DataFrame({"salary": [30000, 45000, 60000, 75000, 100000,
120000]})
df.with_columns(
    pl.col("salary").qcut([0.25, 0.75], labels=["low", "med", "high"]).
alias("qcut")
)
print(df)
Output:
shape: (6, 1)
┌────────┐
│ salary │
│ ---    │
│ i64    │
╞════════╡
│ 30000  │
│ 45000  │
│ 60000  │
│ 75000  │
│ 100000 │
│ 120000 │
└────────┘
```

Choosing Appropriate Bin Sizes for Analysis

The choice of bin size is crucial for effective bucketing, as it influences how much information is lost or retained in the process. If the bin sizes are too large, you may oversimplify the data, which can lead to the loss of valuable detail. Conversely, if the bins are too small, the analysis may become overly complex, and the bins may not represent significant patterns in the data. The ideal bin size depends on the dataset, the analysis objective, and the trade-off between simplicity and precision. A common approach is to use domain knowledge to define meaningful bin ranges, or alternatively, statistical methods such as the Freedman-Diaconis rule can be applied to determine optimal bin sizes for continuous variables.

Normalizing Numerical Data

Normalization is a data preprocessing technique used to scale the features of numerical data so that they have a common range, typically between 0 and 1. This transformation ensures that different features in the data contribute equally to the analysis or modeling process, especially when those features have varying scales. For example, in datasets where one feature is in the range of thousands (for example, income), while another is in the range of tens (for example, age), normalization ensures that the larger values do not dominate the analysis. This is particularly important when using ML algorithms that rely on distance calculations, such as K-Nearest Neighbors (KNN), Support Vector Machines (SVM), and gradient-based optimization methods such as neural networks.

Standardization vs. Normalization: Key Differences

While both normalization and standardization aim to scale data, they do so in different ways, and the choice of which method to use depends on the algorithm being applied. Normalization adjusts the values of a numerical attribute to fit within a specific range, usually [0, 1], which is useful when you need to ensure that all features contribute equally. On the other hand, standardization transforms the data to have a mean of 0 and a standard deviation of 1. This technique is particularly useful when the distribution of data is not uniform and has significant deviations (outliers), as it does not bound the data within a specific range but rather adjusts it to fit a normal distribution.

For example, when applying linear regression, support vector machines, or neural networks, standardization is generally preferred as it centers the data around 0 and scales it based on the spread (standard deviation). Normalization, on the other hand, is preferred when you are working with methods such as KNN or algorithms that are sensitive to the magnitude of the data. The key difference lies in the fact that normalization compresses data into a range (for example, [0, 1]), while standardization creates a standard scale based on statistical measures of the data.

Scaling Techniques for Numerical Attributes

Scaling techniques are essential when working with numerical attributes that vary in magnitude, units, or range. These techniques ensure that all features contribute equally to the modeling process, while preventing some features from disproportionately affecting the output. The most commonly used scaling techniques are min-max scaling (normalization), z-score scaling (standardization), and robust scaling. Min-max scaling compresses data into a specific range, while z-score scaling centers the data around 0 and scales it based on standard deviation. Robust scaling is less sensitive to outliers, as it uses the median and interquartile range (IQR) for scaling, which makes it more suitable for datasets with significant outliers.

In practice, you can choose the scaling technique based on the nature of the data and the algorithm you are applying. For instance, min-max scaling is ideal when you need the data to fit within a known range (for example, for neural networks where inputs are expected to be in a range), whereas robust scaling is useful for datasets that contain outliers, as it is less sensitive to extreme values. Standardization, on the other hand, is suitable when you want to center the data and ensure that all features contribute equally, regardless of their initial scale. Choosing the appropriate scaling technique is crucial for the performance of ML models.

Impact of Normalization on Machine Learning Models

The impact of normalization on ML models is significant, particularly when the models are sensitive to the scale of input features. For example, in distance-based algorithms such as K-Nearest Neighbors (KNN), normalization ensures that all features have the same impact on distance calculations. Without normalization, features with larger numerical ranges may dominate the distance calculation, which can potentially skew the results. Similarly, gradient-based optimization techniques used in models such as neural networks and logistic regression can converge faster when the features are normalized, as it avoids the algorithm's reliance on larger feature values.

Moreover, normalization is especially important when features vary in units or range. For example, when dealing with features such as height (in cm) and weight (in kg), without normalization, the height feature will dominate any analysis or model training. By normalizing, both features are scaled to a common range, which allows the model to learn the relationships between them more effectively. However, normalization can have a negative impact in certain scenarios, especially if there are extreme outliers or skewed distributions. In such cases, standardization may be more appropriate, as it reduces the impact of outliers and helps in preserving the relationships between features.

Working with Nested Data

Nested data refers to data that has multiple levels of hierarchy or layers within itself. In other words, it is data that contains one or more fields that are themselves lists, dictionaries, or other complex data structures. Such data can arise in various scenarios, such as when working with JSON, XML, or when data is retrieved from APIs or database systems that store related entities together in a structured format. In ML or data analysis, nested data structures often need to be flattened or transformed into a simpler format for easier analysis.

A common example of nested data is a JSON file, where each record can have subrecords, arrays, or nested attributes. Handling this kind of data in traditional flat file formats such as CSV becomes challenging due to the complexity and richness of the relationships within the data. However, tools such as Polars allow you to work with these nested structures efficiently. With Polars, you can flatten the nested structures or extract specific elements from these nested fields, which can then be processed and analyzed more easily.

Understanding Hierarchical and Nested Structures

Hierarchical or nested data structures typically involve data that can be represented in a tree-like form, where each record can have multiple attributes or sub-records associated with it. For instance, in a dataset representing employees in a company, you might have a field for the department, and each department could contain a list of employee records. Another example is a product catalog, where each product could have a list of categories or attributes (for example, size, color, specifications, and so on).

Working with nested data in a relational database would typically involve multiple tables with relationships like "one-to-many" or "many-to-many". However, when these structures are stored as nested entities (such as in JSON), handling them requires special care. Polars supports working with nested data types such as lists and structs. This allows for operations such as unwrapping, extracting, or reshaping the data, so that it can be analyzed in a tabular format. This makes it easier to apply typical data analysis workflows.

Flattening and Extracting Meaningful Information

Flattening nested data involves transforming the hierarchical structure into a flat table where each nested element or attribute becomes its own column. This is useful when dealing with JSON data, API responses, or other data formats that involve records with embedded lists or dictionaries. Flattening the data allows you to extract relevant details and enables you to work with them in the same way you would work with flat files, such as performing aggregations, transformations, and visualizations.

In Polars, you can flatten hierarchical data by accessing specific elements in nested lists or structs and then using functions like `explode()` or `unnest()` to transform the nested structures into flat columns. Additionally, extracting meaningful information from nested data often involves applying functions that allow you to parse and access individual elements from lists or structs, which can be done efficiently with Polars' built-in expressions.

Here is an example of how you can work with nested data in Polars:

```
import polars as pl

# Sample data with nested structures (lists and structs)
df = pl.DataFrame({
    "City": ["New York", "Los Angeles", "Chicago"],
    "Weather": [
        {"Temperature": 25, "Humidity": 65},
        {"Temperature": 28, "Humidity": 70},
        {"Temperature": 20, "Humidity": 75}
    ],
    "Hourly_Temperature": [
        [22, 23, 24, 25],
        [27, 28, 29, 30],
        [19, 20, 21, 22]
    ]
})
print("Original DF")
print(df)
# Flatten the nested structs in the 'Weather' column
df_flattened = df.with_columns(
    pl.col("Weather").struct.field("Temperature").alias("Temperature"),
    pl.col("Weather").struct.field("Humidity").alias("Humidity")
)

# Flatten the 'Hourly_Temperature' list into separate rows using explode
df_exploded = df_flattened.explode("Hourly_Temperature")

# Show the final flattened DataFrame
print("flattened DF")
print(df_exploded)
```

```
Output:
Original DF
```

```
shape: (3, 3)
```

City --- str	Weather --- struct[2]	Hourly_Temperature --- list[i64]
New York	{25,65}	[22, 23, … 25]
Los Angeles	{28,70}	[27, 28, … 30]
Chicago	{20,75}	[19, 20, … 22]

```
flattened DF
shape: (12, 5)
```

City --- str	Weather --- struct[2]	Hourly_Temperature --- i64	Temperature --- i64	Humidity --- i64
New York	{25,65}	22	25	65
New York	{25,65}	23	25	65
New York	{25,65}	24	25	65
New York	{25,65}	25	25	65
Los Angeles	{28,70}	27	28	70
…	…	…	…	…
Los Angeles	{28,70}	30	28	70
Chicago	{20,75}	19	20	75
Chicago	{20,75}	20	20	75
Chicago	{20,75}	21	20	75
Chicago	{20,75}	22	20	75

In this example, the DataFrame df contains a mix of nested structures, including a Weather column, which is a struct with Temperature and Humidity fields, and an Hourly_Temperature column, which is a list of hourly temperature readings. The goal is to flatten this data into a format suitable for analysis.

- **Flattening the Weather struct:** The `struct.field()` function is used to extract individual fields from the struct, which are then added as separate columns (Temperature and Humidity). This allows you to access the individual elements of the struct and work with them as separate columns in the DataFrame.
- **Exploding the Hourly_Temperature list:** The `explode()` function is used to flatten the Hourly_Temperature column, which is a list of values, into separate rows. Each temperature value is extracted and placed into its own row, which allows you to analyze hourly temperatures independently.

The resulting DataFrame has no nested structures, which makes it easier to work with in a flat format suitable for further analysis. This approach can be applied to any type of nested data, such as JSON or XML data, where the goal is to extract meaningful information from hierarchical structures and convert it into a usable tabular format.

Conclusion

In this chapter, we have explored a range of fundamental techniques used in data processing, including grouping, aggregating, and joining datasets. Grouping data allows for meaningful summaries and insights through aggregation functions such as sum, mean, and count, while multi-level grouping and custom aggregations provide more flexibility in handling complex datasets. We also examined the different types of joins—inner, outer, left, and right—as well as their respective use cases for merging datasets. The process of pivoting and unpivoting data, such as reshaping it from wide to long format, has also been crucial for better data analysis and representation. Additionally, we delved into the intricacies of handling time-series data through resampling and the importance of proper transformations when combining datasets.

Moving forward, we also discussed several techniques for data transformation and normalization, including window functions, outlier detection, and working with categorical and numerical data. We explored various window operations such as rolling, expanding, and cumulative functions, for trend analysis and handling time-series data. Addressing outliers in datasets is essential for accurate analysis, as they can significantly impact analytical models. Finally, understanding how to handle date-time data, perform bucketing and binning, and apply appropriate normalization techniques is key in ensuring that data is in the right form for ML and analysis. With these tools and techniques, you can confidently work with diverse datasets, extract valuable insights, and make informed decisions based on data. In the next chapter, we will address data visualization with Polars.

Exercises

Groupby

- Basic Grouping: You are given a dataset containing information about sales transactions with columns: Product, Region, Quantity_Sold, and Sales_Price. Write a query to find the total quantity sold and total sales price for each product.
- Multiple Aggregations: Using the same dataset, calculate the average sales price and total quantity sold for each region.
- Custom Aggregation: For a dataset containing employee records where each employee has a Department and Salary, calculate the highest and lowest salary per department and also determine the average salary for each department.

Pivot and Unpivot

- Pivot Data: You have a dataset containing City, Date, and Temperature columns. Pivot the data so that each column represents a date and the values are the corresponding temperatures.
- Unpivot Data: You are given a wide-format dataset where each column represents a different year and the rows contain data for different regions. Unpivot the data so that you have columns for Region, Year, and Temperature.

Joins

- Inner Join: You have two datasets: one with Customer_ID and Name, and another with Customer_ID and Order_ID. Write a query to get the list of customers along with their corresponding orders.
- Left Join: In a dataset containing Employee_ID and Department, and another with Employee_ID and Salary, write a query to display the employee details along with their salary, including employees who may not have a recorded salary.
- Multiple Joins: Given two datasets—one with Student_ID and Name, and another with Student_ID, Course, and Grade—write a query to list all students along with their courses and grades, ensuring every student is included.

Bucketing

- Categorize Data: You have a dataset with Age and Income columns. Create bins for different age groups (for example, 18-30, 31-45, 46-60, 61+) and assign each record to its appropriate bucket.

- Salary Bucketing: Given a dataset of employee salaries, create salary buckets such as Low, Medium, and High based on specific ranges (for example, Low: < 50k, Medium: 50k-100k, High: > 100k). Assign each employee to the appropriate salary bucket.

Window Functions

- Rolling Average: You are given a dataset with Date and Stock_Price. Calculate the 7-day rolling average for stock prices.
- Rank Function: Using a dataset with Salesperson, Sales_Amount, and Date, rank the salespersons based on their sales for each month.
- Cumulative Sum: You have a dataset of City and Monthly_Sales. Calculate the cumulative sum of sales for each city across months.

Nested Data

- Flatten Nested Data: You are given a dataset where each row contains a list of Order_Items, with each item containing Product_ID, Quantity, and Price. Flatten the dataset so that each item is displayed as a separate row, but with the Order_ID repeated for each item.
- Extracting Nested Data: Using a dataset with a column Details containing nested dictionaries (for example, {"Address": "123 Main St", "Phone": "123-456-7890"}), extract the Address and Phone into separate columns.

These exercises will give you a hands-on experience on the key concepts of data manipulation and processing, while using groupby, pivot/unpivot, joins, bucketing, window functions, and working with nested data structures.

CHAPTER 6
Data Visualization

"If a picture is worth a thousand words,
a data visualization is worth a thousand data points."

Ben Shneiderman

Introduction

Data visualization plays a crucial role in making complex datasets more understandable and insightful. This chapter explores various plotting techniques using hvPlot, Altair, Seaborn, and Plotly, while demonstrating their capabilities in creating both static and interactive visualizations. By leveraging these powerful libraries, users will be able to efficiently represent data through different chart types, uncover patterns, and enhance data storytelling.

The chapter covers a range of visualization techniques, including bar plots, scatter plots, line plots, box plots, area plots, histograms, and candlestick charts using hvPlot and Altair. Additionally, it introduces heatmaps, violin plots, and map-based visualizations with Seaborn and Plotly, while providing a diverse set of tools for effective data representation.

Each section is designed with practical examples, ensuring a hands-on approach to learning. Thus, whether creating simple statistical charts or interactive dashboards, this chapter equips readers with the knowledge to present data in a compelling and meaningful way.

Structure

In this chapter, we will discuss the following topics:

- Visualizing Data with hvPlot and Altair
    - Basic Plots: Bar Plots, Line Plots, Scatter Plots
    - Statistical Plots: Histograms, Area Plots
    - Customization of Plots
- Advanced Visualization with Seaborn
    - Statistical Data Visualizations: Pair Plots and Heatmaps
- Interactive Visualizations with Plotly
- Map-Based Visualizations
    - Choropleth Maps with Plotly
- Comparing Visualization Libraries
    - Strengths and Weaknesses of hvPlot, Altair, Seaborn, and Plotly
    - Using Libraries According to Use Cases

Visualizing Data with hvPlot and Altair

Polars can efficiently handle large datasets, which makes it an excellent choice for data analysis and visualization. When combined with hvPlot and Altair, Polars enable users to create interactive and highly customizable visualizations while maintaining fast data processing capabilities. hvPlot, built on HoloViews, provides an easy-to-use API for generating dynamic charts such as bar plots, scatter plots, line charts, box plots, and histograms directly from Polars DataFrames. Its seamless integration with Polars allows for efficient plotting without converting datasets into Pandas, while maintaining performance benefits when working with large-scale data.

Altair, a declarative statistical visualization library, pairs well with Polars by enabling users to create complex, layered visualizations using a concise syntax. Altair's grammar of graphics approach allows for intuitive chart-building, which makes it easy to define data encodings, transformations, and interactive elements. By leveraging Polars' fast query execution and data manipulation capabilities, Altair can efficiently render interactive scatter plots, area charts, and heatmaps, while ensuring smooth visualization of even the largest datasets. Together, hvPlot, Altair, and Polars form a powerful trio for high-performance, scalable, and interactive data visualization.

In this chapter, we will use a weather dataset for visualization. Weather data consists of various atmospheric parameters recorded over time, including temperature, humidity, wind speed, and precipitation. This data is crucial for forecasting weather patterns, analyzing climate trends, and making informed decisions in agriculture, transportation, and disaster management. The weather data collected from sources like weather stations, satellites, and sensors helps researchers and analysts identify seasonal variations, extreme weather events, and long-term climate changes. With advancements in data processing tools like Polars, hvPlot, and Altair, weather data can be efficiently analyzed and visualized to uncover meaningful insights.

Let us create a box plot with weather data and analyze the results:

```
import polars as pl
# Load dataset using Polars
df = pl.read_csv("weather_data.csv", try_parse_dates=True)
import hvplot.polars
import matplotlib.pyplot as plt
# Extract month from the date
df = df.with_columns(df["date"].dt.strftime("%B").alias("month"))

# Compute monthly average temperature
monthly_avg_temp = df.group_by("month").agg(pl.col("temperature").
mean())
bar_plot
```

output :

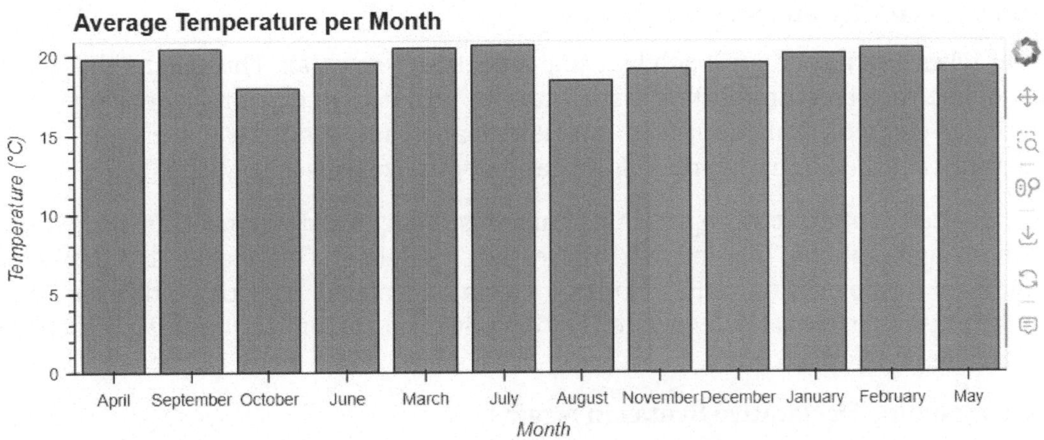

Figure 6.1: *Box Plot Showing Monthly Average Temperature Data*

The code loads a weather dataset using Polars and extracts the month from the date column. It then calculates the average temperature per month by grouping the data accordingly. Using hvPlot, it generates a bar plot to visualize the average temperature trends across months. Finally, the plot can be displayed interactively.

hvPlot vs. Altair: A Comparative Analysis

Data visualization is an essential component of data analysis, which enables users to explore patterns, trends, and insights effectively. hvPlot and Altair are two powerful Python libraries that simplify the process of creating interactive and high-quality visualizations. While hvPlot is built on top of HoloViews and integrates seamlessly with Polars, Pandas, and Xarray, Altair is a declarative statistical visualization library based on Vega and Vega-Lite. Both libraries provide user-friendly interfaces and support for interactive visualizations, which make them popular choices among data analysts and scientists.

hvPlot: Simplicity and Versatility

hvPlot is particularly useful for quick and interactive visualizations without the need for extensive coding. It provides a high-level API for generating plots directly from Polars, Pandas, and Dask DataFrames and facilitates seamless integration with large datasets. Unlike Matplotlib, which requires multiple lines of code for styling and interactivity, hvPlot makes it possible to generate powerful visualizations with a single function call.

One of the biggest advantages of hvPlot is its tight integration with interactive dashboards using Panel and HoloViews, which makes it an excellent choice for Exploratory Data Analysis (EDA). However, when it comes to declarative and statistical plotting, Altair offers more structured control.

Altair: Declarative and Statistical Power

Altair takes a different approach by using a declarative syntax. This means that users can define the structure of their visualizations, rather than explicitly specifying each graphical element. This approach enables cleaner and more readable code, while ensuring that the library handles visualization optimizations automatically.

One of Altair's greatest strengths is its built-in support for statistical transformations such as aggregations, binning, and regression modeling. This makes it a preferred choice for complex data visualizations involving advanced statistical analysis. Since Altair is based on Vega and Vega-Lite, it offers powerful customization and interactivity with minimal effort.

Understanding Declarative Syntax in Altair

Declarative syntax is a programming approach where you describe what you want to achieve, rather than specifying how to do it step by step. In Altair, you define the structure and relationships of the visualization, and the library automatically handles rendering, scaling, and optimizations.

For example, in Altair, you define a chart using a combination of:

- Data Source (the dataset)
- Mark Type (bar, line, scatter, and so on)

- Encodings (X-axis, Y-axis, color, tooltip, and so on)
- Properties (title, width, height, and so on)

hvPlot follows an imperative approach, where you directly call a function on a DataFrame to generate a plot. Unlike Altair, hvPlot does not separate chart definition from data transformation; instead, it generates the visualization directly from the DataFrame.

Comparison: hvPlot vs. Altair

Feature	hvPlot	Altair
Approach	Imperative (simplifies plotting from DataFrames)	Declarative (focuses on defining relationships in data)
Ease of Use	Very easy to use, minimal code needed	Requires a structured approach but results in cleaner code
Best For	Quick interactive visualizations, EDA, dashboards	Statistical analysis, publication-quality plots
Interactivity	High interactivity, supports HoloViews and Panel	Supports interactivity through Vega-Lite
Statistical Capabilities	Basic statistical visualizations	Advanced statistical transformations (binning, aggregations, regression)
Customization	Limited but integrates well with other HoloViz tools	High level of customization for reports and presentations
Best Use Case	Exploratory Data Analysis (EDA), dashboards, interactive apps	Research reports, advanced data visualization, statistical modeling

***Table 6.1**: Comparison of HvPlot and Altair*

We will focus more on Altair going forward in this chapter as it is the recommended data visualization engine for lightweight charts creation with Polars. We will now implement the box plot using Altair instead of hvPlot.

```
import polars as pl
import altair as alt
# Load dataset
df = pl.read_csv("weather_data.csv", try_parse_dates=True)

# Extract month from the date
df = df.with_columns(df["date"].dt.strftime("%B").alias("month"))

# Compute monthly average temperature
monthly_avg_temp = df.group_by("month").agg(pl.col("temperature").
mean())
```

```
# Create bar plot using Altair
bar_plot = alt.Chart(monthly_avg_temp).mark_bar().encode(
    x=alt.X("month:O", title="Month"),
    y=alt.Y("temperature:Q", title="Temperature (°C)"),
    tooltip=["month", "temperature"]
).properties(
    title="Average Temperature per Month",
    width=800,
    height=300
)

bar_plot
```

output :

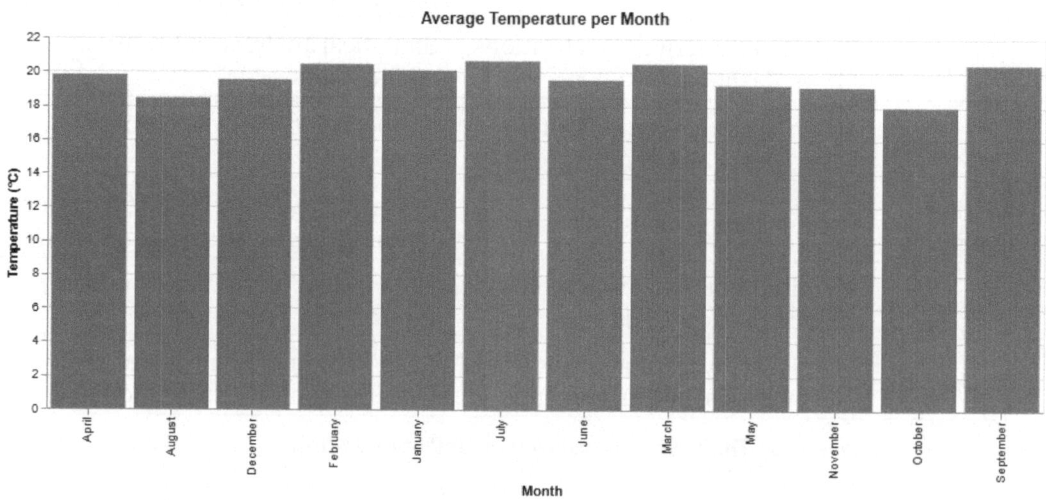

Figure 6.2: *Box Plot: Monthly Average Temperature Data Using Altair*

For trend analysis, we can utilize the line chart. Let us check it out with an example:

```
import altair as alt

# Line plot using Altair
line_chart = alt.Chart(df).mark_line().encode(
    x="date:T",
    y="temperature:Q",
    tooltip=["date", "temperature"]
).properties(
    title="Daily Temperature Trend",
    width=800,
```

```
    height=300
)

line_chart
```

Output:

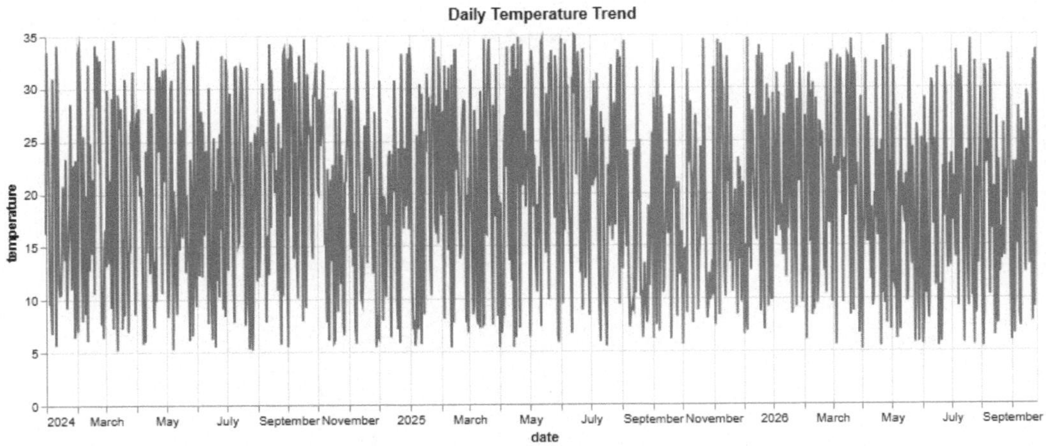

***Figure 6.3**: Line Chart: Daily Temperature Trend*

A scatter plot is used to visualize the relationship between two numerical variables where each point represents an individual data entry. This makes it useful for identifying patterns, correlations, and outliers. In contrast, a box plot summarizes the distribution of a dataset by displaying key statistics such as the median, quartiles, and outliers. Therefore, it is ideal for understanding data spread and variability. On the other hand, a line plot is primarily used for time-series analysis, connecting data points to show trends, patterns, and fluctuations over time. Let us have a look at a scatter plot made using Altair and Polars:

```
import polars as pl
import altair as alt

# Load dataset
df = pl.read_csv("weather_data.csv", try_parse_dates=True)

# Create scatter plot using Altair
scatter_plot = alt.Chart(df).mark_circle().encode(
    x=alt.X("temperature:Q", title="Temperature (°C)"),
    y=alt.Y("humidity:Q", title="Humidity (%)"),
    tooltip=["temperature", "humidity"]
).properties(
    title="Temperature vs Humidity",
```

```
    width=800,
    height=600
)

scatter_plot
```

Output:

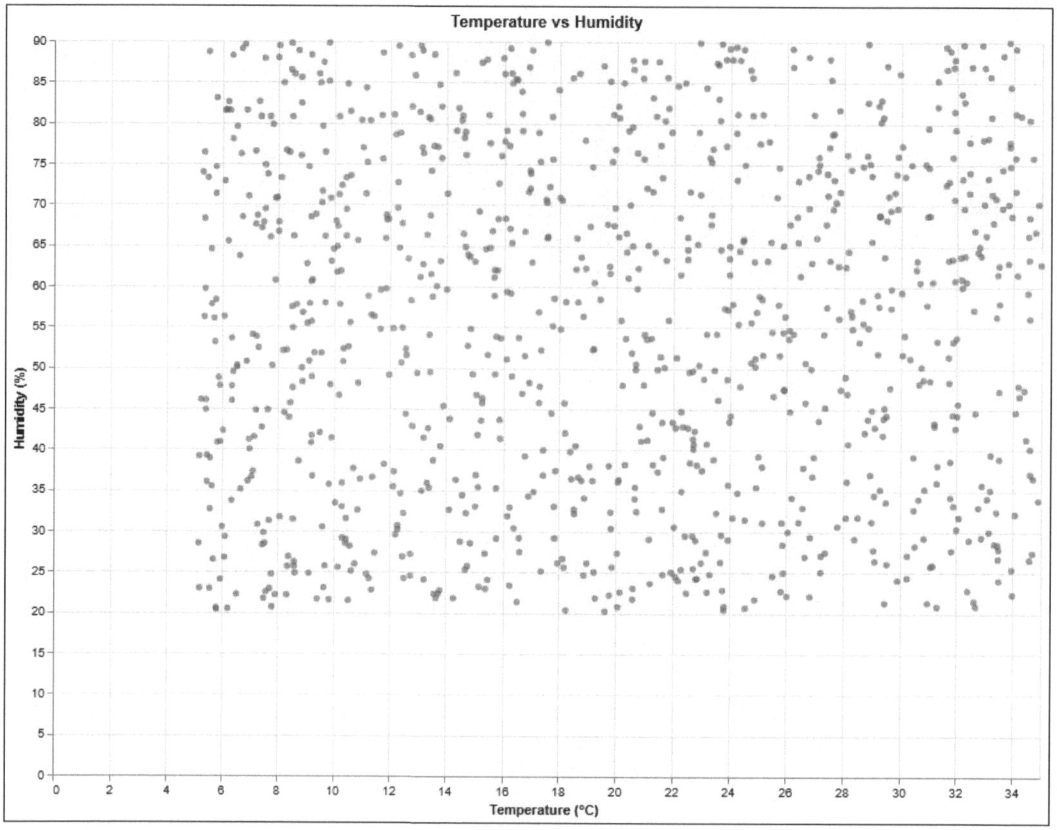

Figure 6.4: *Scatter Plot: Relationship between Humidity and Temperature*

By looking at the plot, we can conclude that there is no major correlation between temperature and humidity.

Statistical Plots: Histograms, Area Plots, and Box Plots

Statistical plots play a crucial role in analyzing and interpreting data by revealing patterns, trends, and distributions. Among the most commonly used statistical plots are histograms, area plots, and box plots, where each serves a distinct purpose in statistical analysis. These plots help summarize large datasets, identify outliers, and understand variable relationships, which makes them essential for data-driven decision-making.

Histograms: Analyzing Data Distribution

A histogram is a graphical representation of the frequency distribution of numerical data. It consists of bars where the height represents the number of data points falling within each bin (interval). Unlike bar charts, histograms display continuous data, which makes them particularly useful for understanding data dispersion, skewness, and central tendency. Histograms help detect whether a dataset follows a normal distribution, is skewed, or contains multiple modes. For example, in a weather dataset, a histogram of daily temperatures can reveal whether temperatures tend to cluster around a specific range, or if extreme temperatures occur frequently.

Area Plots: Visualizing Trends over Time

An area plot is an extension of a line plot where the area under the line is filled with color, emphasizing the magnitude of changes over time. It is particularly useful for tracking cumulative values and comparing multiple variables. Area plots are commonly used in time-series analysis, such as monitoring temperature variations, humidity trends, or precipitation levels over months or years. By shading the area under the curve, this plot makes it easier to compare values at different time points and recognize seasonal patterns. In financial and climate studies, area plots help illustrate overall trends, ensuring that variations in data are clearly represented.

Box Plots: Identifying Outliers and Data Spread

A box plot (box-and-whisker plot) is a powerful visualization tool used to summarize data distribution through five key statistics: minimum, first quartile (Q1), median, third quartile (Q3), and maximum. The plot also highlights outliers, which appear as points beyond the whiskers. Box plots are essential in statistical analysis because they provide insights into data variability, skewness, and the presence of extreme values. For instance, in weather data analysis, a box plot of daily temperatures across different months can reveal whether some months have a wider temperature variation or if certain days experienced extreme weather conditions. Unlike histograms, box plots do not show the shape of the distribution but are excellent for comparing multiple datasets side by side.

Significance of Statistical Plots in Data Analysis

Statistical plots are essential for understanding data characteristics, identifying anomalies, and making data-driven decisions. Histograms help determine the shape of data distribution, area plots visualize changes over time, and box plots highlight variability and outliers. These plots provide an intuitive way to summarize and interpret complex datasets without relying solely on numerical statistics. Thus, by leveraging these visualizations, analysts can detect hidden patterns, assess data quality, and ensure more accurate predictions in fields like finance, healthcare, meteorology, and economics.

Let us explore different statistical plotting with polars dataframes starting with histograms:

```
# Create histogram
histogram = alt.Chart(df).mark_bar().encode(
    x=alt.X("temperature:Q", bin=True, title="Temperature (°C)"),
    y=alt.Y("count():Q", title="Frequency"),
    tooltip=["count()"]
).properties(
    title="Temperature Distribution",
    width=800,
    height=300
)

histogram
```

Output:

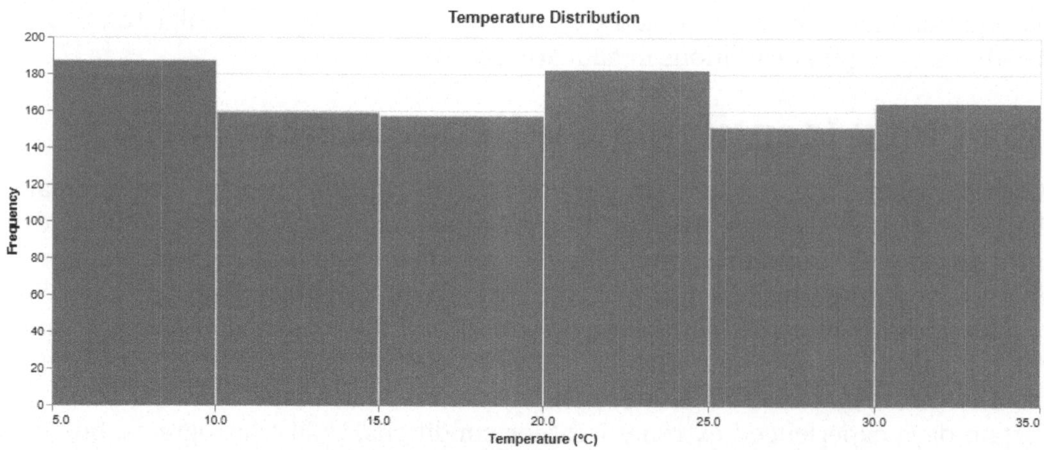

Figure 6.5: *Histogram of Temperature*

This histogram helps in understanding the temperature spread. There are no extreme outliers; the temperatures are evenly spread between 5°C and 35°C.

We will now try to analyze the data using area chart, and visualize temperature trend over time.

```
# Create area plot.
area_plot = alt.Chart(df).mark_area(opacity=0.5).encode(
    x=alt.X("date:T", title="Date"),
    y=alt.Y("temperature:Q", title="Temperature (°C)"),
    tooltip=["date", "temperature"]
).properties(
    title="Temperature Trends Over Time",
    width=1000,
    height=300
)

area_plot
```

Output:

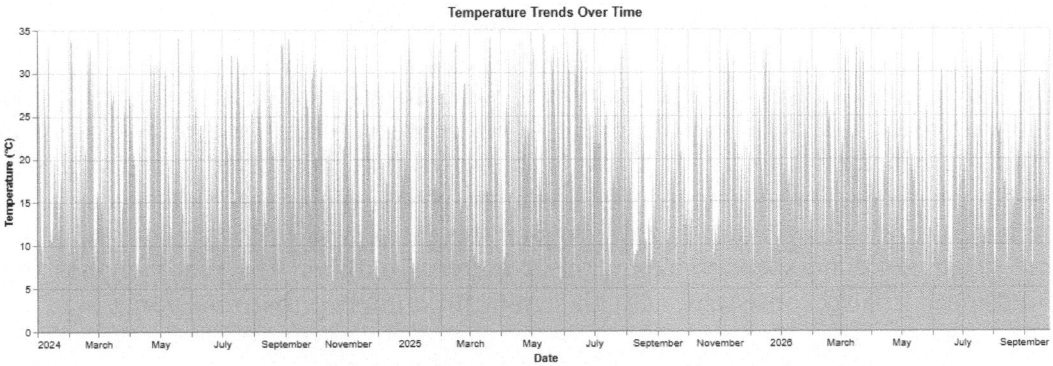

Figure 6.6*: Area Chart of Temperature Trend*

The chart exhibits frequent spikes, indicating rapid fluctuations in temperature over time and likely representing daily or seasonal variations. Despite these short-term changes, the overall pattern suggests that temperature variations remain within a stable range across multiple years, without extreme long-term shifts.

We will now use box plot find outliers for wind speed.

```
box_plot = alt.Chart(df).mark_boxplot().encode(
    x=alt.X("wind_speed:Q", title="Wind Speed (km/h)")
).properties(
    title="Distribution of Wind Speed",
    width=800,
    height=300
)

box_plot
```

Output:

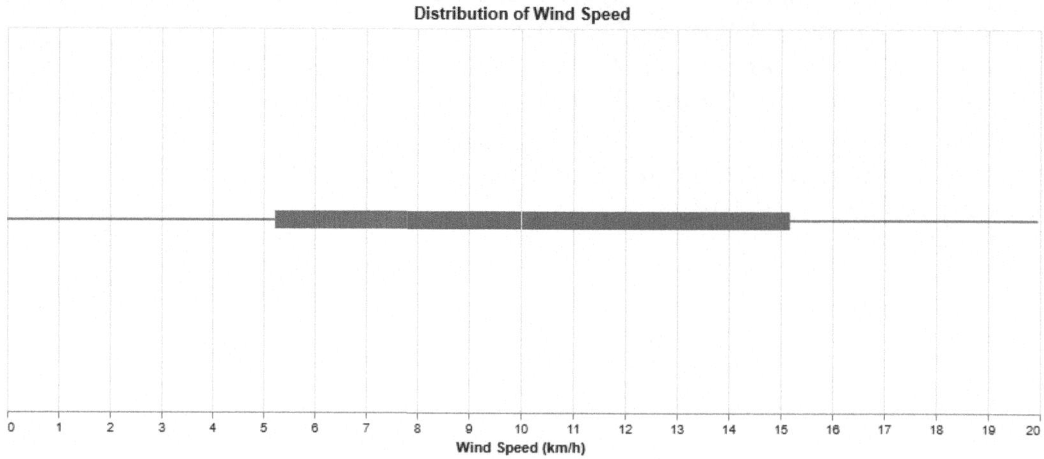

Figure 6.7: *Box Plot of Wind Speed*

The box plot illustrates the distribution of wind speed (km/h), showing its spread and variability. The interquartile range (IQR), represented by the blue box, spans from approximately 5 km/h to 15 km/h, indicates that most wind speed values lie within this range. The median (central line in the box) suggests the middle value of the dataset. The whiskers extend slightly beyond this range, while covering the minimum and maximum wind speed values without extreme outliers. The plot suggests that wind speed is fairly consistent, with no significant outliers or extreme variations.

Customization Options in Altair

Altair provides a declarative and flexible approach to data visualization and allows users to customize various aspects of their charts with ease. Customization in Altair is essential for enhancing readability, improving aesthetics, and making visualizations more effective for analysis. By adjusting chart properties, colors, labels, tooltips, and interactivity, users can tailor their visualizations to meet specific needs.

- Customizing Chart Titles and Axes

  Titles play a vital role in making a visualization understandable. In Altair, the .properties() method allows users to set a title for the chart, while the .encode() function helps customize axis labels. Axes can be modified using alt.X() and alt.Y() parameters, which allow renaming, setting scales, and formatting tick values. These features help in making charts more intuitive and self-explanatory.

- Adjusting Color Schemes and Opacity

  Color plays a critical role in differentiating categories, highlighting trends, and improving visual appeal. Altair allows users to set colors explicitly using the **`.mark_*().encode(color="column_name:N")`** function. Users can also apply predefined color palettes like "category10", "viridis", or "magma" for better visualization. Additionally, opacity settings (opacity=0.6, for example) can be used to control transparency, which is particularly useful in scatter plots with overlapping points.

- Customizing Tooltips and Labels

  Altair provides an easy way to include interactive tooltips, which display additional information when hovering over data points. This is done using **`tooltip=["column1", "column2"]`** inside the **`.encode()`** function. Tooltips are especially useful in dense scatter plots and time series visualizations, where labels might clutter the graph. Adding labels to specific points can also enhance interpretability. They can be displayed using **`text="column_name"`** encoding.

- Modifying Line Styles and Markers

  For line charts, users can customize stroke width, dash styles, and marker shapes. For instance, in a time-series visualization, users can make a line thicker using .mark_line(strokeWidth=3), or they can differentiate multiple lines using dashed patterns by applying .mark_line(strokeDash=[5,2]). For scatter plots, different marker shapes and sizes can be applied using .mark_point(size=50, shape="circle"). These options help in distinguishing various data series clearly.

- Adding Faceting and Multi-Panel Views

  Altair supports faceting, which allows breaking down a dataset into multiple subplots based on categorical variables. This is done using .facet(column="category"), which creates small multiples of the same chart for different groups. This feature is particularly useful in comparative analysis, such as visualizing temperature trends across different cities or comparing sales performance by region.

- Using Interactive Features

  One of Altair's most powerful customization options is interactivity, which allows users to filter, pan, zoom, and highlight elements dynamically. The selection feature can be used to enable interactive filtering of data points. For example, users can define a selection using alt.selection_single() and link it to other charts, while enabling drill-down functionality. This makes dashboards and reports more engaging and insightful.

- Adjusting Gridlines and Background Styles

  Altair also provides options to modify gridlines, background colors, and overall chart themes. Users can disable gridlines using .configure_axis(grid=False) or customize them with different line styles and colors. Background colors can be changed using .configure_view(background="lightgray"), which makes the chart stand out in presentations.

- Exporting High-Quality Visualizations

  Finally, Altair allows users to export charts in high resolution for reports and publications. The `.save()` method enables saving charts as PNG, SVG, or HTML files with a specified scale factor for higher quality. This is especially useful for academic research and business reports, where crisp, high-resolution images are necessary for presentations and documents.

Advanced Visualization with Seaborn

Pair plots and heatmaps are two powerful visualization techniques that help in understanding relationships, correlations, and patterns within a dataset. These plots are particularly useful in exploratory data analysis (EDA), where analysts need to examine multiple variables simultaneously. Using Seaborn and Polars, we can efficiently generate these visualizations from our weather dataset.

Understanding Pair Plots

A pair plot (also called scatterplot matrix) is a collection of scatter plots arranged in a grid. It allows us to visualize pairwise relationships between numerical variables. Each scatter plot represents the relationship between two features and helps us identify correlations, clusters, and outliers. Pair plots also include diagonal plots, which typically display histograms or kernel density estimates (KDE) for univariate distributions.We use dataframe exchange protocol to use polars dataframe with Seaborn.

Use Cases of Pair Plots

- **Feature Selection**: Helps in identifying which variables have strong relationships and aids in feature selection for machine learning models.
- **Outlier Detection**: Unusual data points that do not fit the general pattern can be spotted.
- **Cluster Identification**: If data naturally forms groups, these clusters can be visually identified.
- **Trend Exploration:** Shows how changes in one variable affect another.

```
import polars as pl
import seaborn as sns
import matplotlib.pyplot as plt

# Load dataset
df = pl.read_csv("weather_data.csv", try_parse_dates=True)

# Convert Polars DataFrame to Pandas for Seaborn compatibility
df_pandas = df.to_pandas()

# Create pair plot
sns.pairplot(df_pandas, diag_kind="kde", plot_kws={"alpha": 0.6})

plt.show()
```

Output :

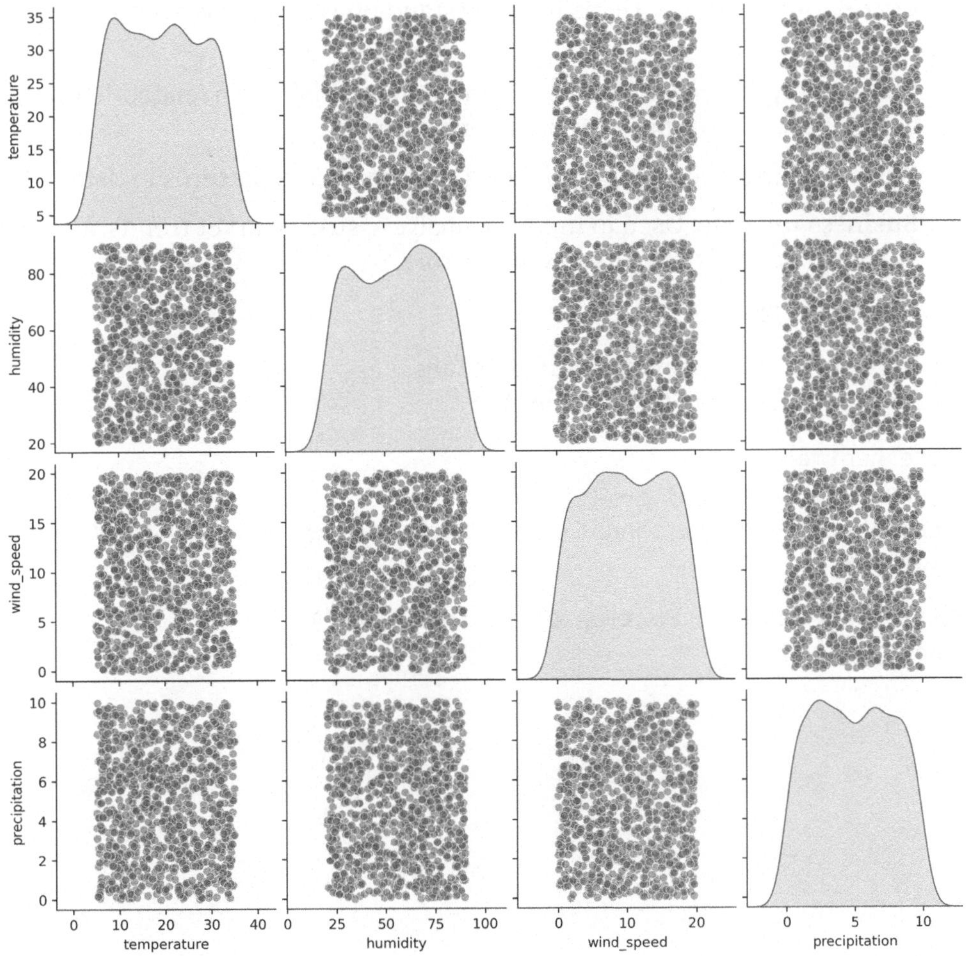

***Figure 6.8**: Pair Plot*

In this pair plot, each cell represents a scatter plot of one variable against another. The diagonal plots show KDE distributions and provides insight into the spread of each variable. The off-diagonal scatter plots reveal correlations and clusters.

Understanding Heatmaps

A heatmap is a two-dimensional representation of data where colors indicate values. It is commonly used to visualize correlations between numerical variables by computing a correlation matrix and displaying it as a color-coded grid. The intensity of the color represents the strength of the correlation, with positive correlations in one color (for example, dark red) and negative correlations in another (for example, dark blue).

Use Cases of Heatmaps

- **Correlation Analysis**: Helps in understanding relationships between multiple variables in a dataset
- **Feature Engineering:** Identifies redundant or highly correlated features that can be removed for better model performance
- **Data Cleaning**: Highlights anomalies or unexpected patterns in data
- **Business Insights:** Used in financial analysis, stock market trends, and climate studies to identify key influencing factors

```
import numpy as np

# Compute correlation matrix using Polars
corr_matrix = df.to_pandas().corr()

# Create heatmap
plt.figure(figsize=(10,6))
sns.heatmap(corr_matrix, annot=True, cmap="coolwarm", fmt=".2f",
linewidths=0.5)

plt.title("Correlation Heatmap of Weather Data")
plt.show()
```

Output:

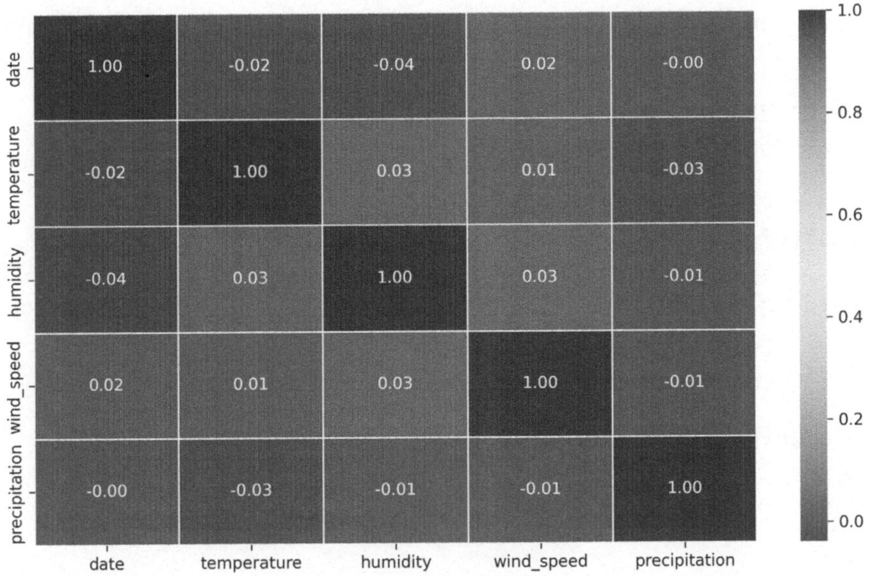

Figure 6.9: *Heatmap Plot*

Interactive Visualizations with Plotly

Plotly is a powerful Python library for creating interactive and high-quality visualizations. It is widely used in data science, business intelligence, and web applications due to its ability to generate interactive charts such as scatter plots, bar charts, line graphs, heatmaps, and even 3D plots. One of its key strengths is its seamless integration with Dash, which is a Python framework that allows users to build web-based analytical applications and dashboards. Unlike traditional static plots, Plotly enables users to zoom, pan, hover, and filter data points, which makes it a preferred choice for real-time data visualization. Additionally, it supports multiple programming languages, including Python, R, and JavaScript. This makes it versatile to use across different environments.

Let us have a look at a simple interactive bar plot using which is created via Plotly and Polars:

```
import polars as pl
import plotly.express as px

# Load weather dataset
df = pl.read_csv("weather_data.csv", try_parse_dates=True)

# Extract month from date column
df = df.with_columns(df["date"].dt.strftime("%B").alias("month"))
```

```
# Compute average temperature per month
monthly_avg_temp    =    df.group_by("month").agg(pl.col("temperature").
mean())

# Convert to Pandas for Plotly compatibility
df_pandas = monthly_avg_temp.to_pandas()

# Create a bar plot using Plotly Express
fig = px.bar(df_pandas, x="month", y="temperature",
             title="Average Temperature per Month",
            labels={"temperature": "Temperature (°C)", "month": "Month"},
             color="temperature",
             color_continuous_scale="viridis")

# Show the interactive plot
fig.show()
```

output:

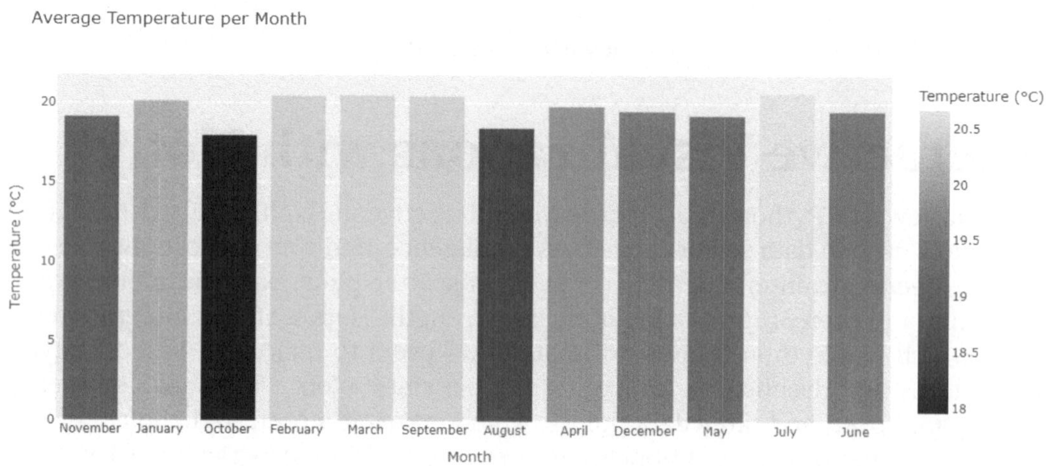

Figure 6.10: *Bar Plot Made Using Plotly*

You may have noticed that Plotly provides additional interaction features compared to Altair and offers more flexibility in exploring and analyzing data visually. This might make you wonder why we are specifically focusing on Plotly in this context. The primary reason for exploring Plotly is its seamless integration capabilities with Polars, which is crucial for building high-performance, scalable data pipelines. Additionally, Plotly is widely used in conjunction with Dash, which is a popular framework for developing interactive web-based dashboards. By understanding how to incorporate Polars within a Plotly-Dash ecosystem, we can enhance the efficiency of existing production dashboards and ensure faster data processing and rendering, while leveraging the advantages of both Polars' high-speed computation and Plotly's interactivity.

Map-Based Visualizations

Geospatial data visualization plays a crucial role in analyzing and interpreting location-based information. It enables businesses, researchers, and policymakers to make data-driven decisions. Maps provide an intuitive way to represent complex spatial data and make it easier to identify patterns, trends, and relationships across geographic regions. Whether tracking population density, climate variations, disease outbreaks, or supply chain logistics, geospatial visualization enhances our ability to understand spatial distributions and interactions. Tools like Plotly, Folium, Altair, and GeoPandas allow for the creation of dynamic and interactive maps. They help users explore data with geographical context. By leveraging choropleth maps, heatmaps, and point maps, organizations can uncover insights that would be difficult to discern from raw numerical data alone. As geospatial data continues to grow in importance, maps remain one of the most effective tools for translating vast amounts of information into actionable insights. We will use sugar production data to explore different types of geospatial data visualizations.

Choropleth Map: Global Sugar Production

A choropleth map is useful for comparing sugar production levels across different countries by representing the data using color intensity. In the example that follows, we load the sugar production dataset using Polars and use Plotly Express to create a map where each country is color-coded based on its total sugar production (in million tons). The iso_alpha column is used for country codes and a continuous color scale (YlGnBu) visually distinguishes high and low production regions.

```
import polars as pl
import plotly.express as px

# Load sugar production dataset using Polars
df = pl.read_csv("sugar_production_data.csv")

# Create a choropleth map
fig = px.choropleth(
    df.to_pandas(),  # Convert Polars DataFrame to Pandas as Plotly
expects Pandas
    locations="iso_alpha",
    color="sugar_production_million_tons",
    hover_name="country",
    color_continuous_scale="YlGnBu",
    title="Global Sugar Production (Million Tons)"
)

fig.show()
```

output:

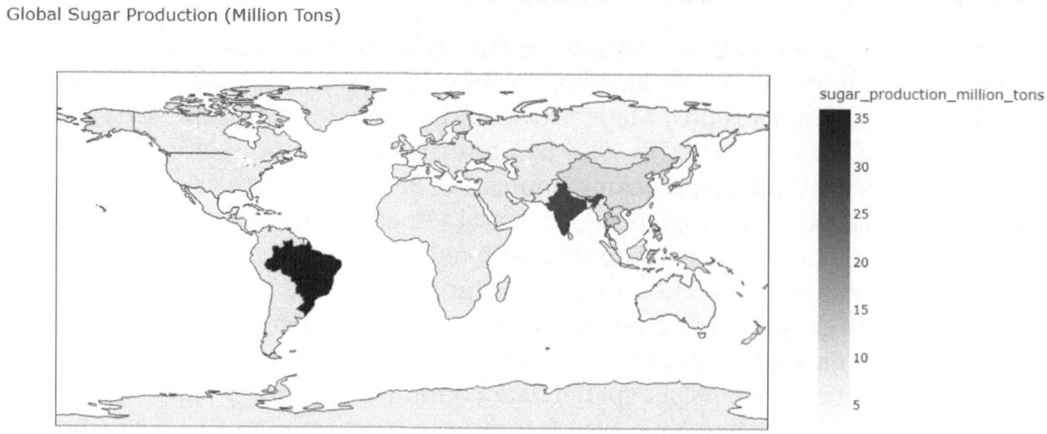

***Figure 6.11**: Choropleth: Sugar Production*

Scatter Geo Map: Sugar Production Distribution

A scatter geo map allows us to plot sugar production levels as points on a world map, where the size of each marker corresponds to the production volume in million tons. This visualization is useful to quickly identify major sugar-producing countries by marking them with larger circles. Using Plotly Express, we project country locations on a "natural earth" map and scale the marker size, based on production figures.

```
fig = px.scatter_geo(
    df.to_pandas(),
    locations="iso_alpha",
    size="sugar_production_million_tons",
    hover_name="country",
    projection="natural earth",
    title="Sugar Production Distribution"
)

fig.show()
```

output:

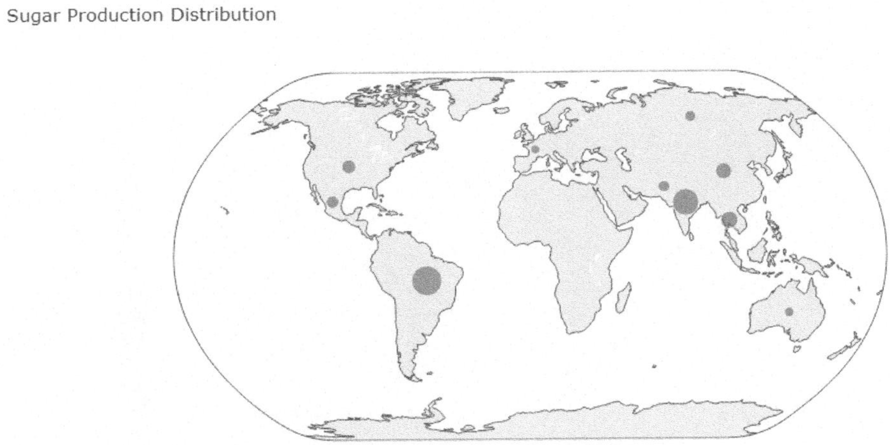

***Figure 6.12**: Scatter Geo Map*

Density Heatmap: Sugar Production Hotspots

A density heatmap helps in identifying geographical hotspots of sugar production, where areas with higher production appear more intensely colored. Instead of country-level aggregates, this visualization focuses on specific regions within countries where sugar production is concentrated. Using latitude and longitude data, we will create a heatmap overlay on a map with Plotly's density_mapbox and highlight areas with the highest sugar production intensity.

```
fig = px.density_mapbox(
    df.to_pandas(),
    lat=[-14.2, 20.6, 23.5, 35.9, 15.0, 19.4, 30.4, 55.7, -25.2, 46.6],
# Approx. latitudes
    lon=[-51.9, 78.9, 82.9, 104.2, 100.5, -99.1, 69.3, 37.6, 133.7,
2.2],  # Approx. longitudes
    z="sugar_production_million_tons",
    radius=20,
    mapbox_style="carto-positron",
    title="Sugar Production Hotspots"
)

fig.show()
```

output:

Figure 6.13: *Density Heatmaps*

Geospatial maps are powerful tools for visualizing data distribution across different regions, as they provide valuable insights into spatial patterns and trends. Choropleth maps highlight regional variations, scatter geo maps display location-specific data points, and density heatmaps reveal concentrated hotspots. These visualizations are widely used in fields like agriculture, business analytics, and urban planning for better decision-making.

Comparing Visualization Libraries

Data visualization is a crucial aspect of analysis. Several libraries in Python offer diverse capabilities for creating insightful charts. hvPlot, Altair, Seaborn, and Plotly are among the most widely used tools, each with its unique strengths and intended use cases. hvPlot provides a high-level interface that integrates well with data science libraries like Pandas and Polars, which make it easy to generate interactive plots with minimal code. Altair, on the other hand, follows a declarative approach, where users define the relationships between data and visualization elements. This approach makes Altair ideal for statistical graphics. Seaborn is built on top of Matplotlib and specializes in statistical data visualization. It helps in creating aesthetically pleasing and informative plots for data exploration. Plotly excels in interactive and web-based visualizations, which make it particularly useful for dashboards and web applications.

Strengths and Weaknesses of hvPlot, Altair, Seaborn, and Plotly

Each of these libraries has its advantages and limitations depending on the context in which they are used. hvPlot simplifies complex plotting tasks and is well-suited for exploratory data analysis. However, it may not provide the same level of fine-grained customization as other libraries. Altair ensures high-quality statistical visualization with a concise syntax, but struggles with large datasets due to its reliance on Vega-Lite. Seaborn produces visually appealing plots with built-in support for complex statistical relationships, but lacks interactivity. This can be a drawback for dynamic analysis. Plotly is the best choice for interactive, browser-based visualizations, but comes with a steeper learning curve when you are customizing plots.

Using Libraries According to Use Cases

Choosing the right visualization library depends on the use case and data requirements. If the goal is quick exploratory analysis, hvPlot is a great choice due to its concise and intuitive API. For statistical analysis and publication-quality figures, Altair and Seaborn are well-suited as they provide structured, insightful representations of data trends. Plotly is ideal for interactive dashboards, web applications, and real-time data visualization, as it allows users to zoom, hover, and interact with the plots. Ultimately, the choice of visualization library depends on the balance between simplicity, interactivity, and customization required for a given project.

Conclusion

Our exploration of Polars-based data visualization covered a wide range of techniques and tools. In this chapter, we demonstrated how libraries like hvPlot, Altair, Seaborn, and Plotly can be effectively used for interactive and statistical visualizations. We examined essential plots such as bar charts, scatter plots, histograms, box plots, heatmaps, and geospatial visualizations, each serving a unique purpose in understanding data patterns and distributions. By integrating Polars with these libraries, we achieved both efficiency and scalability, besides enabling large dataset visualizations with minimal performance overhead.

We also compared the strengths and weaknesses of these visualization libraries, while highlighting their suitability for different analytical needs. Whether it was exploratory data analysis with hvPlot, statistical insights with Altair and Seaborn, or interactive web visualizations with Plotly, each approach offered distinct advantages depending on the context. The ability to visualize trends, correlations, and geographical distributions provides a comprehensive perspective for data-driven decision-making.

In the next chapter, we will explore SQL integration with Polars for seamless querying and transforming large datasets within a powerful dataframe-based workflow.

Exercises

Exercise 1: Exploring Weather Data with hvPlot

Load a weather dataset using Polars and use hvPlot to create the following visualizations:

- A line plot showing temperature trends over time.
- A bar plot representing average humidity for each month.
- A scatter plot comparing wind speed and temperature. Save each plot as a high-resolution image (300 DPI) and analyze the key insights from the visualizations.

Exercise 2: Statistical Analysis with Seaborn and Polars

Using the same weather dataset, perform statistical visualizations with Seaborn:

- Create a histogram to visualize the distribution of temperature values.
- Generate a box plot to analyze variations in humidity across different months.
- Develop a pair plot to observe relationships between temperature, humidity, and wind speed. Interpret the statistical significance of these visualizations in understanding weather patterns.

Exercise 3: Geospatial Data Visualization with Plotly and Polars

Use a dataset related to sugarcane production across different regions and visualize it with Plotly:

- Create a Choropleth map to show sugarcane production across states/ countries.
- Use scatter geo to represent production data points with varying marker sizes.
- Generate a density heatmap to highlight high-production regions. Discuss how geospatial visualization helps in identifying agricultural trends and decision-making.

CHAPTER 7
SQL Integration with Polars

"SQL is the lingua franca of data."

Andrew Ng

Introduction

In the era of big data, efficient querying and seamless data retrieval are crucial for data analysts and engineers. This chapter explores SQL-based querying within Polars, while leveraging its SQLContext, Expression SQL, and Global SQL features to simplify data manipulation. Readers will learn how to retrieve data from both traditional databases and cloud storage, and make data access more dynamic and flexible.

This chapter also covers integrating Polars with DuckDB, a fast in-memory analytical database, and LanceDB, a high-performance vector database designed for advanced data operations to enhance performance and scalability. These integrations enable users to perform SQL-like queries on structured and semi-structured datasets.

By the end of this chapter, you will have a strong understanding of how to execute fast, SQL-based queries across various data sources. This will help you unlock new possibilities for data analysis and transformation.

Structure

In this chapter, we will discuss the following topics:

- Overview of SQL Querying in Polars
- SQL in Polars
- Expression SQL

- Global SQL
- Getting Data from a Database
- Getting Data from Cloud Storage
- Integration with DuckDB
- Integration with LanceDB

Overview of SQL Querying in Polars

Polars have gained popularity for its ability to handle large datasets efficiently. While Polars are primarily designed for columnar data processing using its native API, it also provides SQL-like querying capabilities, which makes it more accessible to users familiar with SQL. By leveraging SQLContext, Expression SQL, and Global SQL, Polars allows analysts and data engineers to execute SQL queries directly on DataFrames without converting them into another format. This bridges the gap between traditional SQL-based data manipulation and modern, high-speed analytical workflows.

With SQL capabilities in Polars, users can filter, aggregate, and transform data using familiar SQL syntax. This eliminates the need for extensive knowledge of Polars' native expressions, while reducing the learning curve for those transitioning from SQL-based environments like PostgreSQL or MySQL. Furthermore, Polars' optimized execution engine ensures that these queries run efficiently, often outperforming traditional SQL databases for analytical workloads. Whether working with structured tabular data or semi-structured data from cloud storage, Polars provide a seamless SQL querying experience.

Importance of SQL-Like Operations for Data Analysis

SQL has been the dominant query language for decades, as it provides a powerful and intuitive way to interact with relational databases. Even as data processing has evolved with libraries like Pandas and Polars, SQL remains essential for analysts who need to query, filter, join, and aggregate large datasets efficiently. The ability to write SQL-like queries in Polars allow users to work with data more effectively, especially when dealing with large-scale datasets that require high-speed processing.

One of the major advantages of SQL-based querying is its declarative nature, which allows users to specify what they want from the data without worrying about the underlying execution details. Polars leverage this concept by optimizing queries under the hood, while applying lazy evaluation techniques to minimize memory usage and improve performance. Additionally, SQL-based operations allow for better interoperability with existing data pipelines, as many modern workflows involve querying data stored in relational databases or cloud storage before performing in-depth analysis.

By supporting SQL-like operations, Polars enables data analysts, engineers, and scientists to perform data transformations without switching between different tools. Whether performing exploratory data analysis (EDA), reporting, or building machine learning datasets, SQL capabilities in Polars provide an intuitive and efficient way to process large volumes of data.

Enhancing Data Retrieval and Processing via SQLContext, DuckDB, and LanceDB

To further enhance SQL querying in Polars, integrations with SQLContext, DuckDB, and LanceDB provide additional power and flexibility. SQLContext in Polars acts as an in-memory SQL engine, which allows users to run SQL queries directly on Polars DataFrames. This feature simplifies querying structured data, enabling familiar operations such as SELECT, JOIN, GROUP BY, and WHERE without needing to manually write Polars expressions. Expression SQL further extends this by allowing users to define complex calculations and transformations using SQL-like syntax.

While Polars provides efficient SQL-like querying, it can be further enhanced with DuckDB, an in-memory analytical database designed for high-performance query execution. DuckDB excels at processing large datasets quickly, which makes it an ideal companion for Polars when working with tabular data stored in Parquet, CSV, or databases. By integrating Polars with DuckDB, users can execute complex analytical queries using DuckDB's SQL engine while still benefiting from Polars' performance optimizations.

Additionally, LanceDB extends SQL querying capabilities beyond structured data by introducing vector-based operations and high-performance data indexing. Unlike traditional databases, LanceDB is optimized for large-scale data retrieval, which makes it particularly useful for applications such as machine learning (ML), recommendation systems, and search indexing. By integrating LanceDB with Polars, users can efficiently retrieve and manipulate structured and unstructured data, enabling fast, scalable, and SQL-compatible analytics.

Together, SQLContext, DuckDB, and LanceDB provide a powerful ecosystem for SQL-based querying in Polars. They enhance data retrieval, accelerate query execution, and support both structured and unstructured data analysis, which makes Polars an indispensable tool for modern data workflows.

SQL in Polars

Now, let us try to understand the different SQL options available in Polars. We will also have a look at some practical examples.

Understanding SQLContext

SQLContext in Polars acts as an execution environment for running SQL queries directly on Polars DataFrames. It enables users to interact with data using SQL-like syntax, which makes it more intuitive for analysts who are already familiar with traditional relational databases. Unlike conventional SQL engines, SQLContext in Polars operates in-memory and leverages Polars' high-performance query execution model, which allows for efficient filtering, aggregation, and transformation of large datasets.

The primary advantage of SQLContext is that it brings the power of SQL into Polars' lazy execution model, which means that queries are optimized and executed only when needed. This feature is particularly useful for handling large-scale analytical queries, where performance bottlenecks can arise due to inefficient query execution. Additionally, SQLContext allows users to perform complex joins, window functions, and grouping operations without writing verbose Polars expressions.

Creating and Using SQLContext in Polars

To use SQLContext in Polars, users first need to create an instance of it and register DataFrames as SQL tables. This registration allows for seamless querying of Polars DataFrames using standard SQL syntax.

Example: Registering Telecom Data in SQLContext

```
import polars as pl

# Sample telecom dataset - Call Detail Records (CDRs)
cdr_data = pl.DataFrame({
    "call_id": [101, 102, 103],
    "caller": ["+919876543210", "+918765432109", "+917654321098"],
    "receiver": ["+911234567890", "+919898989898", "+918282828282"],
    "duration": [300, 120, 450],  # Duration in seconds
    "call_type": ["Local", "International", "Roaming"]
})

# Initialize SQLContext
sql_context = pl.SQLContext()

# Register CDR dataset as a SQL table
sql_context.register("cdr_logs", cdr_data)

# Run SQL query to get long-duration calls
query = """
    SELECT caller, receiver, duration
    FROM cdr_logs
    WHERE duration > 200
"""

result = sql_context.execute(query).collect()
print(result)
```

Output:

```
shape: (2, 3)
```

caller --- str	receiver --- str	duration --- i64
+919876543210 +917654321098	+911234567890 +918282828282	300 450

Here, we register Call Detail Records (CDRs) as a virtual SQL table and execute a query to filter long-duration calls.

Expression SQL

In Polars, Expression SQL allows users to define complex filtering, aggregations, and transformations directly on DataFrames, while leveraging Polars' optimized query execution. Instead of running full SQL queries, **`polars.sql_expr()`** helps execute individual SQL expressions on columns, which makes it highly efficient for real-time analytics and in-memory computations.

Let us explore **`polars.sql_expr()`** with **real-world telecom datasets**, including **call records (CDRs), customer plans, and network performance data**. Imagine that we have a **CDR dataset** with call durations and want to filter calls that lasted **more than 5 minutes (300 seconds)**.

```
import polars as pl

# Sample Call Detail Records (CDRs) dataset
cdr_data = pl.DataFrame({
    "call_id": [101, 102, 103, 104],
    "caller": ["+919876543210", "+918765432109", "+917654321098",
"+919191919191"],
    "duration": [300, 450, 120, 600],  # Duration in seconds
    "call_type": ["Local", "International", "Local", "Roaming"]
})

# Using polars.sql_expr() to filter high-duration calls
high_duration_calls = cdr_data.filter(pl.sql_expr("duration > 300"))

print(high_duration_calls)
```

output :

```
shape: (2, 4)
```

call_id --- i64	caller --- str	duration --- i64	call_type --- str
102 104	+918765432109 +919191919191	450 600	International Roaming

Instead of writing a full SQL query, we pass the condition "duration > 300" to sql_expr(). This directly applies the filter to the Polars DataFrame without needing SQLContext.

Here is an example that demonstrates both aggregation and transformation using **polars.sql_expr()**. This example is based on telecom data, where we analyze customer call records to compute.

```
import polars as pl

# Sample telecom call records dataset
cdr_data = pl.DataFrame({
    "customer_id": [1, 2, 1, 3, 2, 3, 1],
    "phone_number": ["+919876543210", "+918765432109", "+919876543210",
                     "+917654321098", "+918765432109", "+917654321098",
"+919876543210"],
    "duration": [300, 450, 120, 600, 150, 200, 400],  # Duration in
seconds
    "call_type": ["Local", "International", "Local", "Roaming", "Local",
"International", "Roaming"]
})

# Aggregation: Calculate total and average call duration per customer
aggregated_data = cdr_data.group_by("customer_id").agg([
    pl.sql_expr("SUM(duration)").alias("total_call_duration"),
    pl.sql_expr("AVG(duration)").alias("avg_call_duration")
])

# Transformation: Categorizing customers based on total call duration
aggregated_data = aggregated_data.with_columns(
    pl.sql_expr("""
        CASE
            WHEN total_call_duration > 1000 THEN 'Heavy User'
            WHEN total_call_duration BETWEEN 500 AND 1000 THEN 'Moderate
User'
            ELSE 'Light User'
        END
    """).alias("user_category")
```

```
)
print(aggregated_data)
```

Output:

```
shape: (3, 4)
┌─────────────┬─────────────────────┬───────────────────┬───────────────┐
│ customer_id ┆ total_call_duration ┆ avg_call_duration ┆ user_category │
│ ---         ┆ ---                 ┆ ---               ┆ ---           │
│ i64         ┆ i64                 ┆ f64               ┆ str           │
╞═════════════╪═════════════════════╪═══════════════════╪═══════════════╡
│ 1           ┆ 820                 ┆ 273.333333        ┆ Moderate User │
│ 2           ┆ 600                 ┆ 300.0             ┆ Moderate User │
│ 3           ┆ 800                 ┆ 400.0             ┆ Moderate User │
└─────────────┴─────────────────────┴───────────────────┴───────────────┘
```

Global SQL

Polars' Global SQL enables users to execute SQL queries across different data sources, including:

- Polars DataFrame, LazyFrame, and Series
- Pandas DataFrame and Series
- PyArrow Table and RecordBatch

Both **`polars.sql()`** and SQLContext allow seamless querying across these formats. When non-Polars objects (like Pandas and PyArrow) are used in a query, Polars automatically converts them to DataFrames. For PyArrow-based Pandas data, this conversion can be zero-copy, which ensures high performance. Let us understand it with an example.

In this example, we use Polars DataFrame, Pandas DataFrame, and PyArrow Table to analyze telecom customer call records, network performance data, and billing information. We then run a single SQL query to combine insights from all sources.

```
import polars as pl
import pandas as pd
```

```
import pyarrow as pa

# Telecom Call Detail Records (CDRs) - Polars DataFrame
cdr_data = pl.DataFrame({
    "customer_id": [1, 2, 3, 4],
    "call_duration": [300, 450, 120, 600],  # in seconds
    "call_type": ["Local", "International", "Local", "Roaming"]
})

# Network Performance Data - Pandas DataFrame
network_data = pd.DataFrame({
    "customer_id": [1, 2, 3, 4],
    "dropped_calls": [2, 10, 5, 1],
    "network_quality": ["Good", "Poor", "Average", "Excellent"]
})

# Billing Information - PyArrow Table
billing_data = pa.table({
    "customer_id": [1, 2, 3, 4],
    "total_bill": [50.0, 120.5, 30.0, 200.0],
    "plan": ["Basic", "Premium", "Basic", "Ultra"]
})

# Running a SQL query across Polars, Pandas, and PyArrow data
query = """
    SELECT
        c.customer_id,
        c.call_duration,
        n.network_quality,
        b.total_bill,
        b.plan,
        CASE
            WHEN b.total_bill > 100 THEN 'High Value'
            WHEN b.total_bill BETWEEN 50 AND 100 THEN 'Medium Value'
            ELSE 'Low Value'
        END AS customer_segment
    FROM cdr_data c
    JOIN network_data n ON c.customer_id = n.customer_id
    JOIN billing_data b ON c.customer_id = b.customer_id
    WHERE n.network_quality != 'Poor'
    ORDER BY b.total_bill DESC
"""

# Execute SQL query using pl.sql() and register data sources
```

```
result = pl.sql(
    query
).collect()

print(result)
```

Output :

```
shape: (3, 6)
┌──────────────┬───────────────┬─────────────────┬────────────┬───────┬──────────────────┐
│ customer_id ┆ call_duration ┆ network_quality ┆ total_bill ┆ plan  ┆ customer_segment │
│ ---         ┆ ---           ┆ ---             ┆ ---        ┆ ---   ┆ ---              │
│ i64         ┆ i64           ┆ str             ┆ f64        ┆ str   ┆ str              │
╞══════════════╪═══════════════╪═════════════════╪════════════╪═══════╪══════════════════╡
│ 4           ┆ 600           ┆ Excellent       ┆ 200.0      ┆ Ultra ┆ High Value       │
│ 1           ┆ 300           ┆ Good            ┆ 50.0       ┆ Basic ┆ Medium Value     │
│ 3           ┆ 120           ┆ Average         ┆ 30.0       ┆ Basic ┆ Low Value        │
└──────────────┴───────────────┴─────────────────┴────────────┴───────┴──────────────────┘
```

The SQL query integrates telecom customer data from multiple sources such as Call Detail Records (CDRs) from Polars, network performance data from Pandas, and billing information from PyArrow. All this is done by using **`pl.sql()`**. It joins the three datasets on **`customer_id`**, which ensures seamless data fusion across different formats. The query filters out customers with poor network quality, while prioritizing those with better service experiences. It then categorizes customers based on their **`total_bill`** into "**`High Value`**" (bill > 100), "**`Medium Value`**" (50-100), and "**`Low Value`**" (below 50). Finally, the results are ordered by billing amount in descending order, which allows businesses to quickly identify high-value customers and assess their network quality and call durations.

Getting Data from a Database

Polars provides efficient methods to read from and write to relational databases, which makes it an excellent choice for data analysis. Two primary functions, **`pl.read_database_uri`** and **`pl.read_database`**, allow users to fetch structured data directly into a Polars DataFrame. Similarly, the **`pl.write_database`** function enables seamless data storage.

Difference between read_database_uri and read_database

The pl.read_database_uri function allows direct database connection using a URI connection string. This approach is suitable when working with remote PostgreSQL, MySQL, or other relational databases storing telecom data.

```
import polars as pl
uri = "postgresql://username:password@server:port/telecom_db"
query = "SELECT * FROM call_records"
df = pl.read_database_uri(query=query, uri=uri)
```

On the other hand, pl.read_database is used when working with a database connection engine, such as SQLAlchemy. This method is commonly used for local databases like SQLite, where telecom providers store historical customer interaction data.

```
import polars as pl
from sqlalchemy import create_engine

conn = create_engine("sqlite:///telecom_data.db")
query = "SELECT * FROM call_records"
df = pl.read_database(query=query, connection=conn.connect())
```

While both methods are effective, **`pl.read_database_uri`** tends to be faster since it loads data in an optimized columnar format directly into Polars.

Database Engines for Efficient Data Retrieval

Polars does not manage database connections directly; instead, it relies on external engines for data transfer. Two main engines are used for reading data into Polars:

- ConnectorX (Default Engine)
- Arrow Database Connectivity (ADBC)

ConnectorX: Optimized for Large-Scale Telecom Data

ConnectorX, written in Rust, efficiently fetches data from PostgreSQL, MySQL, SQL Server, and Redshift. It supports zero-copy conversion to the Apache Arrow format, which ensures high-speed data access.

ADBC: Apache Arrow-Based Engine

ADBC (Arrow Database Connectivity) is an emerging standard developed by Apache Arrow for database interaction. While its database support is currently limited, it provides a direct and efficient way to read data from PostgreSQL, SQLite, and Snowflake.

```
uri = "postgresql://username:password@server:port/telecom_db"
query = "SELECT * FROM call_records"
df = pl.read_database_uri(query=query, uri=uri, engine="adbc")
```

Writing Data to Databases Using Polars

Polars allow writing structured data back to a database using the pl.write_database function.

Writing Data Using SQLAlchemy

By default, Polars writes data using the SQLAlchemy engine, which supports a wide range of relational databases. When using SQLAlchemy, Polars first converts the DataFrame to a Pandas DataFrame backed by PyArrow before writing it to the database.

Writing Data Using ADBC

For databases that support ADBC (for example, PostgreSQL and SQLite), analysts can write high-performance analytical results using the ADBC engine.

```
df.write_database(table_name="processed_calls", connection=uri,
engine="adbc")
uri = "postgresql://username:password@server:port/telecom_db"
df = pl.DataFrame({"customer_id": [101, 102, 103], "call_duration":
[300, 450, 500]})

df.write_database(table_name="processed_calls", connection=uri)
```

Now, we will create an end to end read-write cycle for a sqlite database using Polars.

```
import sqlite3
import random
import datetime
import polars as pl
from sqlalchemy import create_engine

# Step 1: Create SQLite Database and Table
db_name = "telecom_data.db"
conn = sqlite3.connect(db_name)
cursor = conn.cursor()

cursor.execute("""
    CREATE TABLE IF NOT EXISTS call_logs (
        call_id INTEGER PRIMARY KEY AUTOINCREMENT,
        customer_id INTEGER,
        call_duration INTEGER,  -- in seconds
        call_type TEXT,  -- 'incoming' or 'outgoing'
        timestamp TEXT
    )
""")
conn.commit()
```

```
# Step 2: Generate Random Telecom Data
def generate_random_calls(n=5):
    call_types = ["incoming", "outgoing"]
    data = {
        "customer_id": [random.randint(1000, 9999) for _ in range(n)],
        "call_duration": [random.randint(30, 900) for _ in range(n)],  #
Duration between 30 sec to 15 min
        "call_type": [random.choice(call_types) for _ in range(n)],
        "timestamp": [datetime.datetime.now().strftime("%Y-%m-%d
%H:%M:%S") for _ in range(n)]
    }
    return pl.DataFrame(data)

# Step 3: Insert Initial Data Using Polars write_database()
engine = create_engine(f"sqlite:///{db_name}")

df_initial = generate_random_calls(5)
df_initial.write_database(table_name="call_logs", connection=engine.
connect(),if_table_exists= "append")

# Step 4: Read Data Using Polars
query = "SELECT * FROM call_logs"
df_loaded = pl.read_database(query=query, connection=engine.connect())

print("Initial Data Loaded into Polars DataFrame:")
print(df_loaded)

# Step 5: Insert More Records Using write_database()
df_new = generate_random_calls(3)
df_new.write_database(table_name="call_logs", connection=engine.
connect(), if_table_exists
="append")

# Reload the data into Polars
df_updated = pl.read_database(query=query, connection=engine.connect())

print("\nUpdated Data Loaded into Polars DataFrame:")
print(df_updated)

# Close the database connection
conn.close()
```

Output:

```
Initial Data Loaded into Polars DataFrame:
shape: (10, 5)
```

```
┌─────────┬─────────────┬───────────────┬───────────┬─────────────────────┐
│ call_id ┆ customer_id ┆ call_duration ┆ call_type ┆ timestamp           │
│ ---     ┆ ---         ┆ ---           ┆ ---       ┆ ---                 │
│ i64     ┆ i64         ┆ i64           ┆ str       ┆ str                 │
╞═════════╪═════════════╪═══════════════╪═══════════╪═════════════════════╡
│ 1       ┆ 4644        ┆ 247           ┆ outgoing  ┆ 2025-03-02 23:21:35 │
│ 2       ┆ 3790        ┆ 546           ┆ outgoing  ┆ 2025-03-02 23:21:35 │
│ 3       ┆ 8793        ┆ 505           ┆ incoming  ┆ 2025-03-02 23:21:35 │
│ 4       ┆ 9765        ┆ 342           ┆ incoming  ┆ 2025-03-02 23:21:35 │
│ 5       ┆ 9798        ┆ 113           ┆ incoming  ┆ 2025-03-02 23:21:35 │
│ 6       ┆ 4848        ┆ 191           ┆ incoming  ┆ 2025-03-02 23:21:56 │
│ 7       ┆ 2103        ┆ 121           ┆ incoming  ┆ 2025-03-02 23:21:56 │
│ 8       ┆ 6053        ┆ 100           ┆ incoming  ┆ 2025-03-02 23:21:56 │
│ 9       ┆ 9293        ┆ 285           ┆ outgoing  ┆ 2025-03-02 23:21:56 │
│ 10      ┆ 7175        ┆ 245           ┆ incoming  ┆ 2025-03-02 23:21:56 │
└─────────┴─────────────┴───────────────┴───────────┴─────────────────────┘
```

Updated Data Loaded into Polars DataFrame:

```
shape: (13, 5)
┌─────────┬─────────────┬───────────────┬───────────┬─────────────────────┐
│ call_id ┆ customer_id ┆ call_duration ┆ call_type ┆ timestamp           │
│ ---     ┆ ---         ┆ ---           ┆ ---       ┆ ---                 │
│ i64     ┆ i64         ┆ i64           ┆ str       ┆ str                 │
╞═════════╪═════════════╪═══════════════╪═══════════╪═════════════════════╡
│ 1       ┆ 4644        ┆ 247           ┆ outgoing  ┆ 2025-03-02 23:21:35 │
```

```
│ 2         ┆ 3790        ┆ 546            ┆ outgoing  ┆ 2025-03-02
23:21:35 │
│ 3         ┆ 8793        ┆ 505            ┆ incoming  ┆ 2025-03-02
23:21:35 │
│ 4         ┆ 9765        ┆ 342            ┆ incoming  ┆ 2025-03-02
23:21:35 │
│ 5         ┆ 9798        ┆ 113            ┆ incoming  ┆ 2025-03-02
23:21:35 │
│ …         ┆ …           ┆ …              ┆ …         ┆ …
│
│ 9         ┆ 9293        ┆ 285            ┆ outgoing  ┆ 2025-03-02
23:21:56 │
│ 10        ┆ 7175        ┆ 245            ┆ incoming  ┆ 2025-03-02
23:21:56 │
│ 11        ┆ 3022        ┆ 482            ┆ outgoing  ┆ 2025-03-02
23:21:56 │
│ 12        ┆ 4075        ┆ 38             ┆ incoming  ┆ 2025-03-02
23:21:56 │
│ 13        ┆ 7715        ┆ 763            ┆ incoming  ┆ 2025-03-02
23:21:56 │
└───────────┴─────────────┴────────────────┴───────────┴──────────────
───┘
```

This code demonstrates how to use Polars to interact with an SQLite database for telecom data analysis. It starts by creating an SQLite database (**`telecom_data.db`**) and a table **`call_logs`** to store telecom-related call records, including **`customer_id`**, **`call_duration`**, **`call_type`**, and timestamp. Random call data is generated using Python's random and datetime modules, and the initial dataset is written to the database using Polars' **`write_database()`** function to ensure efficient batch insertion. The data is then retrieved into a Polars DataFrame (**`pl.read_database`**) for further analysis. Next, additional random records are generated and inserted into the table using **`write_database()`**. Finally, the updated dataset is reloaded into Polars to reflect the new entries.

Best Practices for Efficient Querying of Data to DataFrames from a Database

Querying data efficiently from a database into a Polars DataFrame is essential for optimizing performance, minimizing memory usage, and ensuring smooth data processing. Poorly designed queries can lead to slow execution times, increased resource consumption, and performance bottlenecks. By following the best practices, users can significantly enhance data retrieval and analysis efficiency when working with large-scale datasets.

Optimize Queries with SELECT Statements and Column Filtering

Fetching unnecessary columns significantly increases memory usage and slows down data retrieval. Instead of using `SELECT *`, it is advisable to explicitly specify only the required columns. This reduces the amount of data transferred from the database to the application, which leads to faster query execution and better memory management. For example, using `pl.read_database("SELECT customer_id, plan_type FROM telecom_data", connection=conn.connect())` ensures that only relevant data is retrieved, thereby improving efficiency.

Apply Query Filtering (WHERE and LIMIT) for Reduced Data Load

Filtering data at the database level using the WHERE clause ensures that only relevant records are retrieved, while reducing processing overhead. Additionally, using LIMIT helps control the amount of data loaded into memory, which is especially useful when dealing with large tables. For instance, executing `pl.read_database("SELECT * FROM telecom_usage WHERE data_usage > 100", connection=conn.connect())` allows for selective retrieval of users with high data consumption and prevents unnecessary data transfer.

Use Database Indexes for Faster Query Execution

Indexes play a crucial role in improving query performance by allowing the database engine to locate records quickly rather than scanning entire tables. Indexing commonly queried columns, such as primary keys or timestamp fields, speeds up data retrieval operations significantly. Without proper indexing, queries can become slow and resource-intensive, especially as the dataset grows over time. For example, when executing `pl.read_database("SELECT call_duration FROM telecom_calls WHERE call_type = 'International'", connection=conn.connect())`, indexing the call_type column ensures optimized query performance.

Leverage Lazy Evaluation for Optimized Query Execution

Polars offer lazy execution, which enables query optimization by deferring execution until necessary. Instead of immediately executing transformations on data, lazy execution builds an optimized execution plan that minimizes redundant computations. This is particularly beneficial when applying filters, aggregations, and joins, as it ensures that only the required data is processed efficiently. For instance, we may use:

```
lf = pl.read_database("SELECT customer_id, monthly_bill FROM telecom_
billing", connection=conn.connect()).lazy()
lf = lf.filter(pl.col("monthly_bill") > 500)
df = lf.collect()
```

This approach ensures that the filtering operation is performed efficiently without unnecessary computations.

Batch Processing for Large Datasets

Fetching an entire dataset at once can lead to memory exhaustion and performance degradation. A better approach is to retrieve data in smaller batches or chunks, which ensures efficient resource utilization. This technique is useful when working with high-volume transactional data and prevents excessive memory consumption, while allowing for incremental processing of records. A recommended practice would be to use LIMIT, along with pagination techniques, such as:

```
pl.read_database("SELECT * FROM telecom_usage LIMIT 10000 OFFSET 20000",
connection=conn.connect())
```

This helps in breaking down the data retrieval process into manageable portions.

Convert Database Data to Efficient Storage Formats

Querying data repeatedly from a database can be costly in terms of time and performance. A more efficient approach is to store frequently accessed data in optimized formats such as Parquet or Apache Arrow. These formats allow for faster reads, efficient compression, and reduced storage footprint, which make subsequent data retrieval significantly quicker. For instance, after retrieving data, we may use:

```
df = pl.read_database("SELECT * FROM telecom_plans", connection=conn.
connect())
df.write_parquet("telecom_plans.parquet")
```

Future reads from the Parquet file will be significantly faster than querying the database each time.

Utilize Connection Pooling for Optimized Performance

Opening and closing database connections for every query can cause significant overhead. Using connection pooling ensures that a predefined number of connections are maintained, while reducing latency and improving query execution times. Connection pooling is particularly important in multi-threaded applications where multiple queries need to be executed simultaneously. For example, using SQLAlchemy with Polars:

```
from sqlalchemy import create_engine

conn = create_engine("sqlite:///telecom.db", pool_size=10)
df = pl.read_database("SELECT * FROM telecom_subscribers",
connection=conn.connect())
```

This helps optimize database connections, and improve query performance.

Perform Data Aggregation at the Database Level

Aggregating data within Polars after loading large datasets can be computationally expensive. Instead, pushing down aggregations to the database using GROUP BY and aggregate functions ensures that only processed results are retrieved. This significantly reduces data transfer time and enhances performance, especially when working with large-scale analytical queries. For example:

```
query = "SELECT plan_type, AVG(monthly_bill) as avg_bill FROM telecom_
billing GROUP BY plan_type"
df = pl.read_database(query, connection=conn.connect())
```

This approach ensures that the database performs the aggregation, which reduces the amount of data transferred.

Handle NULL Values Efficiently

Database tables often contain NULL values, which can impact data processing and analytics. Handling missing data properly by replacing NULLs with appropriate default values ensures data consistency. Performing NULL handling at the database level before querying reduces the need for post-processing in Polars. For example:

```
query = "SELECT customer_id, COALESCE(data_usage, 0) AS data_usage FROM
telecom_usage"
df = pl.read_database(query, connection=conn.connect())
```

This ensures that NULL values are replaced with zero before loading into a Polars DataFrame.

Using Parallel Execution for Faster Query Performance

When querying multiple datasets or partitions, parallel execution helps maximize performance. Instead of executing queries sequentially, running them in parallel reduces overall query time, which allows for faster data retrieval. This approach is particularly beneficial in distributed data environments where multiple data sources need to be processed simultaneously. An example of using Python's threading module is shown here:

```
from concurrent.futures import ThreadPoolExecutor

queries = ["SELECT * FROM telecom_usage WHERE month='Jan'", "SELECT *
FROM telecom_usage WHERE month='Feb'"]
with ThreadPoolExecutor() as executor:
    results = list(executor.map(lambda q: pl.read_database(q,
connection=conn.connect()), queries))
```

This ensures that multiple queries execute in parallel, which significantly improves performance.

Getting Data from Cloud Storage

Polars supports seamless integration with cloud storage solutions like AWS S3, Azure Blob Storage, and Google Cloud Storage, which allows for efficient reading and writing of large datasets. To interact with these storage providers, additional dependencies such as fsspec, s3fs, adlfs, and gcsfs may be required. Polars enables users to read various file formats, including Parquet, CSV, IPC, and NDJSON, from cloud storage. This ensures flexibility in data processing. Scanning files with Polars using pl.scan_* functions allows for query optimization through predicate and projection pushdowns, which reduces the amount of data that needs to be downloaded before query execution, thereby enhancing performance significantly.

Authentication for cloud storage can be handled through multiple methods in Polars. Users can pass credentials manually using the storage_options parameter, while leveraging built-in CredentialProvider classes*, or defining custom credential provider functions for specialized authentication workflows such as AWS IAM role chaining. For example, on Google Cloud Storage (GCS), authentication is managed using gcsfs, and users can set up authentication via Google service account credentials. By incorporating proper authentication mechanisms, Polars ensure secure and seamless access to cloud-based datasets.

Polars also supports PyArrow integration for scanning partitioned datasets, such as those using Hive-style partitioning. This is particularly useful when dealing with large-scale data stored in multiple partitions, as PyArrow's dataset API enables efficient lazy evaluation before retrieving the necessary data. Users can first create a PyArrow dataset from cloud storage and then convert it into a Polars LazyFrame, while applying filters and projections before collecting the final DataFrame. This approach helps optimize memory usage and speeds up query execution by limiting the amount of data loaded at once.

For writing data back to cloud storage, Polars provide methods for saving DataFrames in formats like Parquet, CSV, or IPC. This requires using the appropriate filesystem library (s3fs for S3, adlfs for Azure, and gcsfs for GCS). In a Google Cloud Storage (GCS) example, a DataFrame can be written to a Parquet file using gcsfs, while ensuring that structured data is efficiently stored and accessible for future analysis. By leveraging these capabilities, Polars enable efficient cloud-based data workflows, while reducing local storage dependencies and enabling scalable, high-performance data processing across different cloud environments.

Let us look at a practical example. To interact with AWS S3 using Polars, we specify authentication credentials using `storage_options`. Here is an example demonstrating how to **read from and write to an S3 bucket** while providing access keys explicitly.

Reading Data from AWS S3

```
import polars as pl
s3_path = "s3://my-bucket/telecom_data.parquet"

storage_options = {
    "aws_access_key_id": "<secret>",
    "aws_secret_access_key": "<secret>",
    "aws_region": "us-east-1",
}

df = pl.read_parquet(s3_path, storage_options=storage_options)
print(df)
```

Writing Data to AWS S3

```
import s3fs

df = pl.DataFrame({"customer_id": [101, 102, 103], "plan": ["5G", "4G",
"4G"]})

storage_options = {
    "aws_access_key_id": "<secret>",
    "aws_secret_access_key": "<secret>",
    "aws_region": "us-east-1",
}

fs = s3fs.S3FileSystem(**storage_options)
destination = "s3://my-bucket/telecom_data_output.parquet"

with fs.open(destination, mode='wb') as f:
    df.write_parquet(f)
```

Integration with DuckDB

Why Integrate DuckDB with Polars?

DuckDB is a high-performance, in-memory analytical database designed for complex queries on large datasets. When combined with Polars, it provides a powerful and efficient framework for handling structured data using SQL-like queries. DuckDB enables users to perform fast aggregations, complex joins, and window functions, while benefiting from columnar storage and vectorized execution. Unlike traditional databases, DuckDB is optimized for OLAP (Online Analytical Processing) workloads, which makes it a great companion for Polars, as it also leverages Apache Arrow's columnar format. The integration allows users to harness SQL querying capabilities within Polars without needing to migrate data to an external database.

Setting Up DuckDB for SQL Queries

To use DuckDB with Polars, you need to install the duckdb package. Once installed, you can seamlessly execute SQL queries on Polars DataFrames using DuckDB's SQL engine. DuckDB operates both in-memory and as an embedded database. This means that you can execute queries without setting up a server. This flexibility makes it ideal for analysts and data engineers who need quick and efficient data transformations.

Running Analytical Queries Efficiently Using DuckDB

DuckDB supports advanced SQL functionalities such as group-by aggregations, filtering, and window functions, which make it suitable for complex analytical workloads. When integrated with Polars, DuckDB can execute SQL queries on large datasets stored in Polars DataFrames, while avoiding unnecessary data movement. For example, you can register a Polars DataFrame as a temporary DuckDB table and execute queries directly against it. This method significantly enhances performance when working with structured telecom data, as it allows for optimized execution plans, predicate pushdowns, and parallel processing.

Comparing Performance: Polars vs. DuckDB vs. Pandas

When it comes to performance, DuckDB and Polars significantly outperform Pandas, especially for large-scale analytics. Pandas operates row-wise, which can become inefficient as the dataset size increases. In contrast, both Polars and DuckDB leverage columnar storage and lazy execution to optimize performance. While Polars is ideal for in-memory data manipulations and lazy evaluations, DuckDB excels at complex SQL queries and joins. Benchmark tests show that for simple aggregations, Polars can be faster due to its optimized execution engine, while DuckDB shines in multi-table joins and SQL-heavy workloads. By integrating both, users get the best of both worlds—SQL expressiveness and Polars' high-speed DataFrame operations.

Integration with LanceDB

Overview of LanceDB and Its Advantages

LanceDB is an innovative, high-performance database designed specifically for vector search and AI-driven applications. Unlike traditional relational databases, LanceDB is built to handle high-dimensional vector data, which makes it particularly useful for applications such as recommendation systems, similarity searches, and ML model indexing. By integrating LanceDB with Polars, users can perform advanced analytics and vector-based queries on large datasets, while enabling efficient similarity matching, clustering, and real-time AI-driven insights.

Setting Up LanceDB with Polars

To integrate LanceDB with Polars, you first need to install the lancedb package. LanceDB stores data in an efficient columnar format, which aligns well with Polars' internal data structures. The integration allows Polars users to interact with LanceDB seamlessly by reading and writing vector-based data while leveraging Polars' fast DataFrame operations. This setup enables users to manage high-dimensional data within Polars while offloading complex vector computations to LanceDB.

Performing Vector-Based Queries and Advanced Data Operations

LanceDB is optimized for fast nearest-neighbor searches, which is critical for applications such as image recognition, natural language processing (NLP), and personalized recommendations. When combined with Polars, users can process structured telecom data in Polars while storing high-dimensional embeddings in LanceDB for advanced querying. For example, telecom companies can use LanceDB to search for similar customer profiles based on call patterns or data usage. Vector-based indexing and retrieval make it easy to perform semantic searches and AI-driven predictions, thereby further enhancing analytical capabilities.

Real-World Use Cases for LanceDB Integration

The integration of LanceDB with Polars opens up new possibilities in various industries. In telecom analytics, companies can use LanceDB to build real-time fraud detection systems by identifying suspicious activity patterns through vector similarity searches. In customer segmentation, telecom providers can analyze usage data to cluster users with similar behaviors, which allows for targeted marketing and personalized service offerings. Additionally, LanceDB's AI-powered search capabilities can enhance customer support by quickly retrieving relevant information based on user queries. By combining Polars' high-speed data processing with LanceDB's efficient vector search, organizations can unlock powerful AI-driven insights and improve decision-making.

Conclusion

We explored several key integrations that enhance Polars' capabilities for large-scale data analytics. We began by examining efficient database querying techniques to optimize data retrieval into DataFrames, while ensuring minimal overhead and maximum performance. We then looked into cloud storage integration, covering AWS S3, Azure Blob Storage, and Google Cloud Storage, which allow for seamless reading and writing of structured data from cloud environments. Next, we discussed the integration of Polars with DuckDB and highlighted how SQL-based queries can be executed efficiently within Polars for advanced analytics. Finally, we explored LanceDB, a high-performance vector database and showcased its power for AI-driven applications such as similarity searches and recommendation systems.

These integrations make Polars an incredibly versatile tool for both traditional and modern data processing needs, blending SQL capabilities, cloud interoperability, and AI-driven analytics into a unified workflow. Whether handling massive datasets in the cloud, performing high-speed analytical queries with DuckDB, or leveraging vector-based operations in LanceDB, Polars provides a robust foundation for data engineers and analysts alike.

In the next chapter, we will extend Polars using UDFs (User-Defined Functions) and Rust PyO3, while enabling custom functionality and even faster computations by leveraging Rust's performance advantages.

Exercises

Exercise 1: Querying a PostgreSQL Database with Polars

Objective: Connect to a PostgreSQL database, retrieve telecom-related data, and perform SQL-based transformations using Polars.

Task:

1. Set up a PostgreSQL database and create a table named **`call_records`** with columns: **`call_id`**, caller, receiver, duration, and **`call_type`**.
2. Insert at least 10 records into the table with random telecom call details.
3. Use **`pl.read_database_uri()`** to fetch all records from the **`call_records`** table.
4. Filter the DataFrame to show only calls with a duration more than 2 minutes.
5. Group the records by **`call_type`** (for example, Local, International) and calculate the average call duration for each type.
6. Write back the transformed data into a new table called **`aggregated_call_stats`**.

Exercise 2: Running Analytical Queries with DuckDB and Polars

Objective: Integrate DuckDB with Polars to execute SQL queries on large telecom data efficiently.

Task:

1. Create a DuckDB database file and define a table named **`data_usage`** with columns: **`user_id`**, **`session_id`**, **`data_used_MB`**, **`network_type`**, and **`timestamp`**.
2. Insert random records simulating telecom data usage sessions.
3. Use **`pl.read_database()`** with DuckDB to load the entire dataset into a Polars DataFrame.

4. Execute an SQL query within Polars to compute:
    - The total data consumed by each user_id.
    - The percentage of data usage across different network_type (for example, 4G, 5G, Wi-Fi).
5. Compare the execution time of the same operation in Polars LazyFrame and DuckDB to observe performance differences.

Exercise 3: Reading and Writing Telecom Data to Cloud Storage

Objective: Store and retrieve telecom data from AWS S3 using Polars.

Task:

1. Generate a random telecom dataset in a Polars DataFrame with fields: customer_id, plan_type, monthly_usage_GB, billing_amount, and region.
2. Write this dataset to an S3 bucket in Parquet format, using df.write_parquet().

    Use pl.scan_parquet() to read the data back from S3 with cloud authentication parameters:

    ```
    storage_options = {
        "aws_access_key_id": "<secret>",
        "aws_secret_access_key": "<secret>",
        "aws_region": "us-east-1",
    }
    ```
3. Perform the following operations using Polars LazyFrame:
    - Filter customers with a monthly_usage_GB greater than 100.
    - Group by region and compute the average billing amount.
4. Save the processed data back to S3 under a new name, for example, processed_telecom_data.parquet.

Chapter 8
Extending Polars with UDF and PyO3

"You prototype in Python. You scale in Rust"

Unknown

Introduction

Flexibility and performance are often at odds in data analysis and engineering workflows. While high-level abstractions, like those in Polars, allow for rapid development and clean syntax, there are cases where custom logic is required. The said logic is beyond the scope of built-in expressions. This is where User Defined Functions (UDFs) come into play. UDFs empower users to inject bespoke transformation logic into Polars data frames and enable fine-grained control over data manipulation. However, this flexibility comes with trade-offs, particularly regarding execution speed and parallelism, which are critical in large-scale data processing.

To bridge the gap between customization and performance, this chapter introduces the concept of writing Rust plug-ins for Polars using PyO3, a tool that connects Rust and Python seamlessly. By leveraging Rust's speed and memory safety, you can offload performance-critical tasks from Python to native Rust code, while keeping your workflow within the Polars ecosystem. This chapter guides you through writing and applying UDFs, understanding their pros and cons, and building high-performance Rust plug-ins that can be imported into Python like native modules. These techniques allow you to extend Polars beyond its built-in capabilities, while optimizing both expressiveness and efficiency for advanced, domain-specific data processing.

Structure

In this chapter, we will discuss the following topics:

- Understanding User Defined Functions (UDFs) in Polars
  - Comparison with UDFs in Other Frameworks
  - Creating UDFs Using .map* in Polars
  - Combining Multiple Columns
  - Best Practices for Using UDFs
  - Performance Considerations
- Introduction to PyO3 and Rust Integration
  - Why Integrate Rust with Polars?
  - Benefits of Rust: Speed, Safety, Concurrency
  - Overview of PyO3 for Python-Rust Interop
- Setting Up Rust for Python
  - Introduction to maturin, setuptools-rust
  - Creating a Minimal PyO3 Plugin
- Creating Rust Plugins for Polars
  - Plugin Structure and Design
  - Passing Series and DataFrame to Rust and Returning Results Back to Polars
  - Real-World Examples of Rust Plugins
  - Comparing Performance: UDFs vs Plugins vs Native Expressions
  - Error Handling and Debugging
- Packaging and Distribution Using Maturin

Understanding UDF

A User Defined Function (UDF) is a custom function created by the user to perform operations that aren't natively supported by a framework's built-in functions. In the context of Polars, UDFs allow you to define specific row- or column-level transformations using Python functions, which can then be applied to Series or DataFrame objects. They provide the flexibility to embed domain-specific logic directly into your data processing pipeline.

For example, suppose you are working with a dataset containing air pollution readings across different cities. If you want to flag any city-day combination as "high risk" when

PM2.5 levels exceed 150 and NO_2 levels exceed 80, but only on weekdays. This kind of logic would be difficult to express using only built-in expressions. A UDF provides a natural way to encapsulate this conditional logic.

Comparison with UDFs in Other Frameworks

Polars support UDFs similarly to other data frameworks like Pandas, Spark, or Dask, but with some key differences. In Pandas, UDFs are typically applied using .apply() or .map(), but they tend to be slower due to the row-by-row processing in Python. In Spark, UDFs are often written in Python or Scala and can be distributed across nodes, but Python UDFs can become bottlenecks due to serialization overhead.

Polars, on the other hand, uses a lazy evaluation model and operates in Rust under the hood. While Polars supports Python UDFs, using them breaks the optimized query engine and disables multithreading for that operation. This makes them flexible but less efficient. Therefore, while the concept is similar across platforms, in Polars, it is especially important to understand when and how to use UDFs for the best performance.

Creating UDFs Using .map* in Polars

User-Defined Functions (UDFs) in Polars allow you to customize computations beyond built-in expressions. While Polars is highly expressive and optimized for vectorized operations, there are still cases where you may want to apply a custom function; for example, when using a third-party library or a black-box calculation that is not easily expressible using Polars expressions. UDFs can be applied in two main ways: on individual elements using `map_elements()` and on entire Series using `map_batches()`.

Suppose, you are working with pollution level readings across various telecom towers and need to apply transformations. If you want to apply a function to each reading (say, converting a pollution index to a logarithmic scale for plotting or modeling), you can use `map_elements()`. For instance, applying `math.log()` on each reading might look like this:

```
df.select(pl.col("pollution_index").map_elements(math.log, return_
dtype=pl.Float64))
```

This works, but it is slower since Python function calls are expensive and happen for each value.

To enhance performance further, you can use NumPy's ufuncs or even write compiled custom logic using Numba. With Numba's `@guvectorize` decorator, your Python logic such as subtracting the mean pollution index in each telecom region is compiled to machine code and offers significant speedups. These compiled functions accept NumPy arrays, which makes them ideal for operations on batches of data.

It is important to be cautious with missing data when using generalized ufuncs. Since NumPy does not support missing values natively, Polars will raise an error if you try to pass Series with nulls to functions like those compiled with Numba. You should either fill or drop nulls before applying such UDFs.

Here are code examples of UDFs in Polars using both `map_elements()` and `map_batches()`:

```
import polars as pl
import math
import numpy as np
df = pl.DataFrame(
    {
        "tower_id": ["T1", "T1", "T2", "T2"],
        "pollution_index": [20, 50, 35, 80],
    }
)
print(df)
output :
```

```
shape: (4, 2)
```

tower_id --- str	pollution_index --- i64
T1	20
T1	50
T2	35
T2	80

```
def log_transform(value):
    return math.log(value)
```

```
# Per-element UDF
df_log = df.select(
    pl.col("pollution_index").map_elements(log_transform, return_
dtype=pl.Float64)
)
print("Log-transformed pollution index:")
print(df_log)
```

output :

```
Log-transformed pollution index:
shape: (4, 1)
```

```
┌─────────────────┐
│ pollution_index │
│ ---             │
│ f64             │
╞═════════════════╡
│ 2.995732        │
│ 3.912023        │
│ 3.555348        │
│ 4.382027        │
└─────────────────┘
```

```
#Using map_batches() - Whole-series UDF
def subtract_mean(series):
    mean_val = sum(series) / len(series)
    return pl.Series([val - mean_val for val in series])

df_centered = df.select(
    pl.col("pollution_index").map_batches(subtract_mean)
)
print("Pollution index centered by mean:")
print(df_centered)
output :
Pollution index centered by mean:
shape: (4, 1)
┌─────────────────┐
│ pollution_index │
│ ---             │
│ f64             │
╞═════════════════╡
│ -26.25          │
│ 3.75            │
│ -11.25          │
│ 33.75           │
└─────────────────┘
```

Unlike regular Python UDFs which are interpreted and operate row-by-row (for example, via `.apply()` or `.map_elements()`), this Numba UDF is compiled ahead of time and processes full Series in a single call. This drastically reduces the overhead of function calls and benefits from low-level optimizations such as vectorized CPU instructions and better cache usage. When paired with Polars' `map_batches()` API, the result is a scalable and highly efficient pipeline for performing custom transformations on large datasets, which is ideal for numerical operations such as normalization, signal processing, or statistical modeling.

```
import polars as pl
import numpy as np
from numba import guvectorize, float64

# Numba UDF for z-score normalization
@guvectorize([(float64[:], float64[:])], "(n)->(n)", nopython=True)
def zscore(values, result):
    n = len(values)
    mean = 0
    for i in range(n):
        mean += values[i]
    mean /= n

    std = 0
    for i in range(n):
        std += (values[i] - mean) ** 2
    std = (std / n) ** 0.5

    for i in range(n):
        result[i] = (values[i] - mean) / std if std > 0 else 0.0
df = pl.DataFrame({
    "tower_id": ["T1", "T1", "T2", "T2", "T3", "T3"],
    "signal_dbm": [-85, -80, -95, -90, -70, -75],
})

# Standardize globally
df_std = df.select(
    pl.col("signal_dbm").map_batches(zscore)
)
print("Z-score normalized signal (global):")
print(df_std)
output :
Z-score normalized signal (global):
shape: (6, 1)
```

signal_dbm --- f64
-0.29277
0.29277
-1.46385
-0.87831
1.46385
0.87831

This code leverages the power of Numba's `@guvectorize` decorator to create a high-performance user-defined function (UDF) for Z-score normalization, which is designed to operate efficiently with Polars' `map_batches()` method. The core idea is to perform vectorized operations over entire batches of data, rather than iterating over individual elements. The zscore function calculates the mean and standard deviation of a NumPy array and returns the normalized Z-scores for each value. The signature "(n)->(n)" specifies that both input and output are one-dimensional arrays of equal length, and the nopython=True flag ensures that the function is compiled to machine code for optimal speed.

Combining Multiple Columns

We can use the structs available in Polars to combine multiple columns using UDF. Here is a similar example tailored to a telecom use case, where you are summing call volumes and data usage for towers in a single telecom cluster. This simulates how you might aggregate two numeric metrics for each tower; say, call count and data usage (MB)—and then combine them into a single usage score per tower.

```
# Numba UDF to add call volume and data usage
@guvectorize([(int64[:], int64[:], float64[:])], "(n),(n)->(n)")
def combined_usage(call_volume, data_usage, result):
    for i in range(len(call_volume)):
        result[i] = call_volume[i] + data_usage[i]

# Example telecom cluster data
df = pl.DataFrame({
    "tower_id": ["T1", "T2", "T3"],
    "call_volume": [120, 300, 250],
    "data_usage": [1024, 2048, 1536]  # in MBs
})

# Apply Numba UDF using Polars + Struct + map_batches
result = df.select(
    pl.struct(["call_volume", "data_usage"])
    .map_batches(
        lambda s: combined_usage(
            s.struct.field("call_volume"), s.struct.field("data_usage")
        )
    )
    .alias("total_usage_score")
)

print(result)
```

```
output :
shape: (3, 1)
```

total_usage_score --- f64
1144.0
2348.0
1786.0

Column-wise UDFs shine in scenarios where you want to perform computations that require an awareness of the entire column's context.

Best Practices for Using UDFs

When working with user-defined functions (UDFs) in data processing libraries like Polars, it is important to follow best practices to ensure performance, scalability, and maintainability. The first guiding principle is to avoid UDFs unless absolutely necessary. Polars, like many modern data libraries, is highly optimized with native expressions and vectorized operations. Native Polars expressions are compiled to efficient code and run significantly faster than any UDF written in pure Python. Hence, if a task can be accomplished using built-in functions such as `.filter()`, `.with_columns()`, `.group_by()`, or `.agg()`, it is preferable to use those instead of writing a custom UDF.

If you must use a UDF, aim to minimize the use of row-wise functions like `map_elements()` unless your logic truly requires operating on one value at a time. Row-wise functions introduce Python function call overhead for each value, which becomes inefficient at scale. In contrast, column-wise UDFs via `map_batches()` allow you to pass entire Series to your function at once and leverage vectorized operations and reducing overhead. Further optimization can be achieved by offloading these computations to compiled libraries such as NumPy or Numba, especially when performing numerical operations over large arrays. Using Numba's `@guvectorize` decorator is particularly effective for custom numerical operations because it compiles Python code into fast machine code.

Another best practice is to handle missing data explicitly before passing data into your UDFs. When using generalized ufuncs with Numba or NumPy, missing values (nulls) are not supported, and Polars will raise an error if the Series includes them. You can use .fill_null() or .drop_nulls() on columns to clean the data beforehand. Lastly, be clear about the return data type of your UDF. While Polars can infer types, explicitly specifying the output type (for example, `return_dtype=pl.Float64`) helps avoid surprises and improves code readability. Combining these practices ensures that your UDFs are as efficient and robust as possible within a high-performance, expressive Polars pipeline.

Performance Considerations

UDFs come with notable performance trade-offs, particularly in Python. One major limitation is the Global Interpreter Lock (GIL), which prevents multiple native Python threads from executing Python bytecode simultaneously. This restriction limits UDFs from achieving true parallelism on multi-core systems when using pure Python, which makes them a bottleneck in high-throughput pipelines. Additionally, row-wise UDFs like `map_elements()` incur significant overhead due to Python function calls for each value in the column, which is costly when working with millions of records.

Another limitation is that UDFs often bypass many of the optimizations that make libraries like Polars so fast. Polars relies on efficient query planning, lazy evaluation, and Rust-backed parallel execution for native operations. Custom Python UDFs cannot be optimized in this way. Once a UDF is introduced, it may break the optimized execution pipeline. This results in longer runtimes, higher memory usage, and reduced scalability.

To measure UDF performance, the first step is to isolate the part of your pipeline using the UDF and wrap it in a timing block using Python's time module or %timeit in Jupyter. For more detailed profiling, use cProfile or line_profiler to see how much time each function or line of code takes. You can also benchmark UDFs against equivalent vectorized implementations to understand the performance gap. When using Numba or NumPy, comparing execution time before and after applying those optimizations can also demonstrate the benefits of the compiled code.

In summary, UDFs provide essential flexibility but should be treated as a last resort when built-in functions fall short. Their disadvantages in performance, especially due to Python's GIL and lack of compiler-level optimizations, can severely impact data processing efficiency. Developers should always assess the cost of using UDFs, explore alternatives like vectorized Polars expressions or Numba-accelerated batch UDFs. They should also measure the performance impact as part of their development process.

Introduction to PyO3 and Rust Integration

PyO3 is a powerful Rust crate that enables seamless integration between Rust and Python, which allows you to write performant native extensions in Rust and use them as Python modules. It provides tools to convert between Python and Rust types, manage the Python GIL safely, and interact with Python objects from Rust code. This integration is ideal for optimizing performance-critical parts of Python applications, while leveraging Rust's memory safety and speed.

Integrating Rust with Polars

Integrating Rust with Polars offers significant performance and scalability benefits, especially for computationally intensive data processing tasks. Polars itself is written in Rust, which provides a natural synergy when extending its capabilities using Rust plug-ins or custom logic. By offloading critical operations to Rust, developers can bypass the Global Interpreter Lock (GIL) and achieve true multithreading. This results in faster execution and lower memory overhead than Python-based UDFs. Rust's compile-time safety guarantees also reduce runtime errors and ensure more robust code. This integration is particularly useful in domains like telecom or finance, where high-throughput, low-latency data processing is crucial. With tools like PyO3, developers can write Rust code and expose it seamlessly as Python functions or modules, while combining the expressiveness of Python with the performance of Rust.

Benefits of Rust: Speed, Safety, Concurrency

In the context of Polars UDFs, Rust brings a major performance boost by allowing developers to write fast, memory-safe, and concurrent code that can be compiled into plug-ins using PyO3. Unlike Python-based UDFs, which suffer from the Global Interpreter Lock (GIL) and serialization overhead, Rust-based UDFs execute natively and can fully utilize multiple CPU cores. This leads to significantly faster execution, especially for compute-intensive data transformations across large datasets. Additionally, Rust's strong type safety and compile-time checks reduce runtime errors, which make your data workflows more robust and production-ready

Overview of PyO3 for Python-Rust Interop

PyO3 is a powerful Rust crate that enables seamless interoperability between Rust and Python by allowing Rust code to be called from Python and vice versa. At its core, PyO3 provides a bridge between Python's dynamic runtime and Rust's static, compiled nature through bindings to the CPython API. Developers can use PyO3 to expose Rust functions, structs, and even full modules to Python, often with just a few annotations like #[pyfunction] and #[pymodule]. This means you can write performance-critical logic in Rust and easily integrate it into your existing Python projects without changing the overall structure or ecosystem.

One of PyO3's standout features is its ability to compile Rust code into Python extension modules, which can be imported just like native Python modules. It supports automatic type conversions between Python and Rust data types, memory safety guarantees via Rust's ownership model, and integration with Python's error handling and async features. This makes PyO3 an ideal choice for performance-sensitive tasks like custom Polars UDFs, numeric computation, or heavy data parsing, where Python's performance bottlenecks become apparent. With PyO3, you get the best of both worlds: Python's flexibility and ecosystem, and Rust's speed and safety.

Setting Up Rust for Python

To begin using Rust for developing Python extensions or high-performance libraries, you first need to install the Rust toolchain. The official and recommended way to install Rust is via rustup, a Rust installer and version manager that sets up everything you need with a single command or standalone installer in windows.

After completing installation, you can verify it using the following commands:

```
rustc --version
cargo --version
```

This confirms that rustc (the Rust compiler) and cargo (the package manager and build tool) are properly installed. cargo is particularly important because it not only builds your Rust projects but also manages dependencies, runs tests, and handles documentation. If you are planning to use Rust for Python integration (via PyO3), cargo will be your primary tool for compiling the Rust code into shared libraries.

Introduction to Maturin and setuptools-rust

When building Python extensions with Rust, tools like maturin and setuptools-rust simplify the build and packaging process. maturin is a command-line utility specifically designed for building and publishing Rust-based Python packages using PyO3 or rust-cpython. It automatically compiles your Rust code, generates Python wheels, and handles Python packaging metadata. One of its greatest strengths is that it abstracts away the complex boilerplate often involved in cross-language builds. With just a few commands, you can go from Rust code to a fully installable Python package.

On the other hand, setuptools-rust integrates with Python's native setuptools to support Rust extensions as part of traditional Python packages. This is useful when you are already using setup.py or have mixed codebases involving both Python and Rust. It allows you to declare Rust extensions just like C extensions in the setup.py file. While setuptools-rust gives you tight integration within Python packaging workflows, maturin is more modern and typically easier to use for standalone Rust-based Python modules.

Creating a Minimal PyO3 Plugin

To create a basic PyO3 plugin using maturin, start by generating a new Rust library project using cargo new --lib myplugin. Then, update Cargo.toml to include pyo3 as a dependency and enable the extension-module feature. If you are using maturin, you will also need to specify the `crate-type = ["cdylib"]` under the [lib] section and configure metadata for Python compatibility. Here is an example snippet for Cargo.toml:

```
[package]
name = "myplugin"
version = "0.1.0"
edition = "2021"

[lib]
crate-type = ["cdylib"]

[dependencies]
pyo3 = { version = "0.21", features = ["extension-module"] }
```

Next, create a function inside src/lib.rs and annotate it with `#[pyfunction]`, then register it using a #[pymodule] block. For example:

```
use pyo3::prelude::*;

#[pyfunction]
fn double(x: i32) -> i32 {
    x * 2
}

#[pymodule]
fn myplugin(_py: Python, m: &PyModule) -> PyResult<()> {
    m.add_function(wrap_pyfunction!(double, m)?)?;
    Ok(())
   }
```

Now, you can build the module using `maturin develop`, which compiles the Rust code and installs the resulting Python extension into your current environment.

Here is the step-by-step process:

1. Install Prerequisites.
    a. Install Rust (cargo, rustc) using rustup.
    b. Install Python 3.x and ensure that pip is available.
    c. Install maturin using pip.
2. Create a New Rust Library Project.
    a. Open terminal in your project folder.
    b. Run command to create a new library crate.
    c. Navigate into the project directory.
3. Configure Cargo.toml.
    a. Add [lib] section with crate-type = ["cdylib"].
    b. Add pyo3 as a dependency with extension-module feature.

4. Write Rust Code.
    a. Import necessary items from pyo3.
    b. Create Python-exposed functions using #[pyfunction].
    c. Create a module using #[pymodule] and add functions.
5. Set Up Python Virtual Environment.
    a. Create a virtual environment in the project folder.
    b. Activate the virtual environment based on OS.
6. Install Maturin Inside Virtual Environment.
    a. Use pip to install maturin.
7. Build and Install the Python Module.
    a. Run `maturin develop` inside the activated virtual environment.
8. Test in Python.
    a. Open Python interpreter.
    b. Import the module and test the exposed functions.

Creating Rust Plugins for Polars

In this section, we will explore how to create high-performance Rust plug-ins that can be seamlessly integrated with the Polars Python library using PyO3. You will learn how to write Rust functions, expose them to Python, and use them as efficient UDFs (User Defined Functions) within Polars pipelines.

When designing Rust plug-ins for Polars, the goal is to create performant and memory-safe functions that can be called from Python using the PyO3 interface. These plug-ins typically encapsulate computationally intensive logic or operations that benefit from Rust's zero-cost abstractions, strong compile-time guarantees, and concurrency safety. A well-structured plug-in ensures a clear separation of concerns: Rust handles the core data processing, while Python acts as the orchestrator, while calling these fast Rust functions from within a Polars pipeline. By using maturin or setuptools-rust, we can build these Rust crates into Python-compatible modules that can be imported like any regular Python package. Structuring the plug-in correctly from the start is essential for maintainability, reusability, and performance tuning.

Plugin Structure and Design

Use the following steps to design and build your own Rust-based plugins for the Polars library:

1. Install Rust and PyO3 prerequisites.

Ensure that you have the Rust toolchain installed via rustup. Install maturin using the pip: install maturin.

2. Initialize the Rust project.

   Use maturin init --bindings pyo3 to create a new Rust project pre-configured for Python interoperability.

3. Edit Cargo.toml.

   Specify the required dependencies (pyo3, polars, and so on), enable the extension-module crate type, and ensure compatibility with your Python version.

4. Write the core Rust logic.

   Implement the computational logic you want to expose as a UDF; for example, normalization, aggregation, or transformation functions.

5. Expose functions to Python.

   Use #[pyfunction] and #[pymodule] macros from PyO3 to make Rust functions callable from Python.

6. Build and install the plug-in.

   Run `maturin develop` in your project directory to build the shared library and install it into your Python environment.

7. Use the Rust function in Polars.

   Import the plugin in Python and apply the Rust-powered UDF inside Polars expressions using .map_batches() or .map_elements().

8. Test and optimize.

   Profile your plugin using benchmarking tools, validate correctness with test cases, and iterate on performance improvements.

Passing Series and DataFrame to Rust and Returning Results Back to Polars

Passing a Series or DataFrame from Python (Polars) to Rust and returning results back is a powerful technique enabled by the interoperability of PyO3. When using PyO3, you can receive PySeries or NumPy arrays in your Rust function, perform computations in Rust (which is fast, memory-efficient, and thread-safe), and then return the processed data back to Python, where it can be reinserted into a Polars pipeline. This approach leverages Rust's zero-cost abstractions and high-speed processing, while integrating seamlessly into Python's data workflow. Typically, you expose Rust functions as Python-callable via the #[pyfunction] decorator, use maturin to compile the plugin, and use these functions within .map_batches() or .map_elements() in Polars.

Here is a simplified example of how to pass a Polars Series to Rust, compute a square on each element, and return the result:

```
lib.rs
use pyo3::prelude::*;
use numpy::{PyReadonlyArray1, PyArray1};

#[pyfunction]
fn square_array(py: Python, input: PyReadonlyArray1<f64>) ->
Py<PyArray1<f64>> {
    let input = input.as_array();
    let result: Vec<f64> = input.iter().map(|x| x * x).collect();
    PyArray1::from_vec(py, result).into_py(py)
}

#[pymodule]
fn rustplugin(py: Python, m: &PyModule) -> PyResult<()> {
    m.add_function(wrap_pyfunction!(square_array, m)?)?;
    Ok(())
}
```

Python Code :

```
import polars as pl
import numpy as np
from rustplugin import square_array

df = pl.DataFrame({
    "values": [1.0, 2.0, 3.0, 4.0]
})

# Apply Rust function on Series using map_batches
out = df.select(
    pl.col("values")
    .map_batches(lambda s: pl.Series(square_array(s.to_numpy())),
return_dtype=pl.Float64)
    .alias("squared_values")
)
```

Real-World Examples of Rust Plug-ins

Let us walk through a real-world example where we use astronomy data—specifically, brightness measurements of stars over time—and create a PyO3 plug-in in Rust to integrate with Polars for efficient analysis. This plug-in will compute the rolling standard deviation of brightness to detect variability in stars, which is crucial in identifying variable stars or transient phenomena.

Step 1: Write the Rust Plugin with PyO3.

Cargo.toml:

```
[package]
name = "astro_plugin"
version = "0.1.0"
edition = "2021"

[lib]
crate-type = ["cdylib"]

[dependencies]
pyo3 = { version = "0.20", features = ["extension-module"] }
numpy = "0.20"
polars = { version = "0.38", features = ["lazy", "ndarray"] }
```

src/lib.rs:

```
use pyo3::prelude::*;
use polars::prelude::*;
use numpy::{IntoPyArray, PyArray1};
use std::collections::VecDeque;

#[pyfunction]
fn rolling_std_brightness(py: Python, brightness: Vec<f64>, window: usize) -> Py<PyArray1<f64>> {
    let mut result = Vec::with_capacity(brightness.len());
    let mut window_vals = VecDeque::new();

    for &val in &brightness {
        window_vals.push_back(val);
        if window_vals.len() > window {
            window_vals.pop_front();
        }
         let mean = window_vals.iter().sum::<f64>() / window_vals.len() as f64;
           let std = (window_vals.iter().map(|v| (*v - mean).powi(2)).sum::<f64>() / window_vals.len() as f64).sqrt();
        result.push(std);
    }

    result.into_pyarray(py).to_owned()
}

#[pymodule]
fn astro_plugin(_py: Python, m: &PyModule) -> PyResult<()> {
    m.add_function(wrap_pyfunction!(rolling_std_brightness, m)?)?;
    Ok(())
}
```

Step 2: Build and Install with Maturin.

```
maturin develop
```

Step 3 : Use it with Polars

```
import numpy as np
import pandas as pd
import polars as pl

# Parameters
num_stars = 1000
observations_per_star = 1000  # Total: 1000 * 1000 = 1,000,000 rows

# Generate synthetic data
np.random.seed(42)
star_ids = np.repeat(np.arange(1, num_stars + 1), observations_per_star)
timestamps = pd.date_range(start="2024-01-01", periods=observations_per_
star, freq="H")
timestamps = np.tile(timestamps, num_stars)

# Simulate brightness readings with some noise
base_brightness = np.random.normal(loc=12, scale=0.5, size=num_stars)
brightness = np.hstack([
   np.random.normal(loc=base_brightness[i], scale=0.2, size=observations_
per_star)
    for i in range(num_stars)
])

# Create DataFrame in Pandas
df_pd = pd.DataFrame({
    "star_id": star_ids,
    "timestamp": timestamps,
    "brightness": brightness
})

# Convert to Polars DataFrame
df = pl.from_pandas(df_pd)

import polars as pl
import astro_plugin

# Group by star and apply UDF
result = df.group_by("star_id").agg([
    pl.col("brightness").map_batches(lambda s: astro_plugin.rolling_std_
brightness(s.to_list(), 3)).alias("std_brightness")
])
```

```
print(result)
output :
shape: (1_000, 2)
```

star_id --- i64	std_brightness --- list[f64]
280	[0.0, 0.118485, … 0.146988]
819	[0.0, 0.256748, … 0.26337]
18	[0.0, 0.110319, … 0.031141]
938	[0.0, 0.001497, … 0.129259]
548	[0.0, 0.111289, … 0.162981]
…	…
363	[0.0, 0.010988, … 0.097677]
369	[0.0, 0.186245, … 0.133915]
247	[0.0, 0.166005, … 0.109367]
506	[0.0, 0.32456, … 0.081208]
113	[0.0, 0.188129, … 0.175039]

The real strength of this implementation lies in its use of Rust's memory safety and performance guarantees. The algorithm avoids unnecessary allocations by pre-allocating the result vector and uses efficient data structures like VecDeque to manage the moving window. Moreover, the use of f64 and in-place numerical operations ensures minimal overhead. This would be significantly slower in Python using pure loops or standard user-defined functions (UDFs), especially for large datasets. Thus, by converting the final result into a NumPy array using the NumPy crate, the plug-in ensures that the output is compatible with the Python scientific ecosystem.

Finally, the function is wrapped and exposed as a Python module via the #[pymodule] annotation. This makes it callable from Python just like any native function. When combined with tools like maturin, the Rust code compiles to a shared object file that Python can load, which makes distribution and integration straightforward.

Comparing Performance: UDFs vs. Plug-ins vs. Native Expressions

Here is a comparison table outlining the performance and usability differences between Polars native expressions, Python UDFs, and Rust-based plug-ins (via PyO3):

Feature / Metric	Polars Native Expressions	Python UDFs (map_elements/ map_batches)	Rust Plug-ins via PyO3
Performance	Very high (vectorized and optimized)	Low (interpreted, GIL-bound)	High (compiled, close to native speed)
Parallelism	Fully supported (built-in multithreading)	Limited (GIL restricts threading)	Supported (via Rust threads or rayon)
Memory Efficiency	Very efficient (in-memory columnar ops)	Inefficient for large data volumes	Efficient (manual control over memory)
Ease of Development	Very easy (no extra tooling)	Easy (pure Python)	Moderate (requires Rust and PyO3 setup)
Code Readability	High (concise and expressive)	High (Pythonic syntax)	Moderate (Rust syntax with FFI concepts)
Reusability / Portability	High within Polars	Medium (Python-only)	High (can be reused in Rust and Python apps)
Suitability for Complex Logic	Limited (complex logic can be verbose)	High (custom business logic is easy)	High (ideal for compute-heavy tasks)
Compilation Overhead	None	None	Requires compilation (one-time cost)
Turnaround Time (Iteration Speed)	Immediate	Immediate	Slower (rebuild required for changes)

***Table 8.1**: A Comparison of Native Expressions, UDFs, and PyO3 Plug-ins*

Error Handling and Debugging

Error handling and debugging in PyO3 requires careful management of Rust's strict type system along with Python's dynamic nature. When working with optional values (Option<T>) or nullable inputs from Python (like None), PyO3 provides automatic conversion where Option<T> maps cleanly to Python's None and vice versa. For instance, function arguments declared as Option<&str> or Option<PyReadonlyArray1<f64>> allow safe handling of missing or null values without panics. During debugging, it is helpful to leverage Rust's Result<T, E> system to return detailed errors using PyErr, which integrates with Python's exception system. To aid diagnostics, it is good practice to use .expect() or .unwrap() only in early prototyping and replace them with .map_err() or .ok_or_else() in production to generate meaningful Python errors. Logging can be added using the log crate on the Rust side, paired with env_logger or custom integrations to forward logs to Python. Additionally, you can raise Python exceptions using PyErr::new::<pyo3::exceptions::PyValueError, _>(msg) to ensure consistent error messaging. For smooth debugging, compile in debug mode, use dbg!() liberally during development, and run Python scripts with logging and traceback enabled to trace the source of issues in the Rust layer. Combining Rust's safety guarantees with Python's flexibility through PyO3 makes for a powerful but nuanced development flow.

Packaging and Distribution Using Maturin

Packaging and distributing Rust-based Python plug-ins using maturin is a powerful and developer-friendly approach to bridge performance-critical Rust code with Python. At its core, maturin simplifies the process of building Python wheels that include compiled Rust code and expose Python-callable functions using PyO3. The primary goal of maturin is to make it as easy as possible to compile and package Python extensions written in Rust into standard Python wheels, which are the default binary distribution format for Python packages.

To build Python wheels locally using maturin, the typical workflow involves setting up your Cargo.toml file with the necessary PyO3 dependencies and exposing your Python-callable Rust functions using the #[pyfunction] and #[pymodule] attributes. You can then use the command maturin develop to build and install the extension into your local Python environment for testing. Alternatively, maturin build can generate a .whl file, which you can install with pip install <path_to_wheel> or distribute manually.

Once the plug-in is tested and working as expected, publishing to PyPI becomes straightforward. After registering your project and account on PyPI (https://pypi.org), you can use maturin publish --username <your-username> to upload the built wheels directly. Maturin supports building universal wheels for different Python versions and operating systems using CI services like GitHub Actions, and it can even leverage manylinux containers to ensure Linux compatibility.

When it comes to managing dependencies and versions, Rust's Cargo.toml takes care of Rust-side dependencies, which allows you to pin versions, set compatibility ranges, and organize features. On the Python side, maturin allows you to include a pyproject.toml where you can declare Python-level metadata, dependencies, and versioning using standard fields (similar to setuptools). This dual-layered management makes it easy to ensure that both your Rust and Python environments remain stable, and that version mismatches are caught early during builds or installation.

In summary, maturin abstracts away most of the complexity involved in bridging Rust and Python packaging. It enables Python developers to leverage the power of Rust without becoming full-time Rustaceans. It also provides Rust developers a straightforward way to deploy high-performance logic directly into Python ecosystems with production-grade packaging.

Conclusion

In conclusion, integrating Rust with Polars using PyO3 and tools like maturin offers a powerful pathway to unlock the full performance potential of data-intensive Python applications. Throughout this chapter, we explored the motivation behind combining the speed, safety, and concurrency of Rust with the expressive and flexible data handling capabilities of Polars. We built real-world examples, such as analyzing astronomy datasets, and demonstrated how to write, compile, and call Rust plug-ins from Python, while enabling performance-optimized operations like rolling window computations.

We also compared traditional UDFs, native Polars expressions, and Rust plug-ins to highlight where Rust can truly shine in terms of execution speed and computational efficiency. Finally, we covered packaging and distribution using Maturin, which allows you to build, deploy, and publish Rust-powered Python wheels effortlessly. With the knowledge gained from this chapter, you are now equipped to design and integrate your own Rust extensions for Polars, while combining the best of both ecosystems to solve high-performance data processing challenges with elegance and control.

In the next chapter, we will leverage Polars to analyze large volumes of data with efficiency.

Exercise Tasks

1. Set Up the Rust Development Environment
    - Install the Rust toolchain using rustup.
    - Install the maturin build tool to create Python bindings for your Rust code.
    - Verify that both Rust and maturin are properly installed.
2. Initialize a PyO3 Project
    - Create a new Rust project using maturin init with PyO3 bindings.
    - Familiarize yourself with the generated project structure, including Cargo.toml and lib.rs.
3. Implement a Tax Calculation Function in Rust
    - Write a function in Rust that calculates income tax using a basic slab-based system.
        - Income from 0 to 10,000: 0% tax
        - Income from 10,001 to 30,000: 10% tax
        - Income from 30,001 to 60,000: 20% tax

    - Income from 60,001 to 100,000: 30% tax
    - Income above 100,000: 40% tax
- The function should accept a list of incomes and return the corresponding list of taxes.

4. Expose the Function via PyO3
    - Annotate your Rust function so it can be accessed from Python.
    - Create a module that registers your function using PyO3's module system.
5. Build and Install the Plug-in
    - Use `maturin develop` to compile your plug-in and install it into your local Python environment.
    - Ensure that the plug-in is importable from a Python script.
6. Test the Plug-in from Python
    - Use the plug-in from a Python script that reads or creates a Polars DataFrame.
    - Apply your tax calculation function to a column of income data and verify the output.

CHAPTER 9
Working with Large Datasets

"Laziness is a virtue of a good programmer."

Bjarne Stroustrup

Introduction

In the world of large-scale data processing, performance and efficiency are everything. Therefore, this chapter delves into one of Polars' most powerful capabilities—lazy evaluation—and explores how it stands apart from the more traditional Eager API. Hence, by deferring execution until it becomes necessary, Polars can optimize computations under the hood. This helps in creating data pipelines that are faster and more memory-efficient.

In this chapter, we will compare the Lazy and Eager APIs, while highlighting their trade-offs and illustrating why laziness often leads to better performance in complex workflows. You will then be introduced to the Query Optimization Engine, the core intelligence that analyzes and restructures operations to minimize redundant computation and I/O.

The concept of LazyFrames is the key to understand lazy evaluation, as it allows you to construct a sequence of transformations without triggering immediate computation. These transformations are compiled into a Query Plan, which refers to a blueprint used by Polars to optimize the entire workflow before execution begins.

We will also explore streaming mode, a powerful feature for processing data in chunks. This feature is perfect for handling massive datasets that do not fit in memory. Finally, the chapter touches on GPU support, which unlocks faster processing speed as it leverages modern hardware.

By the end of this chapter, you will be able to understand how lazy evaluation in Polars empowers you to write declarative, scalable data transformations that are both concise and lightning-fast.

Structure

In this chapter, we will discuss the following topics:

- Performance in Data Workflows
    - Overview of Lazy vs Eager Evaluation
    - When to choose Lazy API over Eager API
- Lazy vs. Eager API
    - Code Examples Comparing Both Styles
- The Query Optimization Engine
    - Query Optimization Techniques
- Working with LazyFrames
    - Creating and transforming LazyFrames
    - Building Complex Logic Without Immediate Execution
    - Benefits of Deferred Computation
- Understanding the Query Plan
    - How to Inspect Query Plans Using `explain()`
    - Logical vs. Physical Plans
    - How Polars Optimizes Execution Behind the Scenes
- Streaming Mode
    - Handling Large Data in Chunks
    - When and Why to Use Streaming
    - Streaming with LazyFrames and Its Benefits
- Execution: Triggering the Plan
    - Methods like `collect()` and `fetch()`
- GPU Support in Polars
    - Integration with Arrow or CuDF
    - Scenarios where GPU Offers Speed Boosts

Performance in Data Workflows

In modern data-driven environments, the volume and velocity of data have increased exponentially. As organizations collect and process more information from diverse sources like real-time logs, IoT devices, and complex transactional systems, the performance of data workflows becomes a critical factor for consideration. Efficient data pipelines not only save computation time and reduce infrastructure costs, but also enable faster insights and more responsive systems. Poorly optimized workflows, on the other hand, can lead to bottlenecks, delayed decisions, and even system failures, while processing large datasets.

Performance is especially important when working with exploratory data analysis (EDA), machine learning (ML) pipelines, or real-time dashboards. In such use cases, developers and analysts need to iterate rapidly, process data reliably, and work within constrained resources.

Overview of Lazy versus Eager Evaluation

At the heart of Polars' performance advantage lies the concept of lazy evaluation. In an eager evaluation model, operations are executed immediately as they are defined. For example, applying a filter or a group-by operation triggers computation right away and the results are stored in memory before the next operation begins. This can be intuitive and suitable for small, linear workflows, but it becomes inefficient when dealing with complex sequences of transformations, as each step involves unnecessary intermediate computations and uses more memory.

In contrast, lazy evaluation defers execution until the final result is explicitly requested. Rather than computing results immediately, operations on a LazyFrame build up a query plan, which is a blueprint of transformations to be applied later. This deferred approach allows Polars to analyze the entire transformation pipeline and optimize it holistically. Redundant operations can be removed, filters can be pushed down to earlier stages, and memory can be managed more effectively. The result is often a significant improvement in speed and reduced resource consumption.

Choosing Lazy API over Eager API

The choice between Lazy and Eager APIs depends on the nature of your workload and your performance requirements. If you are working on quick experiments, debugging, or analyzing small datasets where execution time is negligible, the Eager API may be more convenient. It provides immediate feedback, is easy to reason about, and behaves similarly to familiar tools like Pandas.

However, for large datasets, complex transformations, or production workflows, the Lazy API is the better choice. It enables Polars to optimize the entire computation pipeline before anything is executed and often leads to orders-of-magnitude performance improvements. Lazy evaluation is also a good fit when working with batch jobs, automated pipelines, or any scenario where throughput and resource efficiency are priorities. Additionally, if you are looking to scale your data analysis without manually tuning performance at each step, LazyFrames offer a smart and declarative approach to getting the job done efficiently.

Ultimately, both APIs are powerful in their own right, but knowing when to leverage lazy evaluation can unlock the true potential of Polars in high-performance data workflows.

Lazy vs. Eager API

The primary difference between Lazy and Eager APIs emerges during computation. In an Eager API, each operation executes immediately and produces an in-memory result before moving on to the next step. This model is straightforward and intuitive, as each line of code corresponds to a concrete result and makes it easy to debug and reason about the intermediate outputs. However, this eager nature can lead to inefficiencies, especially in large data pipelines where intermediate results consume memory and time rather unnecessarily.

The Lazy API, on the other hand, builds a deferred execution plan. When you perform operations on a LazyFrame in Polars, nothing is actually computed right away. Instead, a logical plan is constructed and optimized under the hood. Execution only happens when explicitly triggered using methods like `.collect()` or `.fetch()`. This allows Polars to analyze the entire pipeline and apply powerful optimizations such as predicate pushdown (applying filters earlier), projection pruning (removing unused columns), and operation reordering for efficiency.

Code Examples Comparing Both Styles

Eager API:

```
import polars as pl

df = pl.read_csv("sales_data.csv")
filtered = df.filter(pl.col("region") == "Asia")
result = filtered.groupby("product").agg(pl.sum("revenue"))
```

In this example, each step reads and processes data in memory as it is executed.

Lazy API:

In this code, lazy execution begins when the CSV is read using `.lazy()`, which prevents immediate data loading and instead creates a logical query plan. The filter, `groupby`, and `agg` operations are not executed right away but are added to this plan as transformations. Polars analyzes and optimizes the entire plan before running it, such as pushing filters down to the file scan and reading only required columns. Actual computation happens only when `.collect()` is called, triggering a single, optimized execution of the pipeline

```
import polars as pl

lf = pl.read_csv("sales_data.csv").lazy()
result = (
    lf.filter(pl.col("region") == "Asia")
      .groupby("product")
      .agg(pl.sum("revenue"))
      .collect()
)
```

Query Optimization Engine

One of the most powerful features of Polars' Lazy API is its Query Optimization Engine, which gives the former a significant advantage when it comes to performance. Instead of executing each transformation step-by-step like in eager evaluation, Polars constructs a logical query plan representing the entire transformation pipeline. This plan is then optimized using a variety of strategies meant to reduce memory usage, minimize I/O operations, and improve computation speed. Once optimized, the plan is compiled into a physical execution plan, which is then executed efficiently.

The optimization engine applies multiple passes over the query plan to streamline operations, avoid redundant computations, and restructure execution in ways that yield better performance. These optimizations are especially beneficial when working with large datasets or complex transformations where even small improvements can lead to substantial gains.

Query Optimization Techniques

Let us have a look at different query optimization techniques that Polars perform.

Predicate Pushdown

Predicate pushdown is one of the most effective optimization strategies in Polars. It ensures that filters, such as region == "Europe", are applied as early as possible and ideally at the data source level. Instead of reading the full dataset and filtering afterward, Polars pushes the condition down to the scan level, so that only matching rows are loaded into memory. This drastically reduces I/O and speeds up query execution, especially with large datasets.

Projection Pushdown

Projection pushdown is all about selecting only the necessary columns during the data scan. If your query only uses a few columns from a large table, there is no need to load everything. Polars identifies these relevant columns in advance and limits the scan to just those, saving both memory and time. This is particularly beneficial when working with wide datasets where most columns are not required in a specific operation.

Slice Pushdown

When you are only interested in a specific slice of the data, such as the top 10 rows or a specific range, slice pushdown comes into play. Instead of materializing the full result and then slicing, Polars intelligently applies slicing during the data scan. This is extremely useful in cases like `df.join(...).head(10)`, where only a handful of rows are needed from potentially massive intermediate results. It avoids unnecessary computation and materialization.

Common Subplan Elimination

In complex queries, it is not uncommon for the same sub-computation or file scan to be reused multiple times. With common subplan elimination, Polars detects these shared subplans and caches the results, while avoiding redundant computation. This optimization is especially powerful in joins, unions, or aggregations where the same logic is applied to multiple branches of a query.

Simplify Expressions

The simplification pass goes through your entire query plan and performs constant folding (evaluating constant expressions at compile time), simplifies arithmetic operations, and replaces expensive operations with more efficient equivalents when possible. This optimization runs repeatedly until no more simplifications can be made and is known as reaching a "fixed point." It ensures that the executed plan is as lean as possible.

Join Ordering

When performing joins between datasets of different sizes, the order in which joins are executed can significantly impact performance. Polars uses heuristics and data statistics to reorder joins such that the smallest or most selective branches are joined first, while reducing the overall memory pressure and intermediate result sizes. This results in more efficient join strategies, especially in multi-way joins.

Type Coercion

Type coercion ensures that data types are compatible across operations. If you are joining a string column with an integer, or applying an operation across mixed types, Polars will automatically coerce types to make the operation succeed while using the minimal memory footprint. This optimization is not just about compatibility; it is also about choosing types that lead to more efficient execution.

Working with LazyFrames

LazyFrames are designed for performance at scale—doing less work until it's absolutely necessary. In this section, you will learn how LazyFrames defer execution, optimize query plans, and handle large datasets efficiently. We will explore when and why to choose lazy execution to write faster, cleaner, and more memory-efficient data pipelines.

Creating and Transforming LazyFrames

In Polars, a LazyFrame represents a deferred computation. This means that the operations you apply on it are not executed immediately. Instead, they form a query plan that gets executed only when explicitly triggered, often using `.collect()` or other terminal operations. LazyFrames allow for efficient handling of large datasets by chaining together transformations without actually computing intermediate results until it is absolutely necessary. This approach provides better control over the execution flow and allows for optimization before the computation.

You can create a LazyFrame from any source, such as a CSV file or a DataFrame. For example, using `pl.read_csv("file.csv").lazy()` creates a LazyFrame from a CSV file. After that, you can chain transformations like filtering, joining, or aggregating. However, unlike the eager approach, these transformations are not executed immediately. Instead, Polars builds a logical and physical query plan in the background. This provides users an opportunity to combine complex logic without worrying about inefficient intermediate computations.

```
lazy_df = pl.read_csv("data.csv").lazy()
filtered_df = lazy_df.filter(pl.col("age") > 30)
aggregated_df = filtered_df.groupby("region").agg(pl.col("sales").sum())
```

Here, lazy_df, filtered_df, and aggregated_df are all LazyFrames. The actual computation will not occur until `.collect()` is invoked.

Building Complex Logic Without Immediate Execution

The ability to build complex logic with LazyFrames without triggering immediate execution offers several advantages. When working with large datasets, you may want to combine multiple transformations (for example, filters, joins, and aggregations) into a single query plan rather than executing them one by one. With LazyFrames, you can keep building this complex logic incrementally and optimize the execution plan at the end.

For instance, if you want to apply multiple filters, aggregate data, and join it with another dataset, you can do so in a single LazyFrame chain. Instead of executing each operation as it is applied (which can lead to unnecessary memory usage and time-consuming intermediate results), Polars will wait until the entire pipeline is built and allows it to optimize the whole query. This deferred execution ensures that only the minimal amount of work is done when the query is finally executed.

Here is an example:

```
lazy_df = (
    pl.read_csv("sales_data.csv")
    .lazy()
    .filter(pl.col("region") == "Europe")
    .select(["product", "revenue"])
    .groupby("product")
    .agg(pl.col("revenue").sum())
)
```

In this case, all the transformations are applied without any data being processed yet. When `.collect()` is called, Polars evaluates the entire chain in an optimized manner, while ensuring the best performance possible.

Benefits of Deferred Computation

One of the major benefits of deferred computation is performance optimization. By delaying computation, Polars has the opportunity to optimize the entire query before it is executed. This leads to significant reductions in both memory usage and computation time, since unnecessary steps are avoided. For example, when applying filters and selecting specific columns early in the pipeline, Polars can avoid loading unnecessary data, which is particularly useful when working with large files or datasets.

Another benefit is flexibility. Since the computations are deferred, you can modify or inspect parts of your pipeline without triggering computation until the very end. This allows for easy debugging and adjustment of your queries, especially in complex workflows. You can inspect the query plan with `.explain()`, which will make it easier for you to understand how the final computation will be executed and whether any optimizations have been applied.

Deferred computation also allows you to build complex transformations without worrying about the memory consumption of intermediate results. In an eager evaluation model, each transformation generates intermediate results that can overwhelm memory if the dataset is large. With LazyFrames, however, these intermediate results are not materialized until execution time. This ensures that memory usage is minimized, while improving performance.

Understanding the Query Plan

In Polars, when using the Lazy API, a key feature is the query plan, which is a logical representation of the operations that will be performed on your data. The query plan is initially built based on the operations defined in your pipeline, such as filters, joins, and aggregations. Once the query plan is constructed, Polars applies its optimization engine to transform the logical plan into an optimized physical plan that specifies how the operations should be executed efficiently, including execution strategies like parallelism or caching. Understanding the query plan is crucial for debugging performance issues and ensuring that operations are executed in the most efficient manner.

How to Inspect Query Plans Using explain()

Polars provides the explain() function to allow users to inspect the generated query plan. This function provides a detailed view of the logical query plan, the physical plan, and the transformations that Polars applies to optimize the query. You can use explain() to inspect how Polars interprets your query, what optimizations have been applied, and how the query will be executed under the hood. For example:

```
lazy_df = (
    pl.read_csv("sales_data.csv").lazy()
    .filter(pl.col("region") == "Europe")
    .select(["product", "revenue"])
    .explain()
)
```

The output of `explain()` will show the logical plan first, followed by the physical plan. This can help you identify any inefficiencies, such as unnecessary scans, operations, or projections. If needed, this insight can guide you to rework your query for better performance.

Logical vs. Physical Plans

The logical plan represents the high-level operations that Polars will perform on the data, regardless of how they are executed. It describes the data manipulations (filters, projections, joins) without considering the underlying system optimizations. The logical plan is a blueprint that guides Polars in constructing the query, while ensuring that all operations are logically sound.

The physical plan, however, is the optimized version of the logical plan. After applying optimizations like predicate pushdown, projection pruning, and reordering joins, the physical plan dictates how the operations will actually be executed, focusing on performance improvements. For example, in the case of large datasets, the physical plan might split the operations across multiple threads or apply more memory-efficient strategies. This ensures that the query runs as fast as possible.

Optimizing Execution behind the Scenes with Polars

Polars automatically handles query optimization behind the scenes, but understanding these optimizations helps developers ensure their data processing pipelines are running as efficiently as possible. After constructing the logical plan, Polars applies several optimization techniques such as predicate pushdown, projection pushdown, and common subplan elimination, to minimize memory usage and reduce the number of operations needed to execute the query.

For instance, if the query includes a filter and a projection, Polars might push the filter down to the scan level (predicate pushdown) and ensure only the necessary columns are loaded (projection pushdown). If multiple operations share the same subquery, Polars will cache the result (common subplan elimination) to avoid redundant computations. Once these optimizations are applied, the physical plan is generated, and the execution proceeds according to the optimized strategy, while leveraging techniques such as parallel execution or memory-efficient joins.

The goal of this whole process is to ensure that large datasets can be processed quickly and efficiently, which minimizes memory usage and boosts performance. Understanding how Polars works behind the scenes allows users to write more optimized queries and troubleshoot performance bottlenecks in their data workflows.

Streaming Mode

The streaming mode is a powerful feature in Polars and is designed to handle large datasets that cannot fit entirely into memory. This is accomplished by breaking the data into chunks and processing them one at a time, instead of loading the entire dataset into memory at once. This technique allows Polars to efficiently manage large-scale data without overwhelming system resources. When dealing with massive datasets such as logs, sensor data, or any other time-series data, the streaming mode ensures that the processing happens incrementally and without causing memory issues. It does so by processing the data in small, manageable portions.

Thus, by using streaming mode, you can ensure that your application can scale to handle large datasets, even when available memory is limited. The key idea behind streaming is that, rather than loading the entire dataset into memory and processing it all at once, Polars only loads and processes a small portion of the data at any given time. This allows for continuous data processing while keeping memory usage minimal.

Handling Large Data in Chunks

The ability to handle large data in chunks is particularly important when working with datasets that are too large to fit into memory at once, such as log files, transaction records, or high-frequency market data. When dealing with large files or datasets that can otherwise overwhelm system memory, streaming mode breaks the data into smaller chunks and processes each chunk sequentially.

In Polars, you can use streaming mode by reading data in a manner where the data is consumed in smaller segments instead of all at once. For example, when reading a CSV file, Polars can read it in chunks and apply the transformations incrementally. This can dramatically reduce memory usage and ensure that the application does not crash or slow down due to insufficient memory.

```
# Example of streaming mode for large CSV data:
lazy_df = pl.read_csv("large_file.csv", with_columns=["col1", "col2"]).
lazy().streaming()
```

With this approach, the computation will process each chunk of data before moving on to the next, rather than loading everything into memory at once.

Reasons and Occasions for Using Streaming

Streaming mode is most useful when you are working with large datasets that exceed the available memory. It is particularly beneficial when dealing with real-time data processing or when you need to apply the same transformations repeatedly over large files without needing to load the entire data simultaneously.

Reasons to Use Streaming:

- **Memory Constraints:** When working with large datasets, the entire dataset may not fit into memory. Thus, streaming mode allows you to process the data in smaller, more manageable chunks.
- **Efficiency:** By loading and processing data in chunks, streaming mode ensures that the system is not wasting resources on loading or holding unnecessary data in memory.
- **Real-Time Data Processing:** Streaming mode is ideal for scenarios where you are processing data in a continuous flow, such as log file analysis, real-time analytics, or processing sensor data.
- **Large Data Sources:** When working with datasets that are either too large for traditional batch processing or are too slow to process all at once, streaming allows for quick, incremental processing without running into bottlenecks.

Streaming with LazyFrames and Its Benefits

Combining streaming mode with LazyFrames provides the best of deferred computation and efficient data handling. LazyFrames already allow you to build complex query pipelines without triggering immediate computation. As streaming is enabled, Polars can further optimize data handling by loading and processing the data in chunks as the operations are applied.

By using streaming with LazyFrames, you can build complex data transformations over a large dataset, and only the necessary chunks of data are loaded at any time, while ensuring that memory usage stays low. This is especially useful when building queries that involve multiple stages of filtering, transformation, or aggregation.

The main benefits of combining streaming with LazyFrames include:

- **Improved Memory Efficiency:** Since only small chunks of the data are loaded at any given time, you will not run into memory bottlenecks.
- **Decreased Processing Time:** By processing data in chunks, Polars can reduce the overall time needed to process large datasets by leveraging parallelism and optimizing how chunks are handled.
- **Flexible Data Pipelines:** LazyFrames with streaming allow for flexible, scalable data pipelines where complex logic can be built incrementally and optimized behind the scenes without loading the entire dataset.

Execution: Triggering the Plan

In Polars, LazyFrames allow for deferred computation, where the execution of a query is delayed until explicitly triggered. This gives Polars the flexibility to optimize the entire query plan before executing it, while ensuring that the computation is as efficient as possible. The execution of the query is triggered when you invoke terminal methods, such as `.collect()` or `.fetch()`. These methods serve as the signal for Polars to begin processing the data according to the query plan that has been built and optimized behind the scenes.

The key idea is that until these methods are invoked, Polars only constructs a logical and physical plan for the query but does not execute any of the operations. This allows Polars to apply optimizations like predicate pushdown, projection pruning, and query plan reordering before any data is actually processed. Once you call a method like `.collect()`, Polars takes the constructed query plan, applies the optimizations, and begins executing the operations on the data in an efficient manner.

Methods like collect() and fetch()

The most common methods for triggering the execution of a LazyFrame are `.collect()` and `.fetch()`. Both of these methods instruct Polars to execute the deferred computations, but they differ in how they return the results.

`collect()`: This method is used to trigger the execution of the entire LazyFrame pipeline and return a materialized DataFrame. Once `.collect()` is called, Polars processes the data, applies all transformations and optimizations, and returns the final result as an eager DataFrame. This method is ideal when you want to finalize all the operations and load the entire result into memory.

Example:

```
lazy_df = pl.read_csv("data.csv").lazy()
result_df = lazy_df.filter(pl.col("age") > 30).collect()
```

Here, `.collect()` triggers the query to filter the data and returns the result as an eager DataFrame (result_df). This method is typically used when you are ready to view, manipulate, or analyze the final result.

`fetch()`: The `.fetch()` method, on the other hand, is used to fetch a limited number of rows from the LazyFrame. Unlike `.collect()`, which fetches the entire result, `.fetch()` is useful when you only need a subset of the data; for example, when previewing a dataset or retrieving a sample. It is especially useful for inspecting the first few rows of a large dataset without needing to process all the data.

Example:

```
lazy_df = pl.read_csv("sales_data.csv").lazy()
result_df = lazy_df.groupby("region").agg(pl.col("revenue").sum()).fetch(10)
```

- In this case, `.fetch()` is used after applying .sum(), which limits the result to the first 10 rows. This is efficient when you only need a quick preview of the data without triggering full-scale execution.

Execution Flow and Efficiency

When you use methods like `.collect()` or `.fetch()`, the execution of the LazyFrame involves several stages. First, Polars processes the transformations defined in the query plan and applies the optimizations. After that, it executes the operations in the most efficient order, taking advantage of optimizations like streaming mode (for large datasets) or parallel execution (for faster processing). By deferring the execution until these methods are invoked, Polars ensure that the final computation is not only correct, but also efficient.

The execution triggered by `.collect()` or `.fetch()` also benefits from memory optimizations. Since only the necessary data is processed and loaded into memory at each stage of the query pipeline, Polars minimizes the memory footprint, especially when working with large datasets. This ensures that the system can handle large-scale data efficiently without running into memory bottlenecks.

Overall, using `.collect()` or `.fetch()` provides the flexibility to control when the actual computation occurs and allows Polars to optimize the execution for better performance. Whether you need the entire dataset or just a preview, these methods provide an efficient way to trigger the computation whenever you are ready to process the data.

GPU Support in Polars

Polars offers an in-memory, GPU-accelerated execution engine for the Lazy API in Python, utilizing RAPIDS cuDF on NVIDIA GPUs. This feature, available in Open Beta, is actively being developed. It enables faster data processing by offloading computations to the GPU, which makes it ideal for handling large datasets and computationally intensive operations. Users can trigger GPU-based execution by using `.collect(engine="gpu")` instead of the standard `.collect()`.

Both CPU and GPU engines in Polars use the Apache Arrow columnar memory format, which facilitates rapid data movement between the CPU and GPU. This design ensures smooth interoperability, as files produced by one engine can be accessed by the other. However, GPU execution is currently only available through the Lazy API, which means that materialized DataFrames will reside in CPU memory, once the query execution completes.

When running a query in GPU mode, Polars automatically inspects the query plan to determine if it can be executed on the GPU. If not, the query seamlessly falls back to the CPU without causing an error. This fallback might not result in a performance change. For better visibility into whether the query ran on the GPU, users can enable verbose mode, where unsupported queries will trigger a PerformanceWarning.

Integration with Arrow and cuDF

The integration of Apache Arrow and cuDF is crucial for Polars' GPU support. Arrow's columnar format is highly optimized for data processing, which makes it efficient for transferring data between the CPU and GPU. By leveraging cuDF, a RAPIDS library built for GPU-accelerated DataFrames, Polars can accelerate tasks like aggregations, joins, filters, and string processing on GPUs. This setup allows Polars to optimize query execution, while reducing computation time and improving overall performance.

The cuDF-based execution engine in Polars creates a query plan, dispatches it to the RAPIDS cuDF-based engine, and retrieves the results as a standard CPU-backed Polars DataFrame. This approach offers a seamless experience for users who want to accelerate their workflows without having to manually manage GPU memory or data transfers.

When GPU Offers Speed Boosts

Polars' GPU support is particularly beneficial in scenarios where large-scale computations are required. Here are some scenarios where the GPU engine provides substantial performance improvements:

- **Grouped Aggregations and Joins:** You will see the most significant speedups when working with grouped aggregations and joins. These operations involve repetitive calculations that can benefit from the parallel processing capabilities of GPUs. For instance, large groupby aggregations which can take considerable time on the CPU, can be processed much faster on the GPU.
- **Large-Scale Data Processing**: GPUs are ideal for handling large datasets, though they generally have less RAM compared to CPUs. Consequently, very large datasets may cause out-of-memory errors on GPUs. Datasets between 50-100 GiB fit well with GPUs that have 80 GiB of memory, but larger datasets may not be suitable for GPU execution.
- **I/O Bound Queries**: While GPU acceleration excels in computation-heavy tasks like aggregations, I/O bound queries, such as file reading and writing, typically exhibit similar performance on both the CPU and GPU. If your workload is I/O-bound, switching to GPU may not offer significant performance benefits.
- **Real-Time Analytics**: Real-time data processing benefits significantly from GPU acceleration. The ability to handle incoming data streams faster is critical in scenarios like high-frequency trading or IoT data analytics, where latency and processing speed are crucial.
- **ML Pipelines**: GPUs are ideal for speeding up data preprocessing tasks in ML pipelines. Operations like feature engineering, data transformation, and aggregation can be dramatically accelerated, which allows for faster model training and more efficient pipelines.

System Requirements and Installation

To use the GPU backend in Polars, you will need a NVIDIA Volta™ or higher GPU with compute capability 7.0+, CUDA 11 or 12, and either Linux or Windows Subsystem for Linux 2 (WSL2). To install Polars with GPU support, you can add the GPU feature flag during installation by running:

```
pip install polars[gpu]
```

This enables the use of GPU acceleration in your Lazy API workflows, while optimizing your data processing tasks.

Features Supported on the GPU

Although the GPU engine is in Open Beta and rapidly evolving, it currently supports many core operations, including:

- LazyFrame API
- SQL API
- I/O from CSV, Parquet, ndjson, and in-memory CPU DataFrames
- Operations on numeric, logical, string, and datetime types
- String processing
- Aggregations and grouped aggregations
- Joins
- Filters
- Handling missing data
- Concatenation

However, some operations are not yet supported on the GPU, such as:

- Eager DataFrame API
- Streaming API
- Operations on categorical, struct, and list data types
- Rolling aggregations
- Time series resampling
- Timezones
- Folds
- User-defined functions
- JSON, Excel, and Database file formats

Conclusion

In this chapter, we explored the powerful performance optimizations provided by Polars' Lazy API, including techniques such as query optimization, query plans, GPU acceleration, and streaming mode. These features enable efficient handling of large datasets and complex data workflows and make Polars a robust tool for high-performance data processing. We covered key concepts like Lazy vs Eager evaluation, how query optimization techniques such as predicate pushdown, projection pushdown, and common subplan elimination improve execution efficiency, and how GPU support can accelerate compute-intensive tasks.

Thus, by leveraging the Lazy API, deferred execution, and GPU acceleration, users can significantly optimize the performance of their data workflows, especially in scenarios involving large-scale aggregations, joins, and other computationally expensive operations. Understanding these optimization techniques and their applications in Polars are crucial for efficiently managing large datasets and minimizing memory usage.

In the next chapter, we will dive into practical examples where we apply these optimizations in real-world data processing workflows. Additionally, we will cover profiling techniques to measure and evaluate the performance of your code, and testing methods to ensure that your pipelines are working as expected. By the end of the next chapter, you will gain hands-on experience with these powerful features and understand how to integrate them into your own data analysis pipelines effectively.

Exercise Tasks

1. Exploring Query Optimization Using a large dataset of your choice, experiment with different query optimization techniques such as predicate pushdown, projection pushdown, and common subplan elimination. Try to measure and compare the performance of a query before and after applying these optimizations. Pay attention to memory usage and execution time. Report your findings, highlighting which optimization provided the most significant improvement for your specific use case.

2. GPU Acceleration Exploration Install Polars with GPU support and run a set of grouped aggregation operations (for example, groupby) on a large dataset. First, execute the query using the CPU engine, then trigger the same query using the GPU engine by calling `.collect(engine="gpu")`. Compare the execution times and note any differences in performance. Test this with varying dataset sizes and document when GPU acceleration offers the most noticeable speedup, and when it does not.

CHAPTER 10
Profiling, Optimization, and Testing

"If you cannot measure it, you cannot improve it."

Peter Drucker

Introduction

Efficient data processing is not just about writing performant code; it is also about understanding how your queries behave under the hood. This chapter focuses on profiling and testing techniques in Polars that will help you analyze the performance of DataFrame operations, detect inefficiencies, and apply targeted optimizations. By examining query execution plans and runtime metrics, you will gain insights into detecting and resolving bottlenecks.

We will also explore practical strategies for troubleshooting common issues in Polars workflows, including interpreting errors, validating assumptions, and ensuring correctness through testing. Beyond diagnostics, this chapter introduces powerful data management techniques such as Run-Length Encoding (RLE), compression, and partitioning, which are essential for optimizing storage and improving the speed of data access in large-scale pipelines.

Additionally, we will demonstrate how leveraging LazyFrames and the GPU execution engine can further boost performance, particularly for compute-heavy operations. These tools allow you to defer execution and offload tasks to the GPU when possible, making them critical components of a high-performance data stack. Therefore, by the end of this chapter, you will be equipped with the skills to profile, test, and fine-tune your Polars workflows for maximum efficiency.

Structure

In this chapter, we will discuss the following topics:

- Why Profiling Matters
  - Importance of Performance Visibility
  - Common Pitfalls in Data Workflows
  - Different Profilers in Python
- Profiling LazyFrame Execution
  - Profiling eager dataframes
  - Comparison with lazyframe
- Testing Polars Pipelines
  - Parametric and Strategy Based Testing
  - Writing a Unit Test for Data Pipelines
- Improving Performance with LazyFrames
  - Efficient Chaining of Transformations
- Leveraging the GPU Engine
  - When and How to Use `.collect(engine="gpu")`
  - Understanding Fallbacks and Profiling GPU Execution
- Advanced Data Management Techniques
  - Run-Length Encoding (RLE)
  - Columnar Compression
  - Partitioning for Scalable Workflows

Importance of Profiling

Profiling is a crucial step in developing efficient data pipelines. It provides the visibility needed to understand how long each stage of your computation takes and where performance bottlenecks exist. Without profiling, developers often rely on intuition or guesswork to optimize their code, which can lead to missed opportunities or even make things worse. Especially in large-scale data workflows, even small inefficiencies can snowball into significant slowdowns or increased memory usage. Profiling ensures that you are not just writing the correct code, but also the code that performs well under real-world data volumes.

Importance of Performance Visibility

One of the key benefits of profiling in Polars is the ability to inspect execution plans and runtime behavior, particularly when using LazyFrames. As LazyFrames delay execution, they allow Polars to optimize the full query before any data is touched. Profiling such deferred execution provides insights into how optimizations like predicate pushdown or join ordering affect runtime performance. By analyzing these profiles, developers can validate that the expected optimizations are happening, and that unnecessary work is being avoided.

Common Pitfalls in Data Workflows

Many data workflows suffer from common pitfalls that profiling can help uncover. For instance, eagerly materializing intermediate results can lead to memory bloat. Misaligned data types in joins or filters can cause silent coercion and increased compute overhead. Other examples of suboptimal patterns are using wide DataFrames with unnecessary columns, or performing operations in inefficient order (for example, filtering after a join instead of before). With proper profiling, these issues can be spotted and resolved early. This will make your data pipelines more robust and scalable. The result is often a significant improvement in speed and reduced resource consumption.

Different Profilers in Python

When working with Polars in Python, especially while integrating it into broader analytics pipelines, it is often helpful to go beyond Polars' built-in profiling tools and leverage external profilers. These profilers help diagnose issues in custom functions, surrounding Python code, or non-Polars logic that might influence performance. Three commonly used profiling tools in the Python ecosystem are **`line_profiler`**, **`pyinstrument`**, and **`memory_profiler`**.

`line_profiler`

`line_profiler` is a precision tool for profiling the time spent on each line of a function. You decorate functions with **`@profile`** and then run your script using the kernprof command. This profiler is extremely useful when you want to zoom into the internals of a function to understand exactly which lines are expensive. For example, if you have written a custom transformation function before passing data into Polars, **`line_profiler`** helps you pinpoint the exact lines causing slowdowns. One limitation is that it does not provide a holistic view of the program's call stack or handle asynchronous code well.

`pyinstrument`

pyinstrument provides a hierarchical, flame-graph-style view of where time is being spent during your script's execution. It is perfect for getting an overview of how different parts of your code contribute to total execution time. Unlike **line_profiler**, which focuses on line-level granularity, **pyinstrument** captures the structure of your code's call tree and allows you to spot where the most time is consumed in broader logic. It is especially helpful for understanding how time is distributed across I/O, computation, and library calls. However, it may not provide the same level of line-by-line detail that **line_profiler** does.

memory_profiler

memory_profiler is a tool for analyzing memory usage line-by-line in your Python functions. Just like **line_profiler**, you decorate functions with @profile and execute the script to see how much memory is allocated and retained by each line. This profiler is invaluable when you are dealing with large datasets or noticing memory pressure in your pipeline. For Polars workflows, especially when eagerly collecting or materializing DataFrames, **memory_profiler** helps detect memory leaks or suboptimal memory handling. It is a straightforward but powerful way to understand memory behavior.

Tool	Focus Area	Granularity	Ideal Use Case	Limitations
line_profiler	CPU Time	Per line	Zoom into specific functions	Needs decorated functions, not async-friendly
pyinstrument	CPU Time (Call Tree)	Per function/ call stack	Visualize full program execution	Less detailed per-line info
memory_profiler	Memory Usage	Per line	Detect memory leaks and inefficiencies	Slower execution, limited to memory analysis

Table 10.1: *Comparison of Profilers*

Profiling Execution

Profiling execution helps you understand how your program behaves while it runs, not just whether it works. It reveals where time, memory, and resources are actually spent during execution. By identifying bottlenecks early, profiling enables targeted optimizations and more efficient performance tuning.

Profiling Eager DataFrames

When working with Eager DataFrames in Polars, operations are executed immediately, which makes profiling more straightforward but also more limited in scope. Since each operation is carried out as it is called, the profiling insight you get is tied directly to that specific line of code. Python-level profilers like **line_profiler** or **pyinstrument** can be used to time individual Eager DataFrame operations. However, these tools do not reveal the internal optimization strategies that Polars might apply behind the scenes. The primary benefit of profiling Eager execution is its simplicity; you can instantly measure the cost of any transformation without needing to understand execution plans or query trees.

Comparison with LazyFrame

LazyFrames, in contrast, defer execution until a terminal operation like **`.collect()`** is called. This delayed execution allows Polars to build and optimize a full query plan before any data is processed. As a result, profiling LazyFrames requires a different mindset: you are not profiling line-by-line operations, but analyzing the compiled execution graph. The built-in **`.profile()`** and **`.profile_streaming()`** methods in Polars provide excellent visualizations for understanding how Lazy execution flows. In LazyFrames, you benefit from query optimizations like predicate and projection pushdown, which reduce the work Polars has to do. This means LazyFrames often outperform Eager operations on larger datasets, but require more tooling and interpretation.

Interpreting Execution Times and Stages

Interpreting the execution profile of a LazyFrame involves understanding its logical and physical plans. The output of .explain() shows you how Polars transforms your high-level operations into optimized, low-level execution steps. Profiling tools reveal time spent at different stages (such as file scanning, filtering, joining, aggregation) and how effectively optimizations have been applied. If certain operations dominate the runtime (for example, an expensive join or a slow filter due to lack of pushdown), the profile helps you spot and address them. In the Eager mode, by contrast, you measure execution time per operation, which is easier to interpret but less globally optimized.

Identifying Bottlenecks

Whether you are using Eager or Lazy execution, profiling helps you identify performance bottlenecks. In Eager mode, you might spot repeated scans, excessive memory use, or inefficient chaining of transformations. In Lazy mode, bottlenecks are often tied to suboptimal query plans; for instance, if a filter is not pushed down or a join is performed late in the execution. Tools like .profile() and **`.profile_streaming()`** generate clear breakdowns of time spent in each part of the pipeline. These insights guide you to restructure queries, reduce memory load, or move to streaming or GPU execution where appropriate. With consistent profiling, you can make data workflows that are not only correct, but also fast and scalable.

Now let us look at an example of profiling of Eager Dataframes and Lazy Dataframes:

The following code performs a sequence of data analysis operations using the Polars library on a CSV file named `"synthetic_stars.csv"`. First, it reads the CSV file into a Polars DataFrame. Then, it filters the dataset to include only those rows where the "temperature" column has values greater than 20,000, while focusing on very hot stars. After filtering, the data is grouped by the `"spectral_type"` column, which typically categorizes stars based on their spectra. For each spectral type, the code calculates the mean (average) of the "velocity" values and labels it as `"avg_velocity"`. Finally, the result is sorted in descending order of average velocity, while showing which spectral types have the highest average velocities among the hottest stars.

```
import polars as pl
import pandas as pd
import numpy as np
def avgVelocity():
    df = pl.read_csv("synthetic_stars.csv")
    df =df.filter(pl.col("temperature") > 20000)
    df= df.group_by("spectral_type").agg([pl.col("velocity").mean().
alias("avg_velocity")]).sort("avg_velocity", descending=True)
```

Now, we will first use line profiler for this code. In the Jupyter notebook, we will use the below command to load the line profiler:

```
%load_ext line_profiler
```

Then, we will run below command to get line profiler output:

```
%lprun -f avgVelocity avgVelocity()
```

The output looks like this:

```
Timer unit: 1e-07 s

Total time: 5.89141 s
File: C:\Users\khila\AppData\Local\Temp\ipykernel_22964\3090659567.py
Function: avgVelocity at line 6

Line #      Hits         Time  Per Hit   % Time  Line Contents
==============================================================
     6                                           def avgVelocity():
     7         1   54938779.0    5e+07     93.3      df = pl.read_
csv("synthetic_stars.csv")
     8         1    2801623.0    3e+06      4.8      df =df.filter(pl.
col("temperature") > 20000)
     9         1    1173710.0    1e+06      2.0      df= df.group_
by("spectral_type").agg([pl.col("velocity").mean().alias("avg_
velocity")]).sort("avg_velocity", descending=True)
```

This profiler output shows how long each line of the **`avgVelocity()`** function took to run, while helping us understand which part of the code is the most time-consuming.

Here is a detailed breakdown:

- Total time: The function took about 5.89 seconds to run in total.
- Line 7 (`pl.read_csv`): This line, which reads the CSV file, took the most time – around 5.49 seconds (or 93.3% of the total time). This is expected because reading a file from disk is often slow.
- Line 8 (filtering rows by temperature): This took 0.28 seconds (about 4.8% of the time), which is much faster than reading the file.
- Line 9 (grouping, calculating mean, and sorting): This took 0.12 seconds (about 2.0%) and means that it is the fastest part of the function.

Now let us use Pyinstrument to further profile the code.

```
%load_ext pyinstrument
```

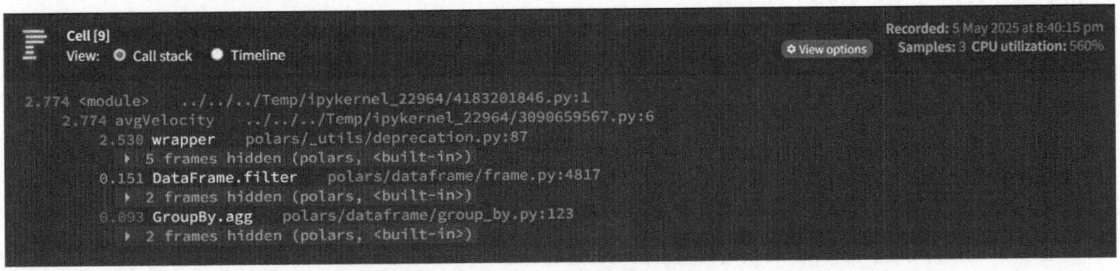

***Figure 10.1**: Pyinstrument Profiling of Eager Dataframe*

This profiler visualization shows a breakdown of where time was spent during the execution of your **`avgVelocity()`** function. Here is what it means in simpler terms:

Key Points:

- Total time (2.774 seconds): The function **`avgVelocity()`** took about 2.77 seconds to run in this profiling session.
- Most time (2.530 s) spent in wrapper: This likely wraps internal Polars logic or deprecated code paths; it might include time spent preparing the function call or doing background work.

Inside avgVelocity():

- DataFrame.filter (0.151 s): Filtering rows where temperature > 20,000 was fast and took just 0.151 seconds.
- GroupBy.agg (0.093 s): Grouping by spectral type and calculating average velocity was also quick, which took only 0.093 seconds.

The visual profiler, powered by PyInstrument, provides a high-level overview of your program's runtime by showing a call tree, which refers to how time is distributed across function calls, including time spent in internal libraries like Polars. It focuses on the structure and flow of execution, while helping you identify which functions or modules dominate execution time. In contrast, `line_profiler` (used via %lprun) gives a fine-grained, line-by-line breakdown of time spent inside a specific function, which makes it ideal for pin-pointing slow lines in critical code. PyInstrument helps you see the big picture (which part of the code to optimize), while `line_profiler` helps with precise tuning (exactly where in the function to optimize). Using both gives a complete performance debugging toolkit.

Now let us focus on the memory profile of our code, and try to identify where memory usage has a spike. We can use the following command to discover memory usage patterns in code:

```
python -m memory_profiler profileTest.py
```

The script looks like this:

```
import polars as pl
import pandas as pd
import numpy as np
from memory_profiler import profile

@profile
def avgVelocity():
    df = pl.read_csv("synthetic_stars.csv")
    df =df.filter(pl.col("temperature") > 20000)
    df= df.group_by("spectral_type").agg([pl.col("velocity").mean().
alias("avg_velocity")]).sort("avg_velocity", descending=True)


if __name__ == '__main__':
    avgVelocity()
```

We will get memory consumption details for the script under test such as:

```
Filename: profileTest.py

Line #    Mem usage    Increment  Occurrences   Line Contents
=============================================================
     6    119.0 MiB    119.0 MiB           1   @profile
     7                                         def avgVelocity():
     8   1748.8 MiB   1629.8 MiB           1       df = pl.read_
csv("synthetic_stars.csv")
     9   2816.8 MiB   1068.0 MiB           1       df =df.filter(pl.
col("temperature") > 20000)
    10   2850.5 MiB     33.7 MiB           1       df= df.group_
by("spectral_type").agg([pl.col("velocity").mean().alias("avg_
velocity")]).sort("avg_velocity", descending=True)
```

This memory profiler output shows how memory usage changes at each step of the `avgVelocity()` function. Initially, the memory usage starts at 119.0 MiB, but after reading the CSV file (`pl.read_csv`), it jumps by ~1.63 GiB, reaching 1748.8 MiB. This indicates that loading the data into memory is the most memory-intensive step. Filtering rows based on the "temperature" column increases memory usage by another ~1.07 GiB, reaching 2816.8 MiB, likely due to Polars creating a new filtered DataFrame rather than modifying in place. The grouping and aggregation step uses relatively little additional memory, which is just ~34 MiB. This suggests that these operations are memory-efficient compared to data loading and filtering. Overall, the majority of memory usage comes from reading the data and filtering it.

Comparison with LazyFrame

When working with data in Polars, users can choose between eager and lazy execution modes, but understanding their performance implications is the key to writing efficient code. Eager execution processes each operation immediately, which can lead to unnecessary memory usage and repeated data scanning. On the other hand, LazyFrames allow Polars to build a full query plan first, then optimize and execute it in the most efficient way possible. This deferred execution model can dramatically reduce runtime and memory consumption, especially for complex pipelines. In this section, we will use profiling tools to compare both approaches and highlight how LazyFrames deliver superior performance through query optimization and reduced resource usage. Let us compare the profiling results of the same operations, but instead of using eager DataFrames, let us use lazyframes. The following is the equivalent LazyFrame script for the operation we performed using an eager DataFrame:

```
def avgVelocity():
    df = pl.scan_csv("synthetic_stars.csv")
    df =df.filter(pl.col("temperature") > 20000)
    df= df.group_by("spectral_type").agg([pl.col("velocity").mean().
alias("avg_velocity")]).sort("avg_velocity", descending=True)
    df = df.collect()
```

If we profile this using same methodology, we will get results like:

Line profiler:

```
Timer unit: 1e-07 s

Total time: 5.5948 s
File: C:\Users\khila\AppData\Local\Temp\ipykernel_22964\3195633586.py
Function: avgVelocity at line 1

Line #      Hits         Time  Per Hit   % Time  Line Contents
==============================================================
```

```
     1                                            def avgVelocity():
     2          1     122730.0 122730.0      0.2      df = pl.scan_
csv("synthetic_stars.csv")
     3          1      17749.0  17749.0      0.0      df =df.filter(pl.
col("temperature") > 20000)
     4          1       3808.0   3808.0      0.0      df= df.group_
by("spectral_type").agg([pl.col("velocity").mean().alias("avg_
velocity")]).sort("avg_velocity", descending=True)
     5          1   55803760.0    6e+07     99.7      df = df.collect()
```

PyInstrument:

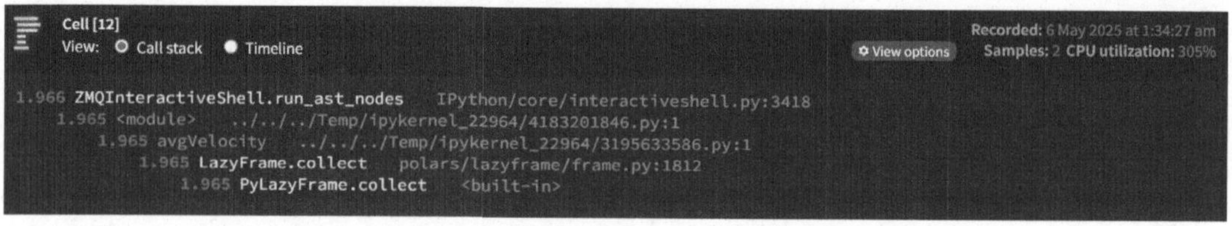

Figure 10.2: *Pyinstrument Profiling of Lazy DataFrame*

Memory Profiler:

```
Filename: lazyProfileTest.py

Line #    Mem usage    Increment  Occurrences   Line Contents
=============================================================
     6    118.8 MiB    118.8 MiB           1   @profile
     7                                         def avgVelocity():
     8    119.1 MiB      0.3 MiB           1       df = pl.scan_
csv("synthetic_stars.csv")
     9    119.2 MiB      0.2 MiB           1       df =df.filter(pl.
col("temperature") > 20000)
    10    119.3 MiB      0.1 MiB           1       df= df.group_
by("spectral_type").agg([pl.col("velocity").mean().alias("avg_
velocity")]).sort("avg_velocity", descending=True)
    11    487.6 MiB    368.3 MiB           1       df = df.collect()
```

As we can see from the profiling output, we drastically reduced the memory consumption using LazyFrame. The execution time has also reduced .The query plan for lazyframe looks like this obtained using `.explain()`:

```
SORT BY [col("avg_velocity")]
  AGGREGATE
      [col("velocity").mean().alias("avg_velocity")] BY [col("spectral_
type")] FROM
    simple π 3/3 ["velocity", "spectral_type", ... 1 other column]
```

```
Csv SCAN [synthetic_stars.csv]
PROJECT 3/20 COLUMNS
SELECTION: [(col("temperature")) > (20000.0)]
```

This Polars query plan shows the optimized steps the LazyFrame will execute. It starts by scanning the CSV file, but only selects 3 of 20 columns needed for the operation; this is efficient column pruning. Then it filters rows where the temperature is greater than 20,000. After filtering, it groups the data by `spectral_type` and computes the mean of velocity, followed by a sort on the resulting `avg_velocity` in descending order. Each step is deferred and reordered for optimal execution before being run.

Testing Polars Pipelines

Polars provide a robust testing module tailored for validating DataFrames and Series in unit tests. Since this module is not imported by default for performance reasons, developers must explicitly import it via `polars.testing` or by directly importing specific functions like `assert_frame_equal` or `assert_series_equal`. These assertion helpers allow comparison of both structure and content between two frames or series, while ensuring correctness in data transformation pipelines. You can assert both equality and inequality, which is useful for regression and edge case testing.

For more dynamic testing, Polars integrate with the Hypothesis library to enable property-based testing. This includes strategies to generate synthetic Polars DataFrames, LazyFrames, Series, lists, and dtypes. Developers can define custom rules and constraints on columns such as data type, nullability, or value range to automatically generate diverse input data. These strategies are critical for testing transformation logic across a wide variety of scenarios, while ensuring reliability without manually crafting each test case.

To control test thoroughness, Polars define parametric test profiles as fast, balanced, and expensive, corresponding to increasing iteration counts and deeper coverage. These profiles can be set or loaded dynamically to fit different testing goals such as quick validation in development or exhaustive testing in CI environments. Taken together, Polars' testing module and Hypothesis integration provide a powerful framework for ensuring the correctness, stability and performance of analytical code in both eager and lazy execution modes.

Basic Parametric Test

This test generates star-like DataFrames with 5 numeric columns simulating physical quantities such as temperature or velocity, and ensures that all columns are of numeric type, while accounting for potential nulls.

```
import polars as pl
from polars.testing.parametric import dataframes
```

```
from polars import NUMERIC_DTYPES
from hypothesis import given

@given(
    dataframes(
        cols=5,
        allow_null=True,
        allowed_dtypes=NUMERIC_DTYPES,
    )
)
def test_star_numeric_columns(df: pl.DataFrame):
    # Check that all columns are numeric (for example, temperature,
velocity, magnitude)
    assert all(df[col].dtype.is_numeric() for col in df.columns)
```

Intermediate Parametric Test

This test generates LazyFrames that resemble realistic star records and ensures that data types and value ranges match expected astronomical properties.

```
import polars as pl
from polars.testing.parametric import column, dataframes
import hypothesis.strategies as st
from hypothesis import given

@given(
    dataframes(
        cols=[
            column("id", strategy=st.text(min_size=3, max_size=6)),
            column("spectral_type", strategy=st.sampled_from(["O", "B",
"A", "F", "G", "K", "M"])),
            column("temperature", strategy=st.integers(min_value=2500,
max_value=40000)),
            column("velocity", strategy=st.floats(min_value=-1000.0, max_
value=1000.0)),
            column("magnitude", strategy=st.floats(min_value=-10.0, max_
value=20.0)),
        ],
        min_size=5,
        lazy=True,
    )
)
def test_star_lazyframe_properties(lf: pl.LazyFrame):
    df = lf.collect()
    assert df.shape[1] == 5  # Should have all specified columns
```

Advanced Parametric Test

This test simulates observational range data for stars (for example, min/max values for temperature, velocity, magnitude, and so on) using lists of UInt16s. It then verifies that the data structure is aligning with the nested range expectations.

```
import polars as pl
from polars.testing.parametric import column, dataframes, lists
import hypothesis.strategies as st
from hypothesis import given

@st.composite
def star_observation_pairs(draw: st.DrawFn):
    obs = lists(pl.UInt16, size=2)
    return [sorted(pair) for pair in zip(draw(obs), draw(obs))]

@given(
    dataframes(
        cols=[
            column("temperature_range", strategy=star_observation_pairs()),
            column("velocity_range", strategy=star_observation_pairs()),
            column("magnitude_range", strategy=star_observation_
pairs()),
        ],
        min_size=3,
        max_size=3,
    )
)
def test_star_range_lists(df: pl.DataFrame):
    assert all(col in df.columns for col in ["temperature_range",
"velocity_range", "magnitude_range"])
```

Reasons to Choose Parametric and Strategy-Based Testing

Parametric testing and Hypothesis library-based strategy testing are powerful techniques for ensuring the robustness and correctness of data processing pipelines, especially in data-intensive contexts like astronomy or financial analytics. Parametric testing allows developers to define test templates that can be automatically run with a wide range of inputs, while enhancing test coverage without redundant code. The Hypothesis library complements this by enabling property-based testing, where tests are written to assert general truths (properties) about data rather than specific outcomes. Hypothesis generates a wide variety of inputs, including edge cases, using customizable strategies such as numeric ranges, nested lists, strings with constraints, or domain-specific values like spectral types. This helps uncover bugs that are often missed by traditional example-based tests, such as those caused by nulls, outliers, or unusual combinations of valid data. Together, these tools lead to more resilient, scalable, and data-agnostic code, which is especially crucial in fields where correctness and data integrity are non-negotiable.

Writing a Unit Test for the Data Pipeline

Unit testing DataFrame transformations is essential for ensuring correctness and stability in data pipelines. Even minor logic errors like incorrect filtering, groupings, or aggregations can silently corrupt downstream analytics. By writing focused tests that validate schema, content, and transformation logic, you catch issues early, increase confidence in refactoring, and protect against regressions as data complexity grows. In short, unit tests serve as safety nets in fast-moving, data-driven development.

Here is an example of a simple unit test case of a polars dataframe where we compare the generated data with the expected data to verify the operation correctness:

```
import polars as pl
from polars.testing import assert_frame_equal

def transform_pipeline(df: pl.DataFrame) -> pl.DataFrame:
    return (
        df.filter(pl.col("temperature") > 20000)
          .groupby("spectral_type")
          .agg(pl.col("velocity").mean().alias("avg_velocity"))
          .sort("avg_velocity")
    )

def test_transform_pipeline():
    input_df = pl.DataFrame({
        "temperature": [15000, 22000, 30000, 18000],
        "velocity": [50.0, 70.0, 120.0, 40.0],
        "spectral_type": ["G", "O", "O", "K"]
    })

    expected_df = pl.DataFrame({
        "spectral_type": ["O"],
        "avg_velocity": [95.0]
    })

    result_df = transform_pipeline(input_df)
    assert_frame_equal(result_df, expected_df)
```

Improving Performance with LazyFrames

We know we can use LazyFrames for boosting performance, but can we do something more to improve the performance further? The answer is yes. We can chain methods to further boost up the performance.

Efficient Chaining of Transformations

Efficient chaining of transformations in data processing involves applying a sequence of operations without creating intermediate copies, while minimizing memory usage and improving performance. Libraries like Polars and Pandas offer built-in support for lazy execution, which allows transformations to be batched and optimized before execution. This approach enables faster data processing, especially with large datasets, by reducing redundant computations. The following is an example and profiling result. We can clearly see by chaining methods we have further reduced memory consumption compared to previous way of performing operations.

```
def avgVelocity():
    df = pl.scan_csv("synthetic_stars.csv").filter(pl.col("temperature") > 20000).group_by("spectral_type").agg([pl.col("velocity").mean().alias("avg_velocity")]).sort("avg_velocity", descending=True).collect()
```

```
Filename: chainlazyProfileTest.py

Line #    Mem usage    Increment  Occurrences   Line Contents
=============================================================
     6    118.9 MiB    118.9 MiB           1   @profile
     7                                         def avgVelocity():
     8    475.6 MiB    356.7 MiB           1       df = pl.scan_csv("synthetic_stars.csv").filter(pl.col("temperature") > 20000).group_by("spectral_type").agg([pl.col("velocity").mean().alias("avg_velocity")]).sort("avg_velocity", descending=True).collect()
```

Leveraging the GPU Engine

Leveraging the GPU engine with Polars enables accelerated data processing by offloading computationally intensive operations to the GPU. This results in significant performance improvements, particularly for large datasets or complex transformations. Polars integrates with libraries like RAPIDS cuDF to provide GPU-accelerated DataFrame operations, which makes it ideal for tasks that require high throughput. By using GPU power, Polars can dramatically speed up data analysis workflows while maintaining ease of use.

Using `.collect(engine="gpu")`

To demonstrate the impact of GPU, we will be using Google collab to use T4 GPU and compare the performance of CPU vs GPU engine for polars.

Let us first create a dataframe for analysis in Collab using the code: cricket player dataset with 10M rows:

```
import polars as pl
import numpy as np

# Number of rows
num_rows = 10_000_000

# Generate random data for the DataFrame
data = {
    "player_id": np.random.randint(1, 1000000, num_rows),  # Player IDs
between 1 and 1,000,000
    "country": np.random.choice(["India", "Australia", "England",
"Pakistan", "South Africa"], num_rows),
    "matches_played": np.random.randint(1, 500, num_rows),
    "runs_scored": np.random.randint(0, 10000, num_rows),
    "wickets_taken": np.random.randint(0, 500, num_rows),
    "highest_score": np.random.randint(0, 300, num_rows),
    "batting_average": np.random.uniform(0, 100, num_rows),
    "bowling_average": np.random.uniform(0, 100, num_rows),
    "strike_rate": np.random.uniform(0, 200, num_rows),
    "economy_rate": np.random.uniform(0, 15, num_rows),
    "hundreds": np.random.randint(0, 100, num_rows),
    "fifties": np.random.randint(0, 200, num_rows),
    "catches": np.random.randint(0, 200, num_rows),
    "stumpings": np.random.randint(0, 100, num_rows),
    "fours": np.random.randint(0, 1000, num_rows),
    "sixes": np.random.randint(0, 500, num_rows),
    "balls_bowled": np.random.randint(0, 10000, num_rows),
    "maiden_overs": np.random.randint(0, 100, num_rows),
    "five_wickets": np.random.randint(0, 20, num_rows),
    "ten_wickets": np.random.randint(0, 5, num_rows)
}
df = pl.DataFrame(data).lazy()
df.head().collect()
```

Now, let us perform a simple aggregation operation to check corresponding CPU and execution times:

```
%%time

import polars as pl
import numpy as np
import time
import psutil

# Start the timer
start_time = time.time()

# Aggregate results country-wise
country_agg = df.group_by("country").agg(
    [
        pl.col("runs_scored").sum().alias("total_runs"),
        pl.col("matches_played").sum().alias("total_matches"),
    ]
).sort("total_runs", descending=True).collect()
output :
CPU times: user 495 ms, sys: 148 ms, total: 643 ms
Wall time: 338 ms
```

Now, let us do the same operation using GPU:

```
%%time

import polars as pl
import numpy as np
import time
import psutil

# Start the timer
start_time = time.time()

# ... (your existing code to create the DataFrame 'df') ...

# Aggregate results country-wise
country_agg = df.group_by("country").agg(
    [
        pl.col("runs_scored").sum().alias("total_runs"),
        pl.col("matches_played").sum().alias("total_matches"),
    ]
).sort("total_runs", descending=True).collect(engine="gpu")
output:
CPU times: user 201 ms, sys: 41.9 ms, total: 243 ms
Wall time: 239 ms
```

We can clearly see from the output that the wall time has reduced with the GPU engine. As mentioned in *Chapter 9*, *Working with Large Datasets*, GPU optimization is available for specific operations and GPUs scale better with large datasets.

Understanding Fallbacks and Profiling GPU Execution

Understanding fallbacks and profiling GPU execution in Polars is crucial to getting the best bang for your buck. Sometimes, even if you invoke **`.collect(engine="gpu")`**, certain operations might quietly fall back to CPU because they are not yet supported on the GPU. After all, not every path is paved in gold. It is important to keep an eye on what is actually running where, and for that, profiling tools or debug logs can be your best indicators. Think of it like checking if the highway is open before starting a long drive. Profiling helps you ensure that your workload is truly riding the GPU wave and not quietly slipping back to CPU behind your back.

Advanced Data Management Techniques

In modern high-performance computing and data engineering, advanced management techniques focus on reducing storage footprints and maximizing CPU efficiency.

Run-Length Encoding (RLE)

RLE compresses columns by representing repeated consecutive values as a single value plus count. It is especially effective on sorted or categorical columns. In storage formats like Parquet, RLE is often automatically applied to columns such as booleans or labels.

Example (Conceptual):

Column [Yes, Yes, Yes, No] becomes [(Yes, 3), (No, 1)] — used internally during Parquet compression.

Columnar Compression

Compression reduces the size of data for more efficient storage and faster transmission. In DataFrame systems, it is commonly applied when saving data to disk formats like Parquet or CSV. Compression algorithms like Snappy, ZSTD, and GZIP can be used to shrink file sizes without changing the logical data. It speeds up both read and write operations by reducing disk I/O.

Example:

```
df.write_parquet("data.parquet", compression="zstd")
```

Lossy Compression

Lossy compression reduces data size by discarding less critical information, while often sacrificing some accuracy. In DataFrames, this could mean converting high-precision floats to lower-precision types or downsampling data in time series. It is suitable when approximate values are acceptable and storage savings are critical.

Example:

Convert float64 to float16 via:

```
df = df.with_columns(pl.col("temperature").cast(pl.Float16))
```

Lossless Compression

Lossless compression reduces data size without losing any information, which makes it ideal for analytics workflows where accuracy is critical. A classic example is replacing repeated categorical strings with binary representations or codes. For instance, instead of storing "Male" and "Female" as strings, you store them as 0 and 1, respectively. This saves space and speeds up processing, especially for columns with repeated values.

Example:

```
df = df.with_columns(
    pl.col("sex").map_elements(lambda x: 0 if x == "Male" else
1).alias("sex_binary")
)
```

Chunking

Chunking breaks a dataset into smaller pieces or "chunks" to reduce memory usage and enable streaming or parallel execution. It is particularly useful when reading massive files that do not fit in memory or when processing can be parallelized for efficiency.

Example:

Read a large CSV file in chunks using Polars:

```
df = pl.read_csv("large_file.csv", low_memory=True)
```

Partitioning for Scalable Workflows

Partitioning divides data into physical subfolders or subsets based on column values, such as date, country, or category. It improves performance by allowing queries to skip irrelevant data. In big data processing (for example, with Spark or DuckDB), partitioned Parquet files enable faster filtering and scanning.

Example:

Partitioning by "year" and "region":

```
df.write_parquet("out/", partition_cols=["year", "region"])
```

Indexing

Indexing involves creating metadata that helps locate and access data efficiently, like an address book for rows. In distributed file systems or columnar formats, indexing can span multiple files; each file could be indexed by a column like **`customer_id`**, which allows fast lookups without scanning every file. Systems like Delta Lake or DuckDB use min/max indexes per file to skip irrelevant data during queries.

Example:

You have many Parquet files partitioned by month. Each file has an index for **`user_id`**:

```
SELECT * FROM data WHERE user_id = 'U123' -- skips unrelated files
```

Conclusion

In this chapter, we explored the essential tools and techniques for profiling, testing, and optimizing data workflows in Polars. We began by demystifying how query execution behaves under the hood, which enables you to spot and resolve performance bottlenecks using lazy evaluation, query plans, and runtime metrics. You learned how to apply practical testing strategies to validate logic and maintain correctness throughout your pipelines.

We also covered powerful data management techniques like compression, partitioning, Run-Length Encoding (RLE), and indexing, which will help scale your workflows by minimizing storage and speeding up access. Additionally, we demonstrated how to harness the GPU execution engine and LazyFrames to unlock significant performance gains for compute-intensive tasks.

Thus, by combining deep observability with structural optimizations, you are now equipped to build robust, efficient, and scalable data pipelines with Polars, which is capable of handling large volumes of data without compromising on speed or correctness. In the next chapter, we will cover practical examples for market data analysis using polars.

Exercise Tasks

Exercise 1: Visualize Memory Profiling in Polars

Objective:

Profile and visualize the memory usage of a Polars workflow to identify memory-intensive operations.

Instructions:

1. Create a large synthetic DataFrame with random numeric, categorical, and datetime columns using pl.DataFrame and pl.arange.
2. Wrap your operations in a LazyFrame chain (for example, filtering, grouping,

joining, and so on).

3. Convert the profile results into a DataFrame and visualize the memory usage per operation using a bar chart (you may use matplotlib or plotly).

Exercise 2: Compare CPU vs GPU Execution Impact

Objective:

Analyze how GPU acceleration affects performance across different operations in Polars.

Instructions:

1. Use a dataset with at least 10 million rows and multiple numeric columns.
2. Define a series of transformations (for example, arithmetic operations, aggregations, joins).
3. Execute the same LazyFrame query twice:
    a. Once with **`.collect(engine="auto")`**.
    b. Once with **`.collect(engine="gpu")`**.
4. Measure and print the execution time for each run.
5. Summarize which operations demonstrate the most benefit from GPU acceleration.

CHAPTER 11
Market Data Analysis Using Polars

"Data beats emotions."

Sean Rad

Introduction

In the fast-paced world of finance, accessing reliable and real-time market data is critical for making informed decisions. Whether you are an analyst, trader, or developer building data-driven financial applications, the ability to collect, clean, and interpret market data efficiently can be a game-changer. This chapter provides a hands-on approach to building a robust market data analysis pipeline using Polars, which is a high-performance DataFrame library built for speed and scalability.

We begin by setting up an API client to fetch market data in real-time or on demand. Once the data is collected, we will demonstrate how to load and manipulate it using Polars, while taking advantage of its lightning-fast query engine. Accurate analysis starts with clean data; therefore, we will delve into cleaning techniques to handle missing values, inconsistencies, and outliers. Finally, we present ways to visualize key market trends, which will allow you to extract actionable insights and communicate findings effectively.

Therefore, by the end of this chapter, you will be equipped with a complete toolkit for market data analysis, which is empowered by Polars' performance and expressiveness.

Structure

In this chapter, we will cover the following topics:

- Setting Up an API for Market Data
  - Overview of Market Data Providers
  - REST API Fundamentals and Authentication python
  - Fetching Real-Time and Historical Data Using Python (Alpha Vantage)
  - Saving API Responses in Structured Formats
- Loading Market Data into Polars
  - Reading Market Data JSON into Polars Dataframes
  - Schema Inspection and Column Selection
  - Converting Timestamps and Financial Datatypes
- Data Cleaning
  - Identifying and Handling Missing or Null Values
  - Filtering Duplicate Records and Incorrect Entries
  - Normalizing Column Names
  - Feature Engineering for Financial Metrics
- Data Visualization
  - Plotting Time Series: Prices, Volume, and Indicators
  - Trend Analysis through Charts
  - Visual Storytelling with Multiple Views and Dashboards

Setting Up an API for Market Data

First, let us set up our API to obtain market data.

Overview of Market Data Providers

Market data providers play a critical role in the financial ecosystem by delivering real-time and historical data on stocks, indices, ETFs, forex, and other financial instruments. These data feeds are essential for traders, analysts, and developers who rely on accurate and timely information to make informed decisions. Depending on the provider, the scope of data may include prices, trading volume, corporate actions, fundamentals, technical indicators, and even alternative datasets such as sentiment or macroeconomic signals.

Some of the most popular market data providers include Alpha Vantage, Yahoo Finance, Polygon.io, IEX Cloud, Quandl, and Tiingo. Each provider offers different levels of access, frequency, and coverage. For instance, Alpha Vantage is widely used for free API access to time-series data and technical indicators, while Polygon.io targets developers who require low-latency data feeds and WebSocket support. Yahoo Finance remains popular for casual investors and offers a user-friendly interface and unofficial APIs. For institutional use or advanced quant research, platforms such as Bloomberg, Refinitiv, and Morningstar provide enterprise-grade data with high reliability and global coverage, albeit at a significantly higher cost.

Choosing the right provider depends on your specific use case: whether it is personal investing, academic research, algorithmic trading, or building data pipelines for financial products. For most entry-level and open-source applications, free or low-cost APIs such as Alpha Vantage or IEX Cloud provide a great starting point.

REST API Fundamentals and Authentication

A Representational State Transfer Application Programming Interface (REST API) is a standardized way for applications to communicate over HTTP. It allows clients like your Python scripts or web applications to request and exchange data with servers that provide services such as market data, news feeds, or financial analytics. REST APIs use simple HTTP methods such as GET, POST, PUT, and DELETE, with GET being the most common for retrieving financial data.

Each API endpoint is typically structured as a URL that represents a resource. For instance, an endpoint like https://api.example.com/stocks/AAPL might return data about Apple Inc.'s stock. Parameters can be passed in the URL as query strings to modify the request, such as specifying the time range, interval, or type of data you want to retrieve. Responses from REST APIs are usually returned in JSON format, which is easy to parse and work with in Python and Polars.

Authentication is a critical component of working with REST APIs, especially when accessing private or rate-limited data. Most market data APIs require an API key, which acts like a password to identify your account and usage. This key is typically passed as a query parameter in your API request (for example, &apikey=YOUR_API_KEY) or included in the HTTP headers.

Some advanced APIs may use OAuth 2.0, which is a more secure and standardized framework for managing access tokens and permissions, which is often seen in institutional-grade data services. However, for most public and free-tier APIs such as Alpha Vantage or IEX Cloud, passing an API key in the query string is sufficient.

It is important to read the documentation of the API provider you are using, as different APIs have different rate limits, endpoints, and authentication mechanisms. Misuse or failure to authenticate properly can result in blocked requests or limited access. For best practices, avoid hardcoding your API key in scripts; consider storing it in environment variables or a configuration file for security and flexibility.

Fetching Real-Time and Historical Data Using Python (Alpha Vantage)

Alpha Vantage offers free access to a wide range of financial market data, including real-time and historical equity data. To begin using it in your data analysis workflow, you first need to obtain a free API key. Please note the free API supports 25 requests per day.

Step-by-Step Guide to Claim Your Free API Key

Step 1: Visit the API Key Page

Go to the Alpha Vantage support page via the following link:

https://www.alphavantage.co/support/#api-key

Step 2: Fill Out the Signup Form

You will see a simple form with the following fields:

Which of the following best describes you?

Choose either:

Investor

Organization (if you are signing up on behalf of a company or institution)

Educator

Software Dev

Organization (Optional):

Enter your company or university name (skip if personal use).

Email:

Enter a valid email address. This is where your API key will be sent.

Step 3: Submit the Form

Click on the **"Get Free API Key"** button. You will immediately see a confirmation message, and your API key will be sent to your inbox.

Step 4: Check Your Email

Look for an email from Alpha Vantage containing your API key. If it does not appear right away, check your spam or promotions folder.

Step 5: Store Your API Key Securely

Save the key in a secure location. You will need it for accessing Alpha Vantage APIs in your code.

Saving API Responses in Structured Formats

Once you fetch data from a market data API, it is good practice to save the response in a structured format. This not only helps preserve the data for offline analysis but also avoids repeatedly hitting the API, which may be rate-limited or subject to changes. Common formats for saving structured data include JSON, CSV, and Parquet, each offering different benefits depending on your use case.

JavaScript Object Notation (JSON) is ideal when you want to preserve the full structure of the API response, especially if it contains nested elements or metadata. It is human-readable and easily parsed by most programming languages. However, for tabular data such as time series (for example, daily stock prices), converting the JSON into a CSV or Parquet format can be more convenient for analysis. CSV files are simple and widely supported, which makes them a good choice for interoperability. On the other hand, Parquet, a columnar binary format, is much more efficient for large datasets, especially when used with high-performance libraries like Polars, as it supports faster reading and selective column loading. Now, let us use the Vantage API to fetch the market data and save it to a file.

```
import requests
import json
# replace the "demo" apikey below with your own key from https://www.
alphavantage.co/support/#api-key
apikey = "<YOUR_APIKEY>"
url = f'https://www.alphavantage.co/query?function=TIME_SERIES_
MONTHLY&symbol=IBM&apikey={apikey}'
r = requests.get(url)
data = r.json()
with open("market_data.json", "w") as f:
    json.dump(data, f, indent=4)
```

The `TIME_SERIES_MONTHLY` function from the Alpha Vantage API provides monthly time series data for a specified global equity, including the open, high, low, close, and volume for the last trading day of each month, with over 20 years of historical coverage. To use this API, you must specify the function=`TIME_SERIES_MONTHLY`, the stock symbol (for example, IBM), and your personal apikey. The optional datatype parameter allows you to choose between JSON (default) and CSV formats for the output.

Loading Market Data into Polars

Let us explore how we can load this data into the Polars DataFrame.

Reading Market Data JSON into Polars DataFrames

Once you have retrieved market data in JSON format from an API like Alpha Vantage, the next step is to load it into a Polars DataFrame for analysis. Since Polars expects tabular data, you will have to extract and transform the relevant portion of the JSON—typically a nested dictionary where each key represents a date and the values contain price and volume information. This data can be converted into a list of records or a dictionary format suitable for Polars. By using Polars' `pl.DataFrame()` constructor or reading from an intermediate format such as CSV or Parquet, you can efficiently load and process large datasets with powerful performance advantages over traditional libraries like Pandas, especially for time series analysis in financial applications.

```
import polars as pl
import json

with open("market_data.json", "r") as f:
    json_data = json.load(f)

# Step 1: Extract "Monthly Time Series"
time_series = json_data["Monthly Time Series"]

# Step 2: Convert to list of dicts with date as a column
records = []
for date, values in time_series.items():
    record = {"date": date}
    record.update({
        "open": float(values["1. open"]),
        "high": float(values["2. high"]),
        "low": float(values["3. low"]),
        "close": float(values["4. close"]),
        "volume": int(values["5. volume"])
    })
    records.append(record)

# Step 3: Create a Polars DataFrame
df = pl.DataFrame(records)
print(df.head())
output :
shape: (5, 6)
```

date --- str	open --- f64	high --- f64	low --- f64	close --- f64	volume --- i64
2025-05-23	241.44	269.28	237.945	258.63	60597210
2025-04-30	248.03	252.79	214.5	241.82	120775331
2025-03-31	254.735	266.45	237.224	248.66	100813990
2025-02-28	252.4	265.72	246.54	252.44	94123851
2025-01-31	221.82	261.8	214.61	255.7	92424171

Schema Inspection and Column Selection

When working with structured data in Polars, it is essential to understand the schema (the structure and data types of the columns) before performing analysis. Schema inspection helps validate that data types are as expected (for example, floats for prices, integers for volume, and strings or dates for timestamps). In Polars, the .schema attribute or the .dtypes method can be used to quickly view the structure of a DataFrame. Once the schema is verified, selective column access is easy using the `select()` method, which allows analysts to focus on relevant fields, such as closing prices or volume, and ignore others for specific tasks such as trend analysis or plotting.

```
# Inspect schema
print(df.schema)  # Shows column names and their data types

# Alternatively, just view data types
print("dtypes" , df.dtypes)
output :
Schema({'date': String, 'open': Float64, 'high': Float64, 'low': Float64, 'close': Float64, 'volume': Int64})
dtypes [String, Float64, Float64, Float64, Float64, Int64]
```

Converting Timestamps and Financial Datatypes

Handling time-series financial data requires converting raw string-based timestamps into an actual date or datetime object. This enables efficient filtering, sorting, and time-based aggregations. Similarly, financial data such as open, high, low, and close prices, and volumes, which is often loaded as strings from JSON, should be explicitly cast to appropriate numeric types such as Float64 or Int64. This ensures mathematical operations and plotting libraries behave as expected. In Polars, the `with_columns()` method is used to apply these transformations efficiently and in a chainable manner. In our current example date has not been inferred correctly, let us rectify it, as shown here:

```
# Convert 'date' to datetime and financial columns to appropriate numeric
types
df = df.with_columns([
    pl.col("date").str.strptime(pl.Date, "%Y-%m-%d").alias("date"),
    pl.col("open").cast(pl.Float64),
    pl.col("high").cast(pl.Float64),
    pl.col("low").cast(pl.Float64),
    pl.col("close").cast(pl.Float64),
    pl.col("volume").cast(pl.Int64)
])
print(df.schema)
output :
Schema({'date': Date, 'open': Float64, 'high': Float64, 'low': Float64,
'close': Float64, 'volume': Int64})
```

Data Cleaning

When working with historical market data, such as the monthly time series of IBM prices, ensuring that the dataset is clean and consistent is a critical first step before conducting any meaningful analysis.

Identifying and Handling Missing or Null Values

One of the most common issues in real-world data is the presence of missing or null values. Although Alpha Vantage generally provides complete datasets, null values might still appear due to market closures, API response errors, or parsing issues. Using Polars, missing values can be identified with `.null_count()` or filtered with `filter(pl.all().is_not_null())`. You may choose to drop rows with missing values or impute them based on logic such as forward-fill or interpolation, depending on the analysis needs.

```
df_clean = df.filter(
    pl.fold(
        acc=pl.lit(True),
        function=lambda acc, col: acc & col.is_not_null(),
        exprs=df.columns
    )
)
```

In the preceding example, `pl.fold()` is used to reduce multiple boolean expressions (like `col.is_not_null()`) into a single boolean by combining them with logical & (AND). This ensures only rows where all values are not null are retained.

Filtering Duplicate Records and Incorrect Entries

Another aspect of cleaning involves removing duplicate records and incorrect entries. Duplicate rows can arise due to repeated API fetches or merging datasets without de-duplication. This can distort time-series calculations such as returns and volatility. Using `.unique()` in Polars helps retain only distinct records. Additionally, sanity checks on fields such as prices (for example, open, close) and volumes can help you detect outliers or nonsensical data, such as negative volumes or prices.

```
# Remove duplicates based on date
df_clean = df_clean.unique(subset=["date"])
```

Normalizing Column Names

Consistency in naming conventions is important for readability and automation. JSON field names such as "1. open" and "5. volume" are better renamed to simpler forms such as open, volume, and so on. This can be done during DataFrame construction or afterward using `.rename()` in Polars.

Feature Engineering for Financial Metrics

With clean data in place, you can now proceed to derive valuable features such as returns, volatility, and moving averages. These features add depth to the raw price data and are often used in algorithmic trading, forecasting, and risk analysis. For instance, simple monthly returns can be calculated as the percentage change in the closing price from one month to the next. Similarly, moving averages smooth out noise and reveal trends, while rolling standard deviations can help quantify volatility.

```
# Sort by date first
df_clean = df_clean.sort("date")

# Calculate monthly return
df_clean = df_clean.with_columns([
      (pl.col("close") / pl.col("close").shift(1) - 1).alias("monthly_
return"),
    pl.col("close").rolling_mean(window_size=3).alias("3M_MA"),
    pl.col("close").rolling_std(window_size=3).alias("3M_volatility")
])

# Sort by date first
df_clean = df_clean.sort("date")

# Calculate monthly return
```

```
df_clean = df_clean.with_columns([
      (pl.col("close") / pl.col("close").shift(1) - 1).alias("monthly_
return"),
    pl.col("close").rolling_mean(window_size=3).alias("3M_MA"),
    pl.col("close").rolling_std(window_size=3).alias("3M_volatility")
])
print(df_clean.head())
```

```
output :
shape: (5, 9)
┌────────────┬─────────┬─────────┬─────────┬─────┬───────────┬────────────────
─┬────────────┬────────────────┐
│ date       ┆ open    ┆ high    ┆ low     ┆ … ┆ volume    ┆ monthly_return
┆ 3M_MA      ┆ 3M_volatility │
│ ---        ┆ ---     ┆ ---     ┆ ---     ┆   ┆ ---       ┆ ---            │
---        ┆ ---           │
│ date       ┆ f64     ┆ f64     ┆ f64     ┆   ┆ i64       ┆ f64            │
f64        ┆ f64           │
╞════════════╪═════════╪═════════╪═════════╪═════╪═══════════╪════════════════
═╪════════════╪════════════════╡
│ 1999-12-31 ┆ 102.56 ┆ 122.12 ┆ 102.25 ┆ … ┆ 158626300 ┆ null           │
null       ┆ null          │
│ 2000-01-31 ┆ 112.44 ┆ 124.75 ┆ 109.62 ┆ … ┆ 175259600 ┆ 0.040604       │
null       ┆ null          │
│ 2000-02-29 ┆ 112.37 ┆ 119.75 ┆ 100.94 ┆ … ┆ 133524400 ┆ -0.084633      │
107.623333 ┆ 4.754801      │
│ 2000-03-31 ┆ 102.0  ┆ 128.25 ┆ 99.5    ┆ … ┆ 194329000 ┆ 0.152019       │
111.123333 ┆ 7.870714      │
│ 2000-04-28 ┆ 120.0  ┆ 128.0  ┆ 101.25 ┆ … ┆ 168464800 ┆ -0.058038      │
110.873333 ┆ 7.828833      │
└────────────┴─────────┴─────────┴─────────┴─────┴───────────┴────────────────
─┴────────────┴────────────────┘
```

These engineered features transform raw market data into actionable insights that are essential for building financial models and visual dashboards. With Polars' performance and expressiveness, these operations are not only simple, but also scalable for large datasets.

Data Visualization

Polars excel at fast and efficient data manipulation, which makes it an ideal preprocessing engine before passing data to visualization libraries like Altair.

Plotting Time Series: Prices, Volume, and Indicators

With the data converted, plotting time series such as open, close, high, low, and volume over time is straightforward. Time series charts help visualize price evolution, while trading volume trends, and market behavior over time. For example, you can use Altair's line and area marks to show stock price changes and volume fluctuations, as shown here:

```
import altair as alt
price_chart = alt.Chart(df_clean).mark_line().encode(
    x='date:T',
    y='close:Q',
    tooltip=['date:T', 'close:Q']
).properties(title='IBM Monthly Closing Price')

volume_chart = alt.Chart(df_clean).mark_area(opacity=0.3).encode(
    x='date:T',
    y='volume:Q'
).properties(title='IBM Monthly Volume')
```

Output:

***Figure 11.1**: IBM Monthly Prices*

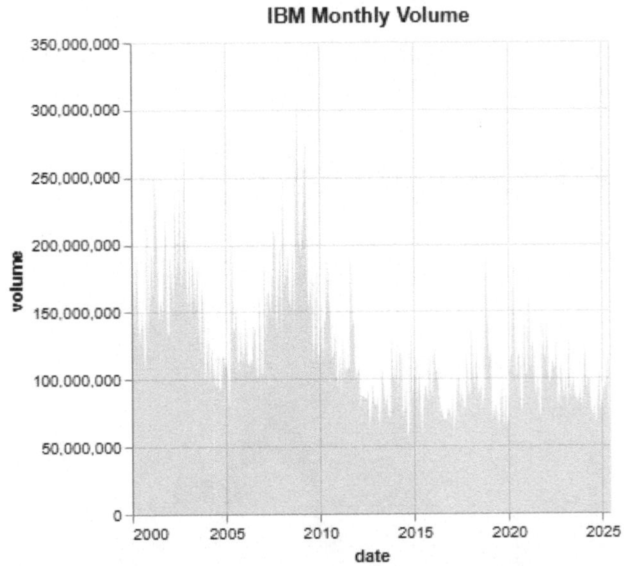

***Figure 11.2**: IBM Monthly Volume*

Trend Analysis through Charts

Candlestick charts are powerful tools for trend analysis in financial time series, offering visual insights into price movements over specific periods. Each candlestick encapsulates the open, high, low, and close (OHLC) prices, which makes it easy to interpret market sentiment at a glance. When plotted sequentially, these candlesticks form recognizable patterns such as bullish engulfing, doji, or hammer formations that signal trend reversals or continuations. Traders and analysts use these patterns to identify bullish or bearish momentum, assess volatility, and confirm breakouts or consolidations. By analyzing clusters of candlesticks and their formations, users can track upward or downward trends over time, detect market shifts, and make more informed trading decisions. Candlestick charts, therefore, not only highlight historical price behavior, but also help anticipate future market direction through pattern recognition.

```
# Rule for high-low, bar for open-close
high_low = alt.Chart(df_clean).mark_rule().encode(
    x='date',
    y='low',
    y2='high'
)

open_close = alt.Chart(df_clean).mark_bar().encode(
    x='date',
    y='open',
```

```
    y2='close',
     color=alt.condition('datum.close > datum.open', alt.value('green'),
alt.value('red'))
)
candlestick = high_low + open_close
```

Output:

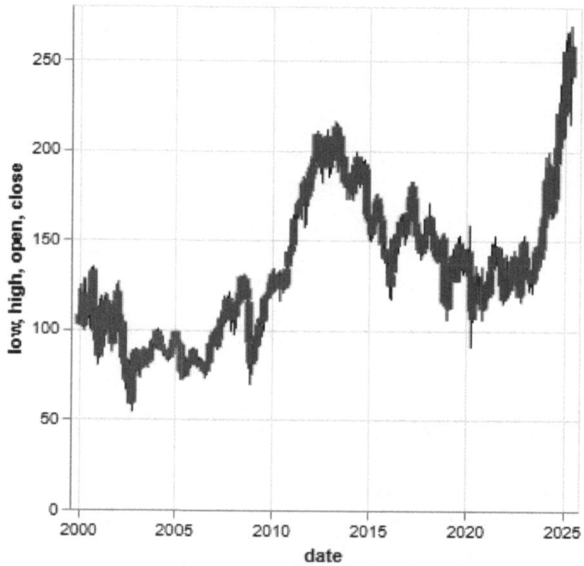

***Figure 11.3**: Candlestick Chart*

Overall Trend (2000–2025):

- **2000–2008:** The market showed a relatively sideways or slightly bearish trend with moderate fluctuations and no strong directional movement.
- **2009–2015:** A clear uptrend is visible, which is marked by a consistent rise in prices. This phase likely reflects a recovery or growth cycle in the underlying asset or index.
- **2016–2020:** The market moved sideways again, forming a consolidation range with multiple pullbacks and short-term rallies.
- **2021–2025:** A strong bullish trend emerged. This period saw a sharp and steady rise in prices, pushing the value above previous highs. This possibly implies renewed investor confidence or positive fundamental changes.

Candlestick Patterns:

- The chart shows green candles dominating during bull phases and red candles during corrections.

- The alternating colors during consolidation phases suggest market indecision and frequent short-term reversals.
- The long wicks in some candles imply volatility, with prices fluctuating significantly within a single period before settling.

Price Volatility:

Noticeable increase in volatility around 2008–2009 and again post-2020. This could correspond to major economic or market events (for example, financial crises, pandemics, policy changes).

The most recent surge in price (2022–2025) also shows larger candle bodies, which indicate strong momentum and high trading volumes.

Visual Storytelling with Multiple Views and Dashboards

Altair's layered and concatenated charts enable the construction of dashboards for exploratory analysis or reporting. You can create a multi-view layout that includes closing prices, trading volume, and technical indicators such as volatility, returns, or moving averages. These dashboards can be used to tell a visual story; for example, how market volatility aligns with macro events or earnings reports.

```
dashboard = alt.hconcat(
    price_chart,
    volume_chart,
    trend_chart
).resolve_scale(
    x='shared'
)
```

Output :

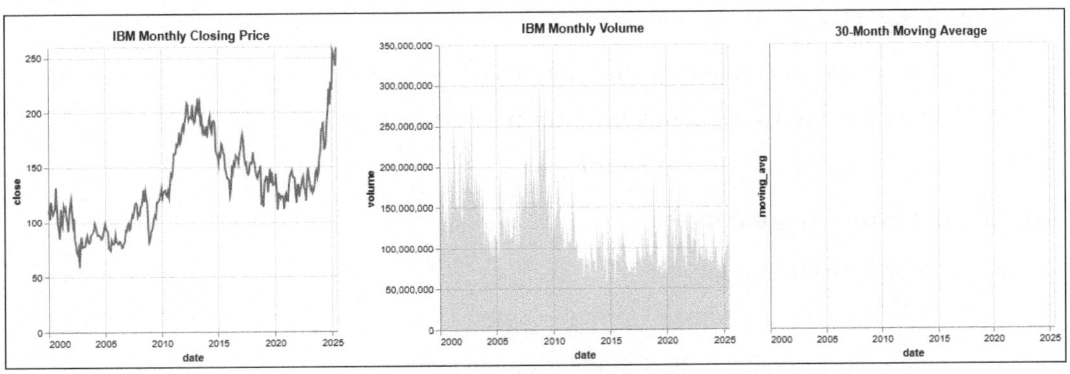

Figure 11.4: *Dashboard View*

Conclusion

In this chapter, we explored a comprehensive data analysis workflow using Polars, while focusing on financial time series. Starting with schema inspection and column selection, we emphasized the importance of understanding dataset structure. We then processed the data through timestamps and financial type conversions to ensure readiness for temporal analysis. Our data cleaning steps tackled missing values, duplicates, and inconsistent types, and laid a strong foundation for accurate insights. We engineered new features such as returns and volatility, thereby enhancing the dataset's analytical value.

With Altair, we created meaningful visualizations—from candlestick charts to anomaly detection using IQR plots, which brought the dataset to life. These visual stories not only revealed historical trends, but also uncovered critical deviations. They ultimately helped us in recognizing patterns and developing strategies.

In the next chapter, we will explore the topic of ML with Polars, where you will learn how to prepare features, build predictive models, and evaluate performance, all while leveraging the speed and efficiency of the Polars engine.

Exercise Tasks

Exercise 1: Fetch Market Data Using Vantage API

a. Sign up and get a free API key from Alpha Vantage.
b. Use the TIME_SERIES_DAILY_ADJUSTED endpoint to download daily stock data (for example, MSFT, AAPL, GOOGL).
c. Convert the API response (JSON or CSV) into a Polars DataFrame.
d. Inspect the schema and preview the first few rows.

Exercise 2: Data Cleaning and Preparation

a. Handle missing or null values.
b. Rename and normalize column names (for example, lowercase, snake_case).
c. Convert string timestamps to datetime types.
d. Cast numeric columns to Float64.

Exercise 3: Feature Engineering

a. Create new columns for:
    - Daily return: (close - open) / open
    - Rolling average (10-day) of close prices

- Rolling volatility (10-day) of returns

b. Filter data between two dates (for example, 2020–2023).

Exercise 4: Data Visualization Using Altair

a. Plot a candlestick chart using open, high, low, and close prices.

b. Plot daily return over time to observe volatility spikes.

c. Create an IQR-based chart to detect outliers in volume.

d. Combine multiple views (prices, volume, trends) in a dashboard layout.

CHAPTER 12
Machine Learning with Polars

"Machine Learning is the science of getting computers to act without being explicitly programmed."

Arthur Samuel

Introduction

In the modern data science workflow, efficiently preparing and modeling data is just as important as selecting the right algorithms. This chapter introduces how to leverage the performance and expressiveness of Polars in combination with Scikit-learn, which is a widely used machine learning toolkit. By using Polars for data manipulation and Scikit-learn for modeling, you can build robust machine learning pipelines that scale with large datasets while maintaining readable and performant code.

We will begin with Exploratory Data Analysis (EDA) to understand the underlying structure and patterns of the data. From there, we will cover data cleaning techniques to address missing or inconsistent values, ensuring the dataset is ready for modeling. Next, we will dive into data transformation, including encoding categorical variables and feature scaling, which are essential steps for preparing data for Machine Learning (ML) models.

Finally, we demonstrate how to integrate Polars with Scikit-learn to build and evaluate models efficiently. Thus, whether you are handling tabular data at scale or building quick prototypes, this chapter will provide a practical foundation for incorporating ML into your Polars-based data analysis projects.

Structure

In this chapter, we will discuss the following topics:

- Introduction to Machine Learning with Polars and Scikit-learn
- Loading and Inspecting Data with Polars
- Exploratory Data Analysis (EDA)
- Data Cleaning with Polars
- Integrating Polars with Scikit-learn
- Building an ML Pipeline Using Polars

Introduction to Machine Learning with Polars and Scikit-learn

ML workflows often involve much more than just selecting a model and training it. A significant portion of the work lies in preparing and transforming the data into a form that models can understand and learn from effectively. In traditional data science pipelines, this preparation is typically handled using libraries like Pandas. However, as datasets grow in size and complexity, performance and scalability become critical. This is where Polars, a high-performance DataFrame library, becomes a powerful alternative. Combined with Scikit-learn, one of the most widely used ML libraries in Python, it is possible to build highly efficient and scalable ML pipelines without sacrificing flexibility or ease of use.

This chapter focuses on bridging the strengths of Polars for data manipulation and Scikit-learn for ML. You will begin by learning how to use Polars to load, explore, and clean datasets efficiently. From there, the chapter guides you through transforming data for modeling, converting it into formats that Scikit-learn can work with, and finally, training and evaluating models. The goal is to provide a seamless and optimized data science workflow by using tools that are expressive and performant.

The motivation for combining Polars and Scikit-learn lies in their complementary design. Polars is designed for high-performance data wrangling and computation, while leveraging Rust under the hood and supporting lazy evaluation and parallel execution. It offers syntax that is both concise and powerful, which makes complex transformations easier to express and execute at scale. On the other hand, Scikit-learn provides a comprehensive suite of ML algorithms, tools for model selection, and utilities for evaluation—all under a unified and well-documented API.

Hence, by using Polars for preprocessing and Scikit-learn for modeling, you gain the ability to handle larger-than-memory datasets, optimize transformation pipelines, and maintain a smooth transition from raw data to deployable model. This approach also promotes modular and reusable code, where the same preprocessing logic can be tested and reused across different models or datasets. In essence, you are building not just models, but sustainable and scalable ML systems.

In the sections that follow, we will walk you through the essential components of this workflow: from exploratory data analysis (EDA), data cleaning, and transformation, to training and evaluating ML models. You will also see how to integrate Polars data structures with Scikit-learn workflows, and how to build end-to-end pipelines that are both readable and efficient. Thus, whether you are working with small experimental data or production-scale pipelines, this approach will enhance both performance and maintainability in your ML projects.

Loading and Inspecting Data with Polars

Before any data analysis or ML can begin, the first step is to load the data and understand its structure. Polars provides a fast and memory-efficient way to read and handle large datasets. It supports a variety of file formats, including CSV, Parquet, JSON, and IPC (Feather), making it well-suited for both raw and pre-processed data. The pl.read_csv() function is commonly used to read tabular data into a DataFrame, and due to Polars' underlying Rust-based engine, it can load even large files significantly faster than traditional libraries like Pandas.

For instance, a simple command like `pl.read_csv("data/loan_data.csv")` returns a Polars DataFrame ready for inspection. If you are working with structured and compressed data formats like Parquet, Polars can read them using pl.read_parquet() with even better speed and lower memory overhead. These read functions support chunked and lazy evaluation modes, which allows developers to load data eagerly into memory or defer execution until needed. This is particularly helpful in performance-sensitive workflows.

Once the dataset is loaded, the next step is to explore its schema and understand the data types of each column. Polars provides a clear view of the column names and their associated data types using the .schema attribute or by simply printing the DataFrame. This is crucial because ML models rely on numerical and categorical data, and misinterpreted types (like treating a numeric column as a string) can lead to model errors or incorrect pre-processing. Polars infers types automatically but also allows manual overrides during reading or transformation.

To get an initial sense of the data, Polars provide several methods for previewing and summarizing the contents of a DataFrame. You can use `.head()` to view the first few rows and `.describe()` to generate summary statistics such as mean, min, max, and standard deviation for numerical columns. Grouped statistics can be obtained using `.group_by()` in combination with aggregation functions like `.mean()` or `.count()`. While Polars is not a visualization library, combining it with Matplotlib or Seaborn enables rich visual EDA, while leveraging Polars' speed and expressiveness for data manipulation.

In summary, Polars make the first step of any ML project not only fast, but also intuitive. Its ability to handle large datasets efficiently, along with clear and concise APIs for schema inspection and basic analysis, makes it an excellent tool for data scientists looking to streamline their ML workflows from the very beginning.

Exploratory Data Analysis (EDA)

Exploratory Data Analysis (EDA) is a crucial step in any data science or ML project. It involves exploring datasets to summarize their main characteristics, often using visual and statistical techniques. With Polars, EDA becomes both efficient and expressive, particularly when working with large or high-dimensional datasets. For this section, we will use a botany-based dataset, such as one containing measurements of various plant species (for example, petal length, leaf area, stem diameter, and moisture content) along with categorical information like species, habitat, or sunlight exposure.

The first step in EDA is to generate summary statistics for numerical features. In Polars, this can be done using the .describe() method, which provides insights into the central tendency, dispersion, and distribution shape of each variable. For example, summary statistics on features like leaf_area and petal_length can quickly reveal skewed distributions or extreme outliers in particular plant species. In a botanical dataset, these values help distinguish between large-leaved tropical plants and small, drought-resistant shrubs.

Grouping and aggregation are essential for uncovering trends across different categories, such as species or environmental conditions. With Polars, you can use .group_by() and aggregation functions like `.mean()`, `.median()`, or `.max()` to analyze patterns. For instance, grouping the data by species and calculating the average moisture_content and stem_diameter allows you to compare physiological traits between species. You might observe that plants found in wetland habitats have higher average moisture content, while desert species show the opposite trend, forming a biologically meaningful pattern.

While Polars excels at data transformation and grouping, visualizations are best handled by complementary libraries like Matplotlib or Seaborn. After computing aggregates with Polars, you can convert the results to Pandas using `.to_pandas()` for visualization. For example, a boxplot of petal_length grouped by species helps visually assess the variance and distribution among plant types. Scatter plots of leaf_area versus moisture_content, colored by habitat, may reveal clusters or linear relationships that could be important for classification tasks.

Identifying correlations and patterns is another core aspect of EDA. You can compute Pearson or Spearman correlations between numeric variables using Polars or external libraries like NumPy. A correlation matrix for features like leaf_thickness, root_depth, and stem_height could reveal strong interdependencies; for instance, deep-rooted plants may tend to have thicker leaves as an adaptation to arid conditions. Understanding these relationships informs which features are likely to be predictive in an ML model.

In summary, EDA with Polars allows for rapid, in-memory analysis even on complex botanical datasets. Its integration with Python's visualization ecosystem makes it easy to gain both numerical and visual understanding of the data, which is essential before you move on to building models. By exploring the data through summary statistics, grouped aggregates, and correlation analysis, you can lay a strong foundation for effective data preprocessing and modeling.

```
import polars as pl
import altair as alt
import pandas as pd

# Step 1: Create a synthetic botany dataset
data = pl.DataFrame({
    "species": [
        "Oak", "Cactus", "Lotus", "Pine", "Cactus", "Lotus", "Oak",
"Pine", "Oak", "Cactus"
    ],
    "leaf_area": [
        120.5, 30.1, 85.7, 95.3, 28.9, 88.0, 122.0, 97.5, 115.0, 31.2
    ],
    "petal_length": [
        5.3, 1.2, 6.0, 3.5, 1.0, 6.2, 5.1, 3.8, 5.7, 1.1
    ],
    "stem_diameter": [
        2.4, 1.5, 2.1, 2.3, 1.4, 2.0, 2.5, 2.2, 2.6, 1.3
    ],
    "moisture_content": [
        45.0, 18.2, 70.0, 40.1, 17.9, 72.5, 46.0, 42.3, 47.2, 19.0
    ],
    "habitat": [
        "Forest", "Desert", "Wetland", "Forest", "Desert", "Wetland",
"Forest", "Forest", "Forest", "Desert"
    ]
})

print("=== Data Preview ===")
print(data.head())

output :
=== Data Preview ===
```

```
shape: (5, 6)
┌─────────┬───────────┬──────────────┬───────────────┬──────────────────
─┬────────┐
│ species ┆ leaf_area ┆ petal_length ┆ stem_diameter ┆ moisture_content
┆ habitat │
│ ---     ┆ ---       ┆ ---          ┆ ---           ┆ ---
┆ ---     │
│ str     ┆ f64       ┆ f64          ┆ f64           ┆ f64
┆ str     │
╞═════════╪═══════════╪══════════════╪═══════════════╪══════════════════
═╪════════╡
│ Oak     ┆ 120.5     ┆ 5.3          ┆ 2.4           ┆ 45.0
┆ Forest  │
│ Cactus  ┆ 30.1      ┆ 1.2          ┆ 1.5           ┆ 18.2
┆ Desert  │
│ Lotus   ┆ 85.7      ┆ 6.0          ┆ 2.1           ┆ 70.0
┆ Wetland │
│ Pine    ┆ 95.3      ┆ 3.5          ┆ 2.3           ┆ 40.1
┆ Forest  │
│ Cactus  ┆ 28.9      ┆ 1.0          ┆ 1.4           ┆ 17.9
┆ Desert  │
└─────────┴───────────┴──────────────┴───────────────┴──────────────────
─┴────────┘
```

Summary and Statistics:

```
print("\n=== Summary Statistics ===")
print(data.describe())

print("\n=== Average Moisture and Stem Diameter by Species ===")
agg = data.group_by("species").agg([
    pl.col("moisture_content").mean().alias("avg_moisture"),
    pl.col("stem_diameter").mean().alias("avg_stem_diameter")
])
print(agg)
```

Output:

```
=== Summary Statistics ===
shape: (9, 7)
┌────────────┬─────────┬───────────┬──────────────┬───────────────┬
──────────────────┬─────────┐
│ statistic  ┆ species ┆ leaf_area ┆ petal_length ┆ stem_diameter ┆
moisture_content ┆ habitat │
│ ---        ┆ ---     ┆ ---       ┆ ---          ┆ ---           ┆ ---
┆ ---     │
```

```
│ str          ┆ str      ┆ f64       ┆ f64          ┆ f64         ┆ f64
┆ str      │
╞══════════════╪══════════╪═══════════╪══════════════╪═════════════╪═══════════
═════════════╪══════════╡
│ count        ┆ 10       ┆ 10.0      ┆ 10.0         ┆ 10.0        ┆ 10.0
┆ 10       │
│ null_count   ┆ 0        ┆ 0.0       ┆ 0.0          ┆ 0.0         ┆ 0.0
┆ 0        │
│ mean         ┆ null     ┆ 81.42     ┆ 3.89         ┆ 2.03        ┆
41.82            ┆ null    │
│ std          ┆ null     ┆ 37.606997 ┆ 2.109476     ┆ 0.471522    ┆
19.567308        ┆ null    │
│ min          ┆ Cactus   ┆ 28.9      ┆ 1.0          ┆ 1.3         ┆ 17.9
┆ Desert   │
│ 25%          ┆ null     ┆ 31.2      ┆ 1.2          ┆ 1.5         ┆ 19.0
┆ null     │
│ 50%          ┆ null     ┆ 95.3      ┆ 5.1          ┆ 2.2         ┆ 45.0
┆ null     │
│ 75%          ┆ null     ┆ 115.0     ┆ 5.7          ┆ 2.4         ┆ 47.2
┆ null     │
│ max          ┆ Pine     ┆ 122.0     ┆ 6.2          ┆ 2.6         ┆ 72.5
┆ Wetland  │
└──────────────┴──────────┴───────────┴──────────────┴─────────────┴───────────
─────────────┴──────────┘

=== Average Moisture and Stem Diameter by Species ===
shape: (4, 3)
┌─────────┬──────────────┬──────────────────┐
│ species ┆ avg_moisture ┆ avg_stem_diameter │
│ ---     ┆ ---          ┆ ---              │
│ str     ┆ f64          ┆ f64              │
╞═════════╪══════════════╪══════════════════╡
│ Oak     ┆ 46.066667    ┆ 2.5              │
│ Cactus  ┆ 18.366667    ┆ 1.4              │
│ Pine    ┆ 41.2         ┆ 2.25             │
│ Lotus   ┆ 71.25        ┆ 2.05             │
└─────────┴──────────────┴──────────────────┘
```

Outlier visualization :

```
# Convert to pandas for Altair

# Create a strip plot (alternative to boxplot)
alt.Chart(data).mark_boxplot(extent='min-max').encode(
    x=alt.X('species:N', title='Species'),
    y=alt.Y('petal_length:Q', title='Petal Length')
).properties(
```

```
    title='Petal Length Distribution by Species',
    width=500,
    height=300
)
```

Output:

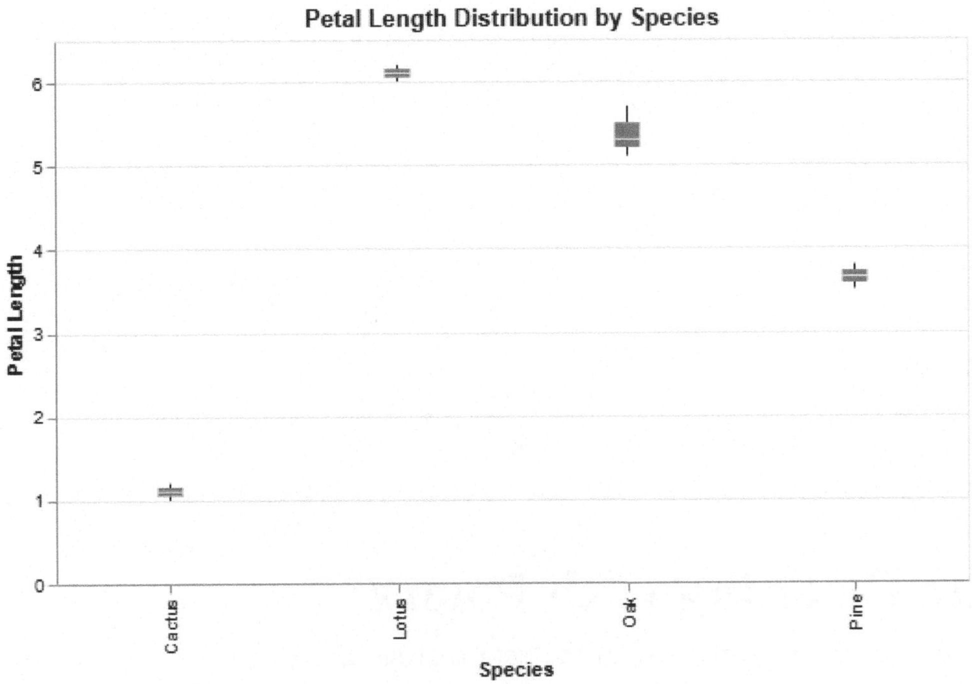

Figure 12.1: *Outlier Visualization Using Box Plot*

Here is an example of a scatter plot to check data characteristics across landscapes:

```
alt.Chart(data).mark_circle(size=100).encode(
    x=alt.X('leaf_area:Q', title='Leaf Area'),
    y=alt.Y('moisture_content:Q', title='Moisture Content'),
    color='habitat:N',
    tooltip=['species', 'leaf_area', 'moisture_content', 'habitat']
).properties(
    title='Leaf Area vs Moisture Content by Habitat',
    width=500,
    height=300
).interactive()
```

output :

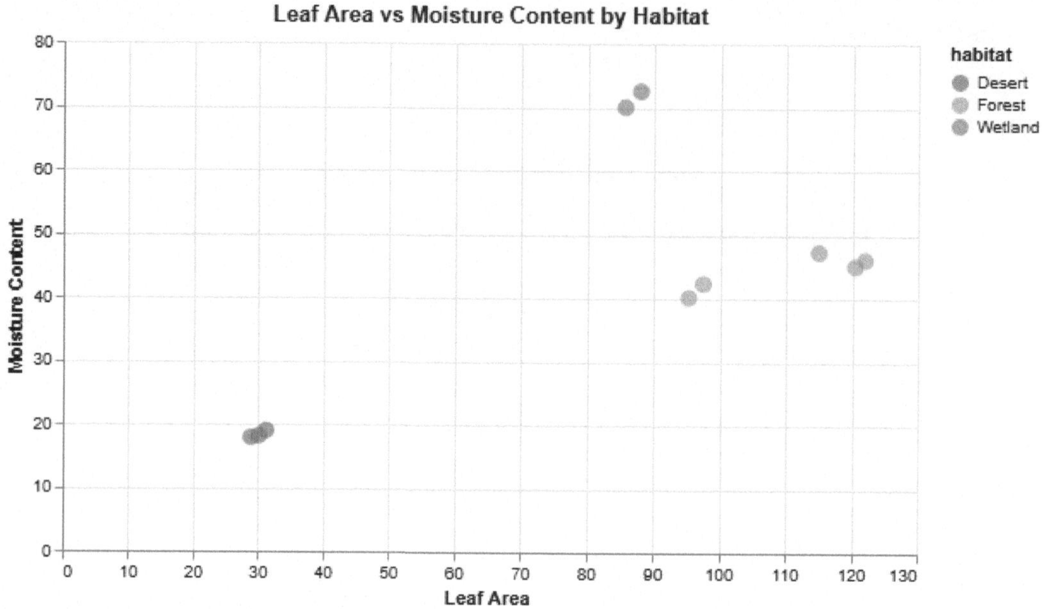

Figure 12.2: *Relationship between Landscapes, Leaf Area and, Moisture Content*

Data Cleaning with Polars

Data cleaning is a critical phase in the data analysis and ML pipeline. Regardless of the domain, real-world datasets often contain inconsistencies such as missing values, outliers, incorrect data types, or improperly formatted entries. In the context of botany or forestry data, messy datasets may include inconsistent units for leaf size, missing moisture readings, or misrecorded timestamps. Polars offers a highly performant and expressive API to handle such irregularities efficiently, especially when dealing with large observational datasets collected in the field.

Detecting and Handling Missing Values

Missing data is common in forest datasets due to sensor malfunctions or human recording errors. For example, a CSV file recording hourly moisture readings might have nulls where the sensor failed. In Polars, missing values (nulls) can be detected using `pl.col("column").is_null()` and handled via `.fill_null()` or `.drop_nulls()`. One might choose to fill missing `moisture_content` values with the median of the column or interpolate values from neighboring timestamps in a time series context.

```
raw = pl.DataFrame({
    "leaf_area (cm2)": [120, None, 30, 9999, 85],
    "moisture": ["45", "NaN", "18.2", "", "70"],
```

```
    "logged_time": ["2024-06-01 08:00:00", "2024-06-01 09:00:00", "",
"2024-06-01 11:00:00", "2024-06-01 12:00:00"]
})

# Clean it
clean = (
    raw
    .with_columns([
        pl.col("leaf_area (cm2)").fill_null(strategy="mean").alias("leaf_
area"),
        pl.col("moisture").str.replace_all("NaN", "").str.strip_chars().
cast(pl.Float64,strict=False).fill_null(0.0),
        pl.col("logged_time").str.strptime(pl.Datetime, format="%Y-%m-%d
%H:%M:%S", strict=False).alias("timestamp")
    ])
    .drop(["leaf_area (cm2)"])
)

print(clean)
```

output :

```
shape: (5, 4)
```

moisture --- f64	logged_time --- str	leaf_area --- i64	timestamp --- datetime[μs]
45.0	2024-06-01 08:00:00	120	2024-06-01 08:00:00
0.0	2024-06-01 09:00:00	2558	2024-06-01 09:00:00
18.2		30	null
0.0	2024-06-01 11:00:00	9999	2024-06-01 11:00:00
70.0	2024-06-01 12:00:00	85	2024-06-01 12:00:00

Integrating Polars with Scikit-learn

As Polars gain popularity for its blazing-fast DataFrame operations, its integration into ML workflows is becoming increasingly seamless. With the release of Scikit-learn 1.4, Polars DataFrames are now natively supported as inputs and outputs for all transformers and as input to estimators. This advancement marks a significant improvement in the ML ecosystem, where developers can now enjoy the performance benefits of Polars and leverage Scikit-learn's mature and well-documented model building capabilities.

One of the most common tasks in ML is fitting simple models like Logistic Regression and Decision Trees. Traditionally, this would involve converting your data from a DataFrame (usually Pandas) to NumPy arrays before model fitting. With native support for Polars in Scikit-learn 1.4, this conversion is no longer necessary. You can pass a Polars DataFrame directly to the fit() method of estimators like LogisticRegression, DecisionTreeClassifier, and pipelines. This simplification reduces overhead, improves readability, and enables the use of Polars' efficient memory management throughout the ML pipeline.

For example, consider a binary classification problem where we predict whether a tree species is drought-tolerant based on features like leaf area, stem diameter, and moisture content. After preprocessing and encoding categorical variables using Polars, the resultant DataFrame can be passed directly to Scikit-learn's logistic regression model without any transformation. This eliminates the need for intermediate Pandas conversions and maintains consistency in data processing.

When working with categorical or datetime features in Polars, it is often helpful to use libraries like skrub, which is designed to simplify encoding and transformation of rich tabular data for Scikit-learn. skrub can automatically convert string columns and datetime fields into numeric encodings suitable for ML models. This complements Polars well, especially since Polars offer excellent support for string and datetime types natively. For instance, you can preprocess your features in Polars, convert them to string or datetime formats, and let skrub handle the encoding before feeding them into Scikit-learn pipelines.

Here is an example:

```
from sklearn.linear_model import LogisticRegression
from sklearn.model_selection import train_test_split
import polars as pl

# Example Polars DataFrame
df = pl.DataFrame({
    "leaf_area": [120, 30, 85, 95, 28, 88, 122, 97],
    "stem_diameter": [2.4, 1.5, 2.1, 2.3, 1.4, 2.0, 2.5, 2.2],
    "moisture_content": [45, 18, 70, 40, 17, 72, 46, 42],
    "drought_tolerant": [1, 1, 0, 0, 1, 0, 0, 0]  # binary target
})

# Train-test split
X = df.drop("drought_tolerant")
y = df["drought_tolerant"]
X_train, X_test, y_train, y_test = train_test_split(X, y, test_
size=0.25)

# Fit logistic regression directly with Polars DataFrame
```

```
model = LogisticRegression()
model.fit(X_train, y_train)
print(model.get_params())
```

output :

```
{'C': 1.0, 'class_weight': None, 'dual': False, 'fit_intercept': True,
'intercept_scaling': 1, 'l1_ratio': None, 'max_iter': 100, 'multi_
class': 'deprecated', 'n_jobs': None, 'penalty': 'l2', 'random_state':
None, 'solver': 'lbfgs', 'tol': 0.0001, 'verbose': 0, 'warm_start':
False}
```

Building an ML Pipeline Using Polars

The Iris dataset is one of the most well-known datasets in data science. It contains 150 records of iris flower measurements from three species: Setosa, Versicolor, and Virginica. In this tutorial, we will walk through how to load, explore, and classify the Iris dataset using Polars for data manipulation and Scikit-learn 1.4+ for modeling.

Each instance in the dataset represents a flower, with four features:

- Sepal length (cm)
- Sepal width (cm)
- Petal length (cm)
- Petal width (cm)

The target variable (label) is one of the three classes mentioned here:

- 0: Setosa
- 1: Versicolor
- 2: Virginica

Scikit-learn 1.4+ supports Polars DataFrames natively for transformers and model input, which allows us to benefit from Polars' blazing-fast performance, while staying within Scikit-learn's ecosystem.

We will use Polars for:

- Loading and transforming data
- Quick exploration and analysis

And Scikit-learn for:

- Splitting data
- Modeling with Logistic Regression
- Evaluation

```
import polars as pl
from sklearn.datasets import load_iris

# Load the iris dataset
iris_raw = load_iris(as_frame=True)

# Convert to Polars DataFrame
df = pl.read_csv("iris.csv")
print(df.head(10))
output :
shape: (10, 5)
```

sepal_length --- f64	sepal_width --- f64	petal_length --- f64	petal_width --- f64	species --- str
5.1	3.5	1.4	0.2	setosa
4.9	3.0	1.4	0.2	setosa
4.7	3.2	1.3	0.2	setosa
4.6	3.1	1.5	0.2	setosa
5.0	3.6	1.4	0.2	setosa
5.4	3.9	1.7	0.4	setosa
4.6	3.4	1.4	0.3	setosa
5.0	3.4	1.5	0.2	setosa
4.4	2.9	1.4	0.2	setosa
4.9	3.1	1.5	0.1	setosa

Let us add a target name column for modelling:

```
species_map = {"setosa" : 0, "versicolor" :1 , "virginica":3}
df = df.with_columns([
    df["species"].replace(species_map).alias("target")
])
print(df.head(10))
```

output :

```
shape: (10, 6)

| sepal_length | sepal_width | petal_length | petal_width | species |
target |
| ---          | ---         | ---          | ---         | ---     |
---    |
```

```
│ f64        ┆ f64        ┆ f64        ┆ f64        ┆ str       ┆
str    │
╞════════════╪════════════╪════════════╪════════════╪═══════════╪
═══════╡
│ 5.1        ┆ 3.5        ┆ 1.4        ┆ 0.2        ┆ setosa    ┆
0      │
│ 4.9        ┆ 3.0        ┆ 1.4        ┆ 0.2        ┆ setosa    ┆
0      │
│ 4.7        ┆ 3.2        ┆ 1.3        ┆ 0.2        ┆ setosa    ┆
0      │
│ 4.6        ┆ 3.1        ┆ 1.5        ┆ 0.2        ┆ setosa    ┆
0      │
│ 5.0        ┆ 3.6        ┆ 1.4        ┆ 0.2        ┆ setosa    ┆
0      │
│ 5.4        ┆ 3.9        ┆ 1.7        ┆ 0.4        ┆ setosa    ┆
0      │
│ 4.6        ┆ 3.4        ┆ 1.4        ┆ 0.3        ┆ setosa    ┆
0      │
│ 5.0        ┆ 3.4        ┆ 1.5        ┆ 0.2        ┆ setosa    ┆
0      │
│ 4.4        ┆ 2.9        ┆ 1.4        ┆ 0.2        ┆ setosa    ┆
0      │
│ 4.9        ┆ 3.1        ┆ 1.5        ┆ 0.1        ┆ setosa    ┆
0      │
└────────────┴────────────┴────────────┴────────────┴───────────┴
───────┘
```

Let us visualize the dataset to identify visible patterns:

```
import altair as alt
import pandas as pd
# Create Altair chart
chart = alt.Chart(df).mark_point().encode(
    x='petal_length',
    y='petal_width',
    color='species',
    tooltip=['species', 'petal_length', 'petal_width']
).properties(
    width=600,
    height=400,
    title='Iris_Flower_Petal_Measurements'
).interactive()

chart.show()
```

output :

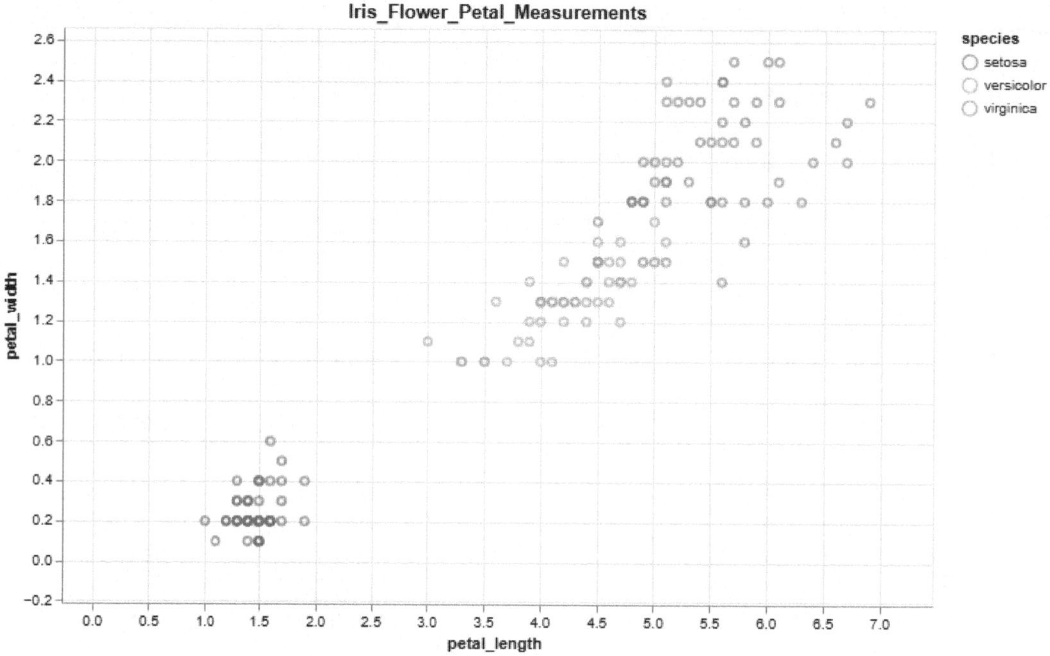

Figure 12.3: *Relationship between Petal Width and Length*

Let us prepare the data for modeling with pipelines:

```
from sklearn.model_selection import train_test_split
from sklearn.pipeline import Pipeline
from sklearn.preprocessing import StandardScaler
from sklearn.compose import ColumnTransformer
from sklearn.linear_model import LogisticRegression

# Select only petal measurements and cast target to integer
X = df.select(["petal_length", "petal_width"])
y = df["target"].cast(int)

X_train, X_test, y_train, y_test = train_test_split(X, y.to_numpy(),
test_size=0.5, random_state=42)

# Create preprocessing and model pipeline
pipeline = Pipeline([
    ("scaler", StandardScaler()),
    ("classifier", LogisticRegression(max_iter=200))
])

# Fit the pipeline
pipeline.fit(X_train, y_train)
```

We need to evaluate the ML model we created using metrics, as shown here:

```
from sklearn.metrics import classification_report, confusion_matrix

# Predictions
train_pred = pipeline.predict(X_train)
test_pred = pipeline.predict(X_test)

print("Training Performance:\n")
print(classification_report(y_train, train_pred))
print(confusion_matrix(y_train, train_pred))

print("\nTesting Performance:\n")
print(classification_report(y_test, test_pred))
print(confusion_matrix(y_test, test_pred))
```

output :

```
Training Performance:

              precision    recall  f1-score   support

           0       1.00      1.00      1.00        21
           1       0.89      0.89      0.89        27
           3       0.89      0.89      0.89        27

    accuracy                           0.92        75
   macro avg       0.93      0.93      0.93        75
weighted avg       0.92      0.92      0.92        75

[[21  0  0]
 [ 0 24  3]
 [ 0  3 24]]

Testing Performance:

              precision    recall  f1-score   support

           0       1.00      1.00      1.00        29
           1       0.96      1.00      0.98        23
           3       1.00      0.96      0.98        23

    accuracy                           0.99        75
   macro avg       0.99      0.99      0.99        75
weighted avg       0.99      0.99      0.99        75

[[29  0  0]
 [ 0 23  0]
 [ 0  1 22]]
```

Let us try to understand the metric performance:

Training Performance

The model scored 92% accuracy on the training set. Here is what the classification report tells us:

Class	Precision	Recall	F1-score	Support
Setosa (0)	1.00	1.00	1.00	21
Versicolor (1)	0.89	0.89	0.89	27
Virginica (2)	0.89	0.89	0.89	27

Precision measures how many predicted members of a class are actually correct. Recall shows how many actual members of a class were correctly predicted. F1-score is the harmonic mean of precision and recall.

Confusion Matrix (Train):

```
             Predicted
              0   1   2
            -----------
Actual  0 | 21   0   0
        1 |  0  24   3
        2 |  0   3  24
```

Testing Performance

On unseen data, the model achieved 99% accuracy, which is extremely high.

Class	Precision	Recall	F1-score	Support
Setosa (0)	1.00	1.00	1.00	29
Versicolor (1)	0.96	1.00	0.98	23
Virginica (2)	1.00	0.96	0.98	23

Confusion Matrix (Test):

```
             Predicted
              0   1   2
            -----------
Actual  0 | 29   0   0
        1 |  0  23   0
        2 |  0   1  22
```

While these results are impressive, it is important to keep things in perspective. These factors are mentioned as follows:

- The Iris dataset is very clean, balanced, and has well-separated classes.
- In real-world datasets, features are often noisy, classes are imbalanced, and boundaries are not this clear.

- Accuracy scores of 90%+ are rare in practical problems unless the data is carefully engineered or the problem is trivial.

Conclusion

In this chapter, we explored how to integrate Polars and Scikit-learn to build efficient and readable ML pipelines. By starting from exploratory data analysis (EDA) and moving on to model evaluation, we demonstrated how Polars' speed and expressiveness can streamline the data preparation process, while Scikit-learn provides a flexible toolkit for model building and validation.

By walking through a full classification example with the Iris dataset, we showed how to handle data transformation, scaling, and pipeline construction using native support for Polars in Scikit-learn 1.4+. While our example used a clean and balanced dataset, real-world data is often more complex and noisy, where achieving high performance requires more careful pre-processing, tuning, and validation.

This foundation equips you to apply similar workflows to larger and more challenging datasets. In the next chapter, we will dive deeper into working with big data using Polars and demonstrate how to apply these same principles at scale.

Exercise Tasks

Exercise: Predict Housing Prices Using Regression

In this exercise, you will use the California Housing dataset to predict house prices. You will work with Polars for data preparation and Scikit-learn for modeling.

1. **Load and explore the data**

   Load the dataset using fetch_california_housing, convert it to a Polars DataFrame, and view the first few rows.

2. **Select features and target**

   Use a few numeric columns (for example, MedInc, HouseAge, AveRooms) as features. Use MedHouseVal as the target and ensure it's a float.

3. **Split the data**

   Use train_test_split with an 80/20 split for training and testing.

4. **Build a regression pipeline**

   Use StandardScaler and LinearRegression (or RandomForestRegressor) in a Scikit-learn pipeline.

5. **Train and evaluate**

   Fit the pipeline and print metrics like MSE and R^2. Optionally, display a few actual vs. predicted values.

CHAPTER 13
Big Data Analysis with Polars

"Big data is not about the data, it is about the insights.
Cloud computing is not about the infrastructure, it is about the agility."

Thomas H. Davenport

Introduction

In today's data-driven world, efficient and scalable data management is the topmost priority for organizations. Cloud platforms, particularly Google Cloud Platform (GCP), offer a robust suite of services designed to handle diverse data workloads. This suit of services comprises simple storage as well as complex analytical processing. This chapter will guide you through integrating with key GCP services: Cloud Storage for durable and scalable data storage; Cloud Functions for event-driven serverless computing; and Google BigQuery for powerful, petabyte-scale data warehousing and analytics.

Beyond individual service integration, we will also explore how to construct a complete Extract, Transform, Load (ETL) pipeline. We will leverage Polars, a high-performance DataFrame library, to efficiently process data, while demonstrating how to seamlessly move and transform data across your cloud environment. By the end of this chapter, you will be able to understand how these components work together to create efficient, scalable data workflows in the cloud.

To solidify your understanding, we will walk through a beginner-friendly project: building an ETL pipeline for farm sensor data. Imagine that you have various sensors deployed across a farm, collecting data like soil moisture, temperature, and humidity. This raw data is already being pushed into your GCP environment. Our goal will be to process this raw data, clean it, aggregate it, and prepare it for analysis. We will ultimately load it into BigQuery for insights into farm conditions and optimal resource management.

Structure

This chapter will cover the following topics:

- GCP Cloud Storage
- GCP Cloud Functions
- Google BigQuery
- ETL Pipeline Using Polars and GCP
- Project: Farm Data ETL

GCP Cloud Storage

Google Cloud Storage (GCS) is a highly scalable, durable, and cost-effective object storage service. It is ideal for storing various data types, including raw sensor data, backups, archives, and large datasets for analytics.

Key Features:

- **Global Reach**: Data is stored across multiple geographic locations.
- **Durability:** Designed for 99.999999999% (11 nines) annual durability
- **Scalability:** Infinitely scalable, handling petabytes of data
- **Security:** Robust security features, including encryption at rest and in transit
- **Lifecycle Management**: Automate data deletion or transition to colder storage classes.

Assuming you have authenticated your environment (for example, via gcloud auth application-default login or by setting GOOGLE_APPLICATION_CREDENTIALS), you can interact with GCS using the google-cloud-storage client library.

Farm Data Context: Raw farm sensor data (for example, `sensor_readings_2024-07-21.csv`) is stored in a GCS bucket.

```
# Import the Google Cloud Storage client library
from google.cloud import storage

def upload_blob(bucket_name, source_file_name, destination_blob_name):
    """Uploads a file to the bucket."""
    storage_client = storage.Client()
    bucket = storage_client.bucket(bucket_name)
    blob = bucket.blob(destination_blob_name)
```

```
    blob.upload_from_filename(source_file_name)
    print(f"File {source_file_name} uploaded to {destination_blob_name}
in bucket {bucket_name}.")

def download_blob(bucket_name, source_blob_name, destination_file_name):
    """Downloads a blob from the bucket."""
    storage_client = storage.Client()
    bucket = storage_client.bucket(bucket_name)
    blob = bucket.blob(source_blob_name)

    blob.download_to_filename(destination_file_name)
    print(f"Blob {source_blob_name} downloaded to {destination_file_
name}.")

def list_blobs(bucket_name):
    """Lists all the blobs in the bucket."""
    storage_client = storage.Client()
    blobs = storage_client.list_blobs(bucket_name)
    print(f"Blobs in bucket {bucket_name}:")
    for blob in blobs:
        print(blob.name)

#Example Usage (replace with your actual bucket and file names)
bucket_name = "your-farm-data-bucket"
local_file_path = "path/to/local/sensor_data.csv"
gcs_blob_path = "raw_data/sensor_readings_2024-07-21.csv"

# # To upload a file:
upload_blob(bucket_name, local_file_path, gcs_blob_path)

# # To download a file:
download_blob(bucket_name, gcs_blob_path, "downloaded_sensor_data.csv")

# # To list files:
list_blobs(bucket_name)
```

GCP Cloud Functions

Cloud Functions is a serverless execution environment for building and connecting cloud services. With Cloud Functions, you can write simple, single-purpose functions that are attached to events emitted from your cloud infrastructure and services. Your function is triggered when an event that it is configured to handle is fired.

Use Cases:

- Responding to file uploads in Cloud Storage

- Processing messages from Pub/Sub
- Handling HTTP requests for webhooks or APIs
- Transforming data in real-time

Farm Data Context: A Cloud Function can be triggered every time a new sensor data file is uploaded to our GCS bucket. This function can then perform initial preprocessing or trigger the next stage of our ETL pipeline.

Creating a Simple Cloud Function (Python)

Here is an example of a Cloud Function that triggers when a new file is uploaded to a specified GCS bucket.

main.py (Cloud Function code):

```
import functions_framework
from google.cloud import storage

# This function is triggered by a new file upload to Google Cloud
Storage.
# The 'data' parameter contains information about the event, including
the bucket and file name.
@functions_framework.cloud_event
def process_new_farm_data(cloud_event):
    """
    Responds to a Cloud Storage event.
    Args:
        cloud_event (google.cloud.functions.Context): The Cloud Event
that triggered this function.
    """
    data = cloud_event.data

    bucket_name = data["bucket"]
    file_name = data["name"]
    event_id = cloud_event["id"]
    event_type = cloud_event["type"]
    time_created = data["timeCreated"]

    print(f"Event ID: {event_id}")
    print(f"Event Type: {event_type}")
    print(f"Bucket: {bucket_name}")
    print(f"File: {file_name}")
    print(f"Time Created: {time_created}")

    # Here you would add your logic to process the new file.
    # For example, you could download the file, parse it, and trigger
```

```
another process.
    # In our ETL, this function could initiate the Polars
transformation.

    # Example: Download the file (optional, depending on your workflow)
    storage_client = storage.Client()
    bucket = storage_client.bucket(bucket_name)
    blob = bucket.blob(file_name)

    try:
            # Define a temporary path to save the downloaded file
        temp_file_path = f"/tmp/{file_name.split('/')[-1]}" # Get just
    the filename
        blob.download_to_filename(temp_file_path)
        print(f"Downloaded {file_name} from {bucket_name} to {temp_
    file_path}")

    except Exception as e:
            print(f"Error downloading file {file_name}: {e}")

    print(f"Successfully processed new file event for {file_name}.")
```

requirements.txt (for Cloud Function deployment):

```
functions-framework==3.*
google-cloud-storage==2.*
```

Deployment Command (Using gcloud CLI):

```
# Replace with your desired function name, region, and bucket
gcloud functions deploy process-farm-data-trigger \
--runtime python310 \
--entry-point process_new_farm_data \
 --trigger-bucket your-farm-data-bucket \
 --region us-central1
```

Google BigQuery

Google BigQuery is a fully managed, serverless enterprise data warehouse that enables super-fast SQL queries using the processing power of Google's infrastructure. It is designed for analyzing petabytes of data in seconds.

Key Features:

- **Serverless:** No infrastructure to manage
- **Scalable:** Automatically scales to handle massive datasets and concurrent queries
- **Cost-Effective:** Pay only for the data you store and the queries you run

- **SQL Interface:** Standard SQL for querying data
- **Machine Learning (ML) Integration:** Direct integration with BigQuery ML

Farm Data Context: After processing our raw sensor data, we will load the cleaned and aggregated data into BigQuery tables. This allows us to run analytical queries to understand trends, identify anomalies, and support decision-making for farm management.

Basic Querying (SQL)

You can interact with BigQuery using the Google Cloud Console, bq command-line tool, client libraries (Python, Java, Node.js, and more), or various BI tools.

```
-- Create a new dataset (if it does not exist)
-- CREATE SCHEMA `your_project_id.farm_analytics`;

-- Create a table for processed sensor data
CREATE TABLE `your_project_id.farm_analytics.daily_sensor_summary` (
    farm_id STRING,
    sensor_id STRING,
    reading_date DATE,
    avg_temperature_celsius FLOAT64,
    avg_humidity_percent FLOAT64,
    avg_soil_moisture_percent FLOAT64,
    record_count INT64
);

-- Insert data (example, typically done via ETL tools like Polars)
INSERT INTO `your_project_id.farm_analytics.daily_sensor_summary` (
    farm_id, sensor_id, reading_date, avg_temperature_celsius, avg_
humidity_percent, avg_soil_moisture_percent, record_count
) VALUES (
    'FarmA', 'Sensor001', '2024-07-20', 25.5, 60.2, 45.1, 1440
);

-- Query data to find average temperature per farm per day
SELECT
    farm_id,
    reading_date,
    AVG(avg_temperature_celsius) AS overall_avg_temp
FROM
    `your_project_id.farm_analytics.daily_sensor_summary`
GROUP BY
    farm_id,
    reading_date
```

```
ORDER BY
    reading_date DESC, farm_id;

-- Find sensors with unusually low soil moisture
SELECT
    farm_id,
    sensor_id,
    reading_date,
    avg_soil_moisture_percent
FROM
    `your_project_id.farm_analytics.daily_sensor_summary`
WHERE
    avg_soil_moisture_percent < 30
ORDER BY
    reading_date DESC;
```

ETL Pipeline Using Polars and GCP

An ETL (Extract, Transform, Load) pipeline is a set of processes that move data from one or more sources to a destination, typically a data warehouse or database, after cleaning and transforming it.

Overview of ETL

- **Extract**: Reading data from source systems (for example, GCS)
- **Transform:** Cleaning, filtering, aggregating, joining, and otherwise manipulating the data to fit the target schema and business requirements (for example, using Polars)
- **Load:** Writing the transformed data to the destination system (for example, BigQuery)

Why Polars?

Polars is a DataFrame library written in Rust, which offers exceptional performance and memory efficiency, especially for large datasets. It is an excellent choice for the transformation step in an ETL pipeline due to the following features:

- **Speed:** Leverages multi-core CPUs and SIMD instructions
- **Memory Efficiency:** Uses columnar storage and lazy evaluation
- **Expressive API:** Intuitive and powerful API for data manipulation

Pipeline Stages with Polars and GCP

We will demonstrate how Polars can be integrated with GCS for extraction and BigQuery for loading.

Farm Data Context: We have raw CSV files in GCS containing sensor readings. Each row might represent a reading at a specific timestamp from a sensor. We want to aggregate this data daily, while calculating averages for temperature, humidity, and soil moisture, before loading it into BigQuery.

```
Example Raw Data Format (sensor_readings_2024-07-21.csv in GCS):
timestamp,farm_id,sensor_id,temperature_celsius,humidity_percent,soil_
moisture_percent
2024-07-21 08:00:00,FarmA,Sensor001,24.5,62.1,45.0
2024-07-21 08:01:00,FarmA,Sensor001,24.6,62.0,45.2
2024-07-21 08:00:00,FarmB,Sensor005,26.1,58.5,38.9
```

Python Code for ETL Pipeline (Using Polars LazyFrames):

```
import polars as pl
from google.cloud import storage
from google.cloud import bigquery
import io
import os

# --- Configuration ---
GCS_BUCKET_NAME = "your-farm-data-bucket" # Replace with your GCS bucket
name
GCS_RAW_DATA_PREFIX = "raw_data/" # Folder where raw CSVs are stored
BQ_PROJECT_ID = "your-gcp-project-id" # Replace with your GCP project ID
BQ_DATASET_ID = "farm_analytics"
BQ_TABLE_ID = "daily_sensor_summary"

def extract_from_gcs(bucket_name, blob_name) -> pl.LazyFrame:
    """
    Extracts a CSV file from GCS, loads it into an eager Polars
DataFrame,
    and then converts it to a LazyFrame for subsequent lazy
transformations.
    """
    print(f"Extracting data from gs://{bucket_name}/{blob_name}")
    storage_client = storage.Client()
    bucket = storage_client.bucket(bucket_name)
    blob = bucket.blob(blob_name)

    # Download the blob into a BytesIO object.
    # This avoids writing to local disk, which is good for serverless
environments
    data_bytes = io.BytesIO()
    blob.download_to_file(data_bytes)
```

```
    data_bytes.seek(0) # Rewind to the beginning of the stream

    # Read the CSV data directly into an eager Polars DataFrame.
    # Then, convert to LazyFrame for lazy operations.
    df = pl.read_csv(data_bytes, infer_schema_length=1000).lazy()
    print(f"Extracted and converted to LazyFrame for {blob_name}")
    return df

def transform_farm_data(ldf: pl.LazyFrame) -> pl.LazyFrame:
    """
    Transforms raw farm sensor data using Polars LazyFrames:
    - Converts timestamp to date
    - Calculates daily averages for temperature, humidity, and soil
moisture
    - Counts records per day per sensor
    """
    print("Starting lazy data transformation with Polars...")
    # Ensure timestamp is parsed as datetime.
    ldf = ldf.with_columns(
        pl.col("timestamp").str.strptime(pl.Datetime, format="%Y-%m-%d
%H:%M:%S").alias("timestamp")
    )

    # Extract date from timestamp.
    ldf = ldf.with_columns(
        pl.col("timestamp").cast(pl.Date).alias("reading_date")
    )

    # Aggregate daily averages per farm_id and sensor_id.
    transformed_ldf = ldf.group_by(["farm_id", "sensor_id", "reading_
date"]).agg(
        pl.col("temperature_celsius").mean().alias("avg_temperature_
celsius"),
        pl.col("humidity_percent").mean().alias("avg_humidity_percent"),
        pl.col("soil_moisture_percent").mean().alias("avg_soil_moisture_
percent"),
        pl.count().alias("record_count") # Count of readings for that
day/sensor
    ).sort(["reading_date", "farm_id", "sensor_id"])

    print("Lazy transformation graph built.")
    return transformed_ldf

def load_to_bigquery(df: pl.DataFrame, project_id, dataset_id, table_
id):
    """
```

```
    Loads an eager Polars DataFrame into a BigQuery table.
    """
    print(f"Loading data to BigQuery table {project_id}.{dataset_id}.
{table_id}")
    client = bigquery.Client(project=project_id)
    table_ref = client.dataset(dataset_id).table(table_id)

    # Convert Polars DataFrame to Pandas DataFrame for BigQuery client's
to_dataframe method.
    # BigQuery client has better integration with Pandas DataFrames.
    # For very large datasets, consider writing to GCS as Parquet/CSV
and then using BigQuery load jobs.
    pandas_df = df.to_pandas()

    job_config = bigquery.LoadJobConfig(
        # Specify the table schema if you want to ensure types.
        # Otherwise, BigQuery will attempt to infer it.
        # schema=[
        #     bigquery.SchemaField("farm_id", "STRING"),
        #     bigquery.SchemaField("sensor_id", "STRING"),
        #     bigquery.SchemaField("reading_date", "DATE"),
        #     bigquery.SchemaField("avg_temperature_celsius", "FLOAT"),
        #     bigquery.SchemaField("avg_humidity_percent", "FLOAT"),
        #     bigquery.SchemaField("avg_soil_moisture_percent",
"FLOAT"),
        #     bigquery.SchemaField("record_count", "INTEGER"),
        # ],
        write_disposition="WRITE_APPEND", # Append new data to existing
table
        # write_disposition="WRITE_TRUNCATE", # Overwrite the table
    )

    try:
        job = client.load_table_from_dataframe(
            pandas_df, table_ref, job_config=job_config
        )
        job.result() # Waits for the job to complete
        print(f"Loaded {job.output_rows} rows into {table_id}.")
    except Exception as e:
        print(f"Error loading data to BigQuery: {e}")
        # Detailed error messages from BigQuery job
        if job.errors:
            for error in job.errors:
                print(f"BigQuery Error: {error}")
```

```
def run_etl_pipeline(bucket_name, blob_name, bq_project, bq_dataset,
bq_table):
    """
    Orchestrates the ETL pipeline for a single farm data file.
    """
    print(f"Running ETL for blob: {blob_name}")
    try:
        # 1. Extract (returns LazyFrame).
        raw_ldf = extract_from_gcs(bucket_name, blob_name)

        # 2. Transform (operates on LazyFrame, returns LazyFrame).
        transformed_ldf = transform_farm_data(raw_ldf)

        # 3. Collect and Load (collects LazyFrame to eager DataFrame
before loading).
        print("Collecting LazyFrame to eager DataFrame...")
        final_df = transformed_ldf.collect()
        print(f"Collected {len(final_df)} rows.")
        load_to_bigquery(final_df, bq_project, bq_dataset, bq_table)
        print(f"ETL pipeline completed successfully for {blob_name}.")
    except Exception as e:
        print(f"ETL pipeline failed for {blob_name}: {e}")]
```

Example of how this might be called, for example, from a Cloud Function or a scheduled job. In a real scenario, you would iterate over new files or specific dates. For demonstration, let us assume '`sensor_readings_2024-07-21.csv`' is the file to process:

```
if __name__ == "__main__":
    # Create a dummy CSV file for demonstration if it does not exist in
GCS.
    # In a real scenario, this file would be uploaded by sensors or other
systems.
    dummy_csv_content = """timestamp,farm_id,sensor_id,temperature_
celsius,humidity_percent,soil_moisture_percent
        2024-07-21 08:00:00,FarmA,Sensor001,24.5,62.1,45.0
        2024-07-21 08:01:00,FarmA,Sensor001,24.6,62.0,45.2
        2024-07-21 08:02:00,FarmA,Sensor001,24.7,62.2,45.1
        2024-07-21 08:00:00,FarmB,Sensor005,26.1,58.5,38.9
        2024-07-21 08:01:00,FarmB,Sensor005,26.0,58.7,39.0
        2024-07-21 08:02:00,FarmB,Sensor005,26.2,58.6,38.8
        2024-07-22 09:00:00,FarmA,Sensor001,25.0,63.0,46.0
        2024-07-22 09:01:00,FarmA,Sensor001,25.1,63.1,46.1
```

```
# To simulate a file upload and trigger the ETL:

 # Create a dummy file locally.
with open("dummy_sensor_data.csv", "w") as f:
   f.write(dummy_csv_content)

# Upload the dummy file to GCS.
upload_blob(GCS_BUCKET_NAME, "dummy_sensor_data.csv", f"{GCS_RAW_DATA_
PREFIX}sensor_readings_2024-07-21.csv")

# Then run the ETL pipeline for that specific blob.
run_etl_pipeline(GCS_BUCKET_NAME, f"{GCS_RAW_DATA_PREFIX}sensor_
readings_2024-07-21.csv",

# Clean up dummy file locally.
If os.path.exists("dummy_sensor_data.csv"):
      os.remove("dummy_sensor_data.csv")
```

requirements.txt (for ETL script):

```
polars==0.*
google-cloud-storage==2.*
google-cloud-bigquery==3.*
pandas==2.* # Required by google-cloud-bigquery for DataFrame loading
```

Project: Farm Data ETL

Goal: To build a basic ETL pipeline that processes raw farm sensor data from Google Cloud Storage, transforms it using Polars, and loads the aggregated results into Google BigQuery for analytical querying.

Assumptions

- You have a GCP project set up.
- You have a GCS bucket (your-farm-data-bucket) where raw sensor data CSV files are uploaded (for example, in a raw_data/ prefix).
- You have created a BigQuery dataset (farm_analytics) and a table (`daily_sensor_summary`) with the schema defined in Section 3.
- Your environment is authenticated to access GCP services (for example, gcloud auth application-default login).

Step-by-Step Guide

1. Set up your GCP Environment:
    a. Create a GCP Project.
    b. Enable the Cloud Storage, Cloud Functions, and BigQuery APIs.

c. Create a GCS bucket (for example, `your-farm-data-bucket`).

d. Create a BigQuery dataset (`farm_analytics`) and the `daily_sensor_summary` table, as shown in Section 3.

2. Simulate Raw Data Upload:

a. Create a dummy CSV file locally named sensor_readings_2024-07-21.csv with the example content provided above in the "Example Raw Data Format" section.

b. Use the `upload_blob` function (from Section 1) or the gsutil cp command to upload this file to your GCS bucket under the `raw_data/` prefix (for example, `gs://your-farm-data-bucket/raw_data/sensor_readings_2024-07-21.csv`).

3. Run the ETL Pipeline Locally (for testing):

a. Install the necessary Python libraries: pip install polars google-cloud-storage google-cloud-bigquery pandas.

b. Copy the `run_etl_pipeline` function and its dependencies (the `extract_from_gcs`, `transform_farm_data`, `load_to_bigquery` functions, and configuration variables) from Section 4 into a Python script (for example, `farm_etl.py`).

c. Crucially, update the `GCS_BUCKET_NAME`, `BQ_PROJECT_ID`, BQ_DATASET_ID, and `BQ_TABLE_ID` variables in the script to match your GCP setup.

d. Uncomment and run the `if __name__ == "__main__":` block in the ETL script to execute the pipeline for the uploaded dummy file.

```
if __name__ == "__main__":
    # Make sure to set these variables correctly for your
GCP project.
    GCS_BUCKET_NAME = "your-farm-data-bucket"
    BQ_PROJECT_ID = "your-gcp-project-id"
    BQ_DATASET_ID = "farm_analytics"
    BQ_TABLE_ID = "daily_sensor_summary"

    # The blob name of the file you uploaded to GCS
    blob_to_process = f"{GCS_RAW_DATA_PREFIX}sensor_
readings_2024-07-21.csv"

    print("Starting local ETL pipeline execution...")
    run_etl_pipeline(GCS_BUCKET_NAME, blob_to_process,
                     BQ_PROJECT_ID, BQ_DATASET_ID, BQ_TABLE_
ID)
    print("Local ETL pipeline execution finished.")
```

Verify Data in BigQuery:

- Go to the BigQuery console in GCP.
- Navigate to your farm_analytics dataset and `daily_sensor_summary` table.
- Run a simple SELECT * FROM `your_project_id.farm_analytics.daily_sensor_summary`` query to see the processed data. You should see the daily aggregated averages.

Automate with Cloud Functions (Optional, but recommended for real-world scenarios):

- Modify the `process_new_farm_data` Cloud Function (from Section 2) to call your run_etl_pipeline function.
- Instead of just printing, the Cloud Function will now extract the bucket_name and file_name from the event data and pass them to `run_etl_pipeline`.
- Deploy the Cloud Function, triggering it on new object finalization in your your-farm-data-bucket bucket, with the `raw_data/` prefix.

Updated `main.py` for Cloud Function:

```
import functions_framework
import polars as pl
from google.cloud import storage
from google.cloud import bigquery
import io
import os

# --- Configuration (same as in your local ETL script) ---
# These should ideally be set as environment variables in the Cloud
Function deployment
# For simplicity, hardcoding them here for the example.
BQ_PROJECT_ID = os.environ.get("BQ_PROJECT_ID", "your-gcp-project-id")
BQ_DATASET_ID = os.environ.get("BQ_DATASET_ID", "farm_analytics")
BQ_TABLE_ID = os.environ.get("BQ_TABLE_ID", "daily_sensor_summary")

# --- ETL Functions (copy paste from your local ETL script) ---
def extract_from_gcs(bucket_name, blob_name) -> pl.LazyFrame:
    print(f"Extracting data from gs://{bucket_name}/{blob_name}")
    storage_client = storage.Client()
    bucket = storage_client.bucket(bucket_name)
    blob = bucket.blob(blob_name)

    data_bytes = io.BytesIO()
    blob.download_to_file(data_bytes)
    data_bytes.seek(0)
```

```
    df = pl.read_csv(data_bytes, infer_schema_length=1000).lazy()
    print(f"Extracted and converted to LazyFrame for {blob_name}")
    return df

def transform_farm_data(ldf: pl.LazyFrame) -> pl.LazyFrame:
    print("Starting lazy data transformation with Polars...")
    ldf = ldf.with_columns(
        pl.col("timestamp").str.strptime(pl.Datetime, format="%Y-%m-%d
%H:%M:%S").alias("timestamp")
    )
    ldf = ldf.with_columns(
        pl.col("timestamp").cast(pl.Date).alias("reading_date")
    )
    transformed_ldf = ldf.group_by(["farm_id", "sensor_id", "reading_
date"]).agg(
        pl.col("temperature_celsius").mean().alias("avg_temperature_
celsius"),
        pl.col("humidity_percent").mean().alias("avg_humidity_percent"),
        pl.col("soil_moisture_percent").mean().alias("avg_soil_moisture_
percent"),
        pl.count().alias("record_count")
    ).sort(["reading_date", "farm_id", "sensor_id"])
    print("Lazy transformation graph built.")
    return transformed_ldf

def load_to_bigquery(df: pl.DataFrame, project_id, dataset_id, table_
id):
    print(f"Loading data to BigQuery table {project_id}.{dataset_id}.
{table_id}")
    client = bigquery.Client(project=project_id)
    table_ref = client.dataset(dataset_id).table(table_id)
    pandas_df = df.to_pandas()
    job_config = bigquery.LoadJobConfig(write_disposition="WRITE_APPEND")
    try:
        job = client.load_table_from_dataframe(pandas_df, table_ref,
job_config=job_config)
        job.result()
        print(f"Loaded {job.output_rows} rows into {table_id}.")
    except Exception as e:
        print(f"Error loading data to BigQuery: {e}")
        if job.errors:
```

```
            for error in job.errors:
                print(f"BigQuery Error: {error}")

def run_etl_pipeline(bucket_name, blob_name, bq_project, bq_dataset,
bq_table):
    print(f"Running ETL for blob: {blob_name}")
    try:
        raw_ldf = extract_from_gcs(bucket_name, blob_name)
        transformed_ldf = transform_farm_data(raw_ldf)
        print("Collecting LazyFrame to eager DataFrame...")
        final_df = transformed_ldf.collect()
        print(f"Collected {len(final_df)} rows.")
        load_to_bigquery(final_df, bq_project, bq_dataset, bq_table)
        print(f"ETL pipeline completed successfully for {blob_name}.")
    except Exception as e:
        print(f"ETL pipeline failed for {blob_name}: {e}")

# --- Cloud Function Entry Point ---
@functions_framework.cloud_event
def process_new_farm_data(cloud_event):
    data = cloud_event.data
    bucket_name = data["bucket"]
    file_name = data["name"]

    print(f"Cloud Function triggered by new file: {file_name} in bucket:
{bucket_name}")

    # Call the main ETL pipeline function
    run_etl_pipeline(bucket_name, file_name, BQ_PROJECT_ID, BQ_DATASET_
ID, BQ_TABLE_ID)
```

requirements.txt for Cloud Function:

```
functions-framework==3.*
polars==0.*
google-cloud-storage==2.*
google-cloud-bigquery==3.*
pandas==2.*
```

Deployment Command for Cloud Function:

```
gcloud functions deploy process-farm-data-etl \
--runtime python310 \
--entry-point process_new_farm_data \
--trigger-bucket your-farm-data-bucket \
```

```
  --trigger-event google.storage.object.finalize \
  --region us-central1 \
  --set-env-vars BQ_PROJECT_ID=your-gcp-project-id,BQ_DATASET_ID=farm_
analytics,BQ_TABLE_ID=daily_sensor_summary \
  --memory=512MB  #Adjust memory as needed for your data size
```

Now, every time a new CSV file is uploaded to `gs://your-farm-data-bucket/raw_data/`, the Cloud Function will automatically trigger and run the ETL pipeline.

Conclusion

This chapter provides a comprehensive overview of integrating with key Google Cloud Platform services such as Cloud Storage, Cloud Functions, and BigQuery for robust data management. We have also demonstrated how to build an efficient ETL pipeline using Polars, while showcasing its power in transforming data at scale. Through the practical example of processing farm sensor data, you have seen how these components can be combined to create automated, scalable, and insightful data workflows in the cloud. This foundational knowledge will enable you to design and implement your own data solutions on GCP.

In the next chapter, we will cover the best practices while using polars for data tasks.

Exercise

Mountain Peak Data Analysis

To reinforce your understanding of the concepts covered in this chapter, let us work through a small exercise using a hypothetical "Mountain Peak" dataset.

Scenario: You have a collection of data files (.csv or .json) in a GCS bucket, each containing information about mountain peaks, such as their name, elevation, mountain range, and country. Your task is to build an ETL pipeline to process this data, identify the highest peaks per mountain range, and load the results into BigQuery for analysis.

Assumptions:

- You have a GCP project and are authenticated.
- You have a GCS bucket (for example, your-mountain-data-bucket) where raw mountain peak data files are uploaded (for example, in a raw_data/mountains/ prefix).

Example Raw Data Format (for example, peaks_europe_2024-07.csv in GCS):

peak_name,elevation_meters,mountain_range,country,first_ascent_year

Mont Blanc,4808,Alps,France/Italy,1786

Matterhorn,4478,Alps,Switzerland/Italy,1865

Mount Everest,8848,Himalayas,Nepal/China,1953

K2,8611,Karakoram,Pakistan/China,1954

Tasks

1. GCS Setup:
    a. Create a new GCS bucket (for example, your-mountain-data-bucket) or use an existing one.
    b. Simulate uploading several dummy mountain peak data files (for example, peaks_europe_2024-07.csv, peaks_asia_2024-07.csv) to a specific prefix within this bucket (for example, raw_data/mountains/).
2. BigQuery Schema Definition:
    a. In your BigQuery project, create a new dataset (for example, mountain_analytics).
    b. Define a new table within this dataset (for example, highest_peaks_summary) with a schema suitable for storing the transformed data (for example, mountain_range, highest_peak_name, highest_elevation_meters, number_of_peaks_in_range).
3. Polars ETL Script Development:
    a. Create a Python script (for example, mountain_etl.py) that includes the following functions:
        i. extract_mountain_data(bucket_name, blob_name) -> pl.LazyFrame: Downloads a mountain data file from GCS and returns a Polars LazyFrame.
        ii. transform_mountain_data(ldf: pl.LazyFrame) -> pl.LazyFrame:
            - Processes the raw data
            - Groups the data by mountain_range
            - For each mountain_range, identify the peak with the highest_elevation_meters.
            - Calculates the number_of_peaks_in_range
            - Selects only the relevant columns for the summary table.
        iii. load_mountain_summary_to_bigquery(df:m pl.DataFrame, project_id, dataset_id, table_id): Loads the transformed Polars DataFrame into your BigQuery highest_peaks_summary table

iv. run_mountain_etl_pipeline(bucket_name, blob_name, bq_project, bq_dataset, bq_table): Orchestrates the E-T-L steps

4. Local Testing:
   a. Run your mountain_etl.py script locally to process one of your dummy mountain data files.
   b. Verify that the highest_peaks_summary table in BigQuery is populated correctly.
5. Cloud Function Automation (Optional, Advanced):
   a. Create a Cloud Function that triggers whenever a new file is uploaded to your raw_data/mountains/ prefix in your-mountain-data-bucket.
   b. The Cloud Function's entry point should call your run_mountain_etl_pipeline function, while passing the bucket and file name from the event trigger.
   c. Deploy the Cloud Function.
   d. Test by uploading a new dummy mountain data file to GCS and observe the BigQuery table updating automatically.

This exercise will give you hands-on experience applying the concepts of GCS, Cloud Functions, BigQuery, and Polars LazyFrames in a new context.

CHAPTER 14

Emerging Trends and Best Practices

"Once a new technology rolls over you,
if you are not part of the steamroller, you are part of the road."

Stewart Brand

Introduction

This chapter provides a comprehensive guide to leveraging Python Polars for efficient data processing, while focusing on best practices, performance optimization, and avoiding common pitfalls. It delves into the symbiotic relationships with PyArrow and Pandas and also offers insights on how to streamline your data analysis workflows.

Structure

This chapter will cover the following topics:

- Emerging Trends for Python Polars
- Best Practices for Working with PyArrow
- Best Practices for Working with Pandas
- Integrating with Modern Data Formats
- Common Anti-Patterns to Avoid with Code Examples

Emerging Trends for Python Polars

Polars, a DataFrame library written in Rust, offers significant speed advantages, especially when working with large datasets. It achieves this performance through an innovative architecture that leverages lazy evaluation and multi-core processing, which allows it to execute operations in parallel and optimize the query plan before computation begins. As datasets continue to grow in size and complexity, Polars' efficiency makes it an increasingly attractive option for data scientists and engineers.

Integration with the Modern Data Stack

Polars is not just a standalone tool; it is a library that is designed to fit seamlessly into modern data stacks. Its foundation on Apache Arrow makes it highly interoperable and enables fast, zero-copy data transfer with other Arrow-based systems. This means Polars can be easily integrated with a wide range of tools for everything from data ingestion to machine learning (ML) model training. For example, you can use Polars to quickly clean and preprocess data before feeding it into an ML pipeline powered by libraries like scikit-learn or PyTorch. This make it a crucial component in contemporary data ecosystems.

GPU Acceleration

A key emerging trend is the ability of Polars to leverage Graphical Processing Units (GPUs) for data manipulation. While Polars is already highly performant on the CPU, a growing number of data science workloads, particularly in ML, are constrained by CPU processing power. By integrating with libraries like NVIDIA's cuDF, which provides a GPU-accelerated DataFrame API, Polars can offload computationally intensive operations to the GPU. This allows for massive parallelization of tasks such as sorting, filtering, and joining. This results in an order-of-magnitude performance increase for a specific class of problems. This is particularly relevant for large-scale data transformations, where the overhead of moving data to the GPU is justified by the speed of computation. As hardware becomes more powerful and accessible, this GPU integration will become a standard feature for high-performance data pipelines.

Polars and Vector Databases

Polars is becoming an essential tool in the AI development landscape, particularly in its role with Vector Databases. Vector databases, such as LanceDB, are specialized databases that store data as high-dimensional vectors, which are central to AI applications like semantic search, recommendation engines, and large language model (LLM) retrieval-augmented generation (RAG) systems. The process of getting data into a vector database often involves several crucial steps such as:

1. **Loading and Preprocessing:** Raw data (for example, text, images) must be loaded and cleaned first.
2. **Feature Extraction and Embedding**: The cleaned data must then be converted into dense numerical vectors (embeddings) using a pre-trained model.

Polars' speed and efficiency are a perfect fit for this pipeline. Its lazy evaluation and parallel processing capabilities allow it to handle the large-scale data loading and pre-processing steps with unmatched performance. You can use Polars to transform raw data, apply filters, and prepare it for the embedding model, all before a single item is sent to the vector database. This efficiency is critical for AI systems that require rapid, large-scale data ingestion and updating. Polars' ability to handle millions of records quickly makes it a foundational component for building and maintaining robust vector-based AI applications.

The Polars Ecosystem

The Polars community is vibrant and growing, contributing to a rich ecosystem of complementary libraries and tools. This includes dedicated packages for reading and writing various data formats, such as polars-json, polars-sql, and polars-io. This expansion of the ecosystem means that Polars is becoming a more complete solution for end-to-end data workflows. This reduces the need for other, less-performant libraries. The active development and community support further solidify Polars' position as a key player in the data science landscape.

Future Directions

The future of Polars is focused on building upon its core strengths. Developers are constantly working on enhanced I/O capabilities to make data loading even faster and more memory-efficient. There is also a strong push for deeper integration with other languages, frameworks, and cloud platforms. As the library matures, we can expect to see new features that will further simplify complex data transformations and push the boundaries of performance, while ensuring that Polars remains at the forefront of data analysis technology.

Best Practices for Working with PyArrow

At the heart of Polars' efficiency is its reliance on **Apache Arrow**. Arrow is a language-independent, in-memory data format that organizes data in a columnar fashion. This structure allows for highly efficient data processing and zero-copy data sharing between different systems and programming languages. By building on Arrow, Polars can perform operations directly on the in-memory data without the overhead of converting data formats, which leads to a significant boost in speed.

Seamless Integration and Code Examples

The integration between Polars and PyArrow is designed to be seamless. You can easily create a Polars DataFrame from a PyArrow Table and vice-versa. This flexibility is incredibly useful when you are working with data from sources that natively use the

Arrow format, such as Parquet files. By sticking to Arrow-native formats, you can avoid unnecessary data conversions and leverage the full power of Polars' query engine.

Here is an example of creating a Polars DataFrame from a PyArrow Table:

```
import polars as pl
import pyarrow as pa

# Create a PyArrow table
pyarrow_table = pa.Table.from_pydict({
    "id": [1, 2, 3],
    "name": ["Alice", "Bob", "Charlie"],
    "score": [85.5, 92.0, 78.2]
})

print("PyArrow Table:")
print(pyarrow_table)

# Convert the PyArrow table to a Polars DataFrame
polars_df = pl.from_arrow(pyarrow_table)

print("\nPolars DataFrame:")
print(polars_df)

# You can also convert back from Polars to PyArrow
pyarrow_again = polars_df.to_arrow()
print("\nConverted back to PyArrow Table:")
print(pyarrow_again)
```

Output :

```
PyArrow Table:
pyarrow.Table
id: int64
name: string
score: double
----
id: [[1,2,3]]
name: [["Alice","Bob","Charlie"]]
score: [[85.5,92,78.2]]

Polars DataFrame:
shape: (3, 3)
```

```
┌─────┬─────────┬───────┐
│ id  ┆ name    ┆ score │
│ --- ┆ ---     ┆ ---   │
│ i64 ┆ str     ┆ f64   │
╞═════╪═════════╪═══════╡
│ 1   ┆ Alice   ┆ 85.5  │
│ 2   ┆ Bob     ┆ 92.0  │
│ 3   ┆ Charlie ┆ 78.2  │
└─────┴─────────┴───────┘

Converted back to PyArrow Table:
pyarrow.Table
id: int64
name: large_string
score: double
----
id: [[1,2,3]]
name: [["Alice","Bob","Charlie"]]
score: [[85.5,92,78.2]]
```

Best Practices for Working with Pandas

While Polars is incredibly powerful, Pandas remains a staple in the data science community, with a vast ecosystem of tools and a large body of legacy code. Fortunately, Polars provides a robust bridge to Pandas, which allows you to convert a polars. DataFrame into a pandas.DataFrame (and vice-versa) with ease. This interoperability is important for building hybrid workflows.

The Right Tool for the Job

Knowing when to use each library is a fundamental skill. You might choose Pandas for its extensive plotting libraries, mature user interface, or when you are working on a project with a small dataset and a well-established Pandas codebase. However, for computationally intensive tasks like complex data cleaning, joining large tables, or aggregating massive datasets, Polars is the clear winner. By understanding the strengths of each, you can select the most appropriate tool for each step of your data analysis.

Performance Conscious Conversion and Hybrid Workflows

When moving data between Polars and Pandas, it is essential to be performance-conscious. It is a common mistake to convert to Pandas for every small operation.

Instead, you must perform all your heavy-duty data transformations in Polars first. Then, you can convert them into a Pandas DataFrame when you need to use a Pandas-specific function or library. This approach allows you to get the best of both worlds without compromising performance.

A great strategy is to build a hybrid workflow. Here is a practical example of a workflow that uses Polars for fast data cleaning and aggregation, and then converts it to Pandas for plotting:

```
import polars as pl
import pandas as pd
import matplotlib.pyplot as plt

# Step 1: Use Polars for efficient data loading and cleaning
# Assume `sales.csv` is a large file
df_pl = pl.read_csv("path/to/sales.csv").lazy()

# Step 2: Perform heavy-duty transformations with Polars' lazy API
sales_agg = df_pl.filter(
    pl.col("date").dt.year() == 2023  # Filter for the last year
).group_by(
    pl.col("product")
).agg(
    pl.col("revenue").sum().alias("total_revenue")
).sort(
    "total_revenue", descending=True
).collect() # Collect the results into a Polars DataFrame

print("Polars Aggregated Data:")
print(sales_agg)

# Step 3: Convert the final, smaller DataFrame to Pandas for plotting
df_pandas = sales_agg.to_pandas()

# Step 4: Use a Pandas-specific plotting library (like Matplotlib)
plt.figure(figsize=(10, 6))
df_pandas.plot(x="product", y="total_revenue", kind="bar", rot=45)
plt.title("Total Revenue by Product in 2023")
plt.xlabel("Product")
plt.ylabel("Total Revenue")
plt.tight_layout()
plt.show()
```

This hybrid approach allows you to achieve both high performance for the core data manipulation and offers full access to the broader Python data science ecosystem.

Integrating with Modern Data Formats

Polars' strong foundation in Apache Arrow makes it a natural fit for working with next-generation data formats. Modern data lakes and warehouses often rely on formats like Delta Lake and Iceberg, which add features like ACID transactions, schema enforcement, and time travel to the standard Parquet format. Polars can easily interact with these formats and allows you to build robust, scalable data pipelines.

Delta Lake Integration

Delta Lake is an open-source storage layer that brings reliability to data lakes. It provides ACID transactions and scalable metadata handling. These features make it a great choice for collaborative data environments. You can use the deltalake Python library to read data into a Polars DataFrame.

Here is an example of reading a Delta Lake table:

```
import polars as pl
from deltalake import DeltaTable

# Path to the Delta Lake table
delta_path = "/path/to/your/delta/table"

# Load the DeltaTable object
delta_table = DeltaTable(delta_path)

# Scan the DeltaTable lazily into a Polars DataFrame
df_pl = pl.scan_delta(delta_table)

# Perform some lazy operations (for example, filter, aggregate)
result_df = df_pl.filter(pl.col("timestamp") > pl.datetime(2023, 1, 1)).
collect()

print("Data from Delta Lake table:")
print(result_df)
```

Apache Iceberg Integration

Apache Iceberg is another open table format that brings reliable transactions to large-scale data sets. It solves problems related to schema evolution and partition management, which makes it an excellent choice for data lakehouse architectures. You can use the pyiceberg library to interact with Iceberg tables.

Here is a simplified example of reading from an Iceberg table:

```
import polars as pl
from pyiceberg.catalog import load_catalog
```

```
# Configure and load the Iceberg catalog
catalog = load_catalog("local", **{
    "warehouse": "/path/to/iceberg/warehouse"
})

# Access a specific Iceberg table
iceberg_table = catalog.load_table("my_database.my_table")

# Read the Iceberg table into a Polars DataFrame
# The pyiceberg library provides a way to read the data as a PyArrow
table, which Polars can then use
arrow_table = iceberg_table.scan().to_arrow()
df_pl = pl.from_arrow(arrow_table)

print("Data from Iceberg table:")
print(df_pl)
```

Common Anti-Patterns to Avoid with Code Examples

Now, we will go through some common anti patterns for dataframes.

Avoiding for Loops

Coming from a Pandas background, it is a common habit to iterate over rows using for loops. In Polars, this is a major anti-pattern. Polars is built for vectorized and expressed-based operations. Using a for loop to apply a function to each row will be incredibly slow and defeats the purpose of using a high-performance library. Instead, you should always aim to write code that operates on entire columns at once, while leveraging built-in expressions or the '.apply()' method for more complex row-wise logic.

Anti-Pattern (Slow):

```
import polars as pl
import random

# Create a sample DataFrame
df = pl.DataFrame({
    "product": ["A", "B", "C"],
    "price": [10.0, 20.0, 30.0]
})

# An inefficient way to apply a discount using a for loop
```

```
discounted_prices = []
for price in df["price"]:
    discounted_prices.append(price * 0.9)

df_slow = df.with_columns(pl.Series("discounted_price_slow", discounted_
prices))
print("Inefficient with a for loop:")
print(df_slow)
```

Best Practice (Fast and Idiomatic):

```
import polars as pl

# Create a sample DataFrame
df = pl.DataFrame({
    "product": ["A", "B", "C"],
    "price": [10.0, 20.0, 30.0]
})

# A fast, vectorized approach using an expression
df_fast = df.with_columns(
    (pl.col("price") * 0.9).alias("discounted_price_fast")
)

print("\nEfficient with a vectorized expression:")
print(df_fast)
```

Improper Use of `to_pandas()`

The `to_pandas()` method is a great utility, but overusing it is a classic anti-pattern. Every time you call this function, Polars has to eagerly execute its query plan and convert the entire dataset to a Pandas DataFrame. If you do this repeatedly, you might lose all the performance benefits of Polars' lazy evaluation and parallel processing. As mentioned before, only use `to_pandas()` when it is necessary.

Anti-Pattern (Overuse):

```
import polars as pl
import pandas as pd

# Assume 'transactions.csv' is a large file
df = pl.read_csv("transactions.csv")

# Inefficient workflow: converting back and forth
df_pandas = df.to_pandas()
df_pandas["new_col"] = df_pandas["old_col"] * 2
df = pl.from_pandas(df_pandas)

# This is extremely slow and memory-intensive for large datasets.
```

Best Practice (Correct Use):

```
import polars as pl

# Use Polars for the whole operation
df = pl.read_csv("transactions.csv")
df = df.with_columns(
    (pl.col("old_col") * 2).alias("new_col")
)

# Convert to Pandas only at the end if needed for a specific library
# for example, for plotting as shown in the previous section
```

Ignoring the Lazy API

The lazy API is a key feature of Polars. Ignoring it is a missed opportunity for performance. The lazy engine can automatically optimize your query, push down filters, and reorganize operations to make the computation as efficient as possible.

Anti-Pattern (Eager Approach on Large File):

```
import polars as pl

# This will read the entire 10GB file into memory
# before applying any filters, which may crash the program
df = pl.read_csv("10gb_data.csv")
filtered_df = df.filter(pl.col("category") == "electronics")
```

Best Practice (Lazy Approach):

```
import polars as pl

# Start a lazy scan, which only builds the query plan
lazy_df = pl.scan_csv("10gb_data.csv")

# The filter is "pushed down" and will be applied while reading
# the file, so only the relevant rows are ever loaded into memory
filtered_df = lazy_df.filter(
    pl.col("category") == "electronics"
).collect()
```

The `with_columns` Trap

Chaining multiple `with_columns` calls can be less efficient because each call triggers an intermediate computation. A more efficient approach will be to combine all your expressions into a single `with_columns` call.

Anti-Pattern (Chained `with_columns`):

```
import polars as pl

df = pl.DataFrame({"a": [1, 2, 3], "b": [4, 5, 6]})

df_inefficient = df.with_columns(
    (pl.col("a") + 1).alias("a_plus_1")
).with_columns(
    (pl.col("b") * 2).alias("b_times_2")
)
```

Best Practice (Single with_columns):

```
import polars as pl

df = pl.DataFrame({"a": [1, 2, 3], "b": [4, 5, 6]})

# All expressions are computed in a single pass
df_efficient = df.with_columns([
    (pl.col("a") + 1).alias("a_plus_1"),
    (pl.col("b") * 2).alias("b_times_2")
])
```

Generating Polars Code with Large Language Models (LLMs)

Large Language Models (LLMs) are becoming an indispensable tool for developers and data scientists. They can significantly accelerate the development process by generating boilerplate code and help you remember complex syntax. LLM can even suggest entire data manipulation pipelines from simple natural language descriptions. This can be especially useful for Polars, as its expression-based syntax can sometimes be less intuitive than Pandas for new users. An LLM can help you quickly translate your analytical thoughts into correct and efficient Polars code.

Best Practices for Prompting

To get the most out of an LLM for Polars code generation, you must provide clear and specific prompts. Simply asking "How do I filter data?" will likely result in a generic answer. A better approach is to be specific: "I have a Polars DataFrame with a sales and region column. Show me the Polars code to filter for all rows where sales is greater than 1000 and the region is 'North'." You can also provide the LLM with a sample of your data's schema, as in: "My DataFrame has columns: user_id: Int32, item_id: String, purchase_date: Date. Can you write a lazy query to find the total number of unique users who made a purchase in the last year?" Being specific about the data schema, the desired output, and the transformation logic will be helpful in getting accurate and efficient code.

Verification and Human-in-the-Loop

While LLMs are powerful, they are not infallible. You should always critically review and verify the generated code. The LLM might hallucinate a function that does not exist, use an outdated syntax, or generate an inefficient approach. Treat the LLM as a highly capable assistant, and not as a source of perfect code. It is your responsibility to ensure the correctness, efficiency, and security of the final product.

Limitations and Pitfalls

Common issues with LLM-generated code include inefficiency, misinterpretation of your query, and hallucinated functions. For instance, an LLM might revert to a for loop-based solution if your prompt is too vague, or it might suggest a syntax that was valid in a previous version of Polars but is now deprecated. By combining your domain knowledge with the LLM's generative power, you can avoid these pitfalls and achieve superior results.

Conclusion

This chapter provides a comprehensive guide to building robust, high-performance data pipelines with Polars by seamlessly integrating it with the wider data science ecosystem. After understanding its core strengths such as lazy evaluation and Apache Arrow integration, and by applying best practices while avoiding common anti-patterns, you can now tackle complex data processing challenges and write clean, maintainable code. The knowledge of how to leverage LLMs is a powerful tool for accelerating your workflow. Since it remains as a critical "human-in-the-loop", it further strengthens your ability to work efficiently and effectively in the modern data landscape.

Index

P

Q

R

S